I0161095

A BLUEPRINT FOR LEADERSHIP SUCCESS

Leadership Wisdom, from Hearts and Minds:
A Public School Miracle

SANDRA DEAN

BALBOA.
PRESS

Copyright © 2010 Sandra Dean

All rights reserved. No part of this book may be used or reproduced by any means, graphic, electronic, or mechanical, including photocopying, recording, taping or by any information storage retrieval system without the written permission of the publisher except in the case of brief quotations embodied in critical articles and reviews.

Balboa Press books may be ordered through booksellers or by contacting:

Balboa Press
A Division of Hay House
1663 Liberty Drive
Bloomington, IN 47403
www.balboapress.com
1-(877) 407-4847

Because of the dynamic nature of the Internet, any Web addresses or links contained in this book may have changed since publication and may no longer be valid. The views expressed in this work are solely those of the author and do not necessarily reflect the views of the publisher, and the publisher hereby disclaims any responsibility for them.

ISBN: 978-1-4525-0014-0 (sc)
ISBN: 978-1-4525-0015-7 (e)

Printed in the United States of America

Balboa Press rev. date: 10/13/2010

To my husband, Ishwar,
For your love, belief, wisdom
and spiritual guidance

ACKNOWLEDGMENTS

My deepest thanks and with more gratitude than you can imagine to:

Jim Giles, Judy Joel and Will McKercher for urging me to write this book.

Diane Allensworth, Mike Bowman, Linda Lopeke, Donna McArthur, Aline Munsch and Debra Wingfield, for editing and feedback.

My family, who love, support, and care for me through the good times and the bad.

My children, Shiva, Lisa, Rishi, and Shalini.

My grandchildren, Nathaniel, Surya and Joshua.

My brothers, Naresh and Ranjie and my sister Shirley.

My parents who always believed in me.

The many people around the world who have supported my work and been so kind to me on my visits.

Contents

Letter to the Reader ix

Chapter 1:   A Dream Fulfilled 1
Chapter 2:   The Task I Was Meant To Do 9
Chapter 3:   A Warm And Loving Place For Learning. 19
Chapter 4:   Loss And Renewal. 49
Chapter 5:   Parenting Voices 83
Chapter 6:   "Not My Kids, Our Kids!" 103
Chapter 7:   The Limits Of Love 121
Chapter 8:   The Right To Be Respected. 151
Chapter 9:   Programs And Progress 171
Chapter 10:   The Circle of Love .193
Chapter 11:   From Worst To First 213
Chapter 12:   The Gifts They Gave Us 237

The way forward 249

The teachers, parents, business and community leaders you will read about in this book are unique, as are all leaders: Their experiences, achievements and accomplishments are theirs alone. They have much in common with the people in your own workplace and in other workplaces and this is vital to your understanding and appreciation of the story about to unfold on the following pages.

The health, well-being, and life success of the people in your family, workplace, and community depend on your thoughts and actions as a leader. Those to whom you are closest may be—and I pray they are—free from undue psychological and emotional stress, confident in your support and guidance, enjoying careers where they are thriving in healthful and inclusionary environments, and feeling fulfilled because they are making a contribution to humanity in some way. People everywhere are vulnerable, more easily hurt than any of us care to admit, and struggling to balance their personal and professional lives.

Many of the people in your workplace are looked upon as leaders in their own spheres of influence- their families and their own communities, yet when they come into the workplace some are treated as less than equal to those who run the organization.

To thrive and prosper as an individual, a leader, and as an organization in these rapidly changing times, leadership has to change and workplaces have to change. People need and want to be recognized as leaders in their own right, to feel more included and appreciated. They need and want to participate and share in the change process and have a voice in what occurs around and to them.

Yes, their role is to help you-the leader-to move the organization forward and your role is to help them by; mentoring them, assisting them to recognize their own talents, strengths and capabilities, awakening them to their own uniqueness, to their own leadership potential. You encourage them to become leaders in their own right, modeling for them how to adopt a leadership heartset and mindset, then lead and serve, regardless of their job description.

This is a task that all leaders should be prepared to fulfill with enthusiasm, with dedication and with love.

During the years I served as principal of South Simcoe Public School, I was privileged to spend time at what I do best and love most: teaching and working with children. I was also fortunate to do so with a dedicated team of leaders who shared my concern and commitment and gave generously of their time and their love. Together we achieved remarkable results, we went from last to first, and our efforts helped the children of South Simcoe Public School to become more resilient, more responsible and better able to embrace their futures.

The message of this book is how to awaken and nurture leaders in your organization.

This expands on the work done in Hearts and Minds: A public School Miracle.

CHAPTER 1

A Dream Fulfilled

The thing I remember most clearly is the strange instant of silence just before my heart leapt at the news. In that fraction of time, everything crystallized for me: the hopes, the frustrations, and the memories of so many tears and, yes, so much laughter too. During that brief moment they all became real again, and the crises and tragedies that often accompanied them were nowhere in sight.

Then the screaming and the shouting started—nineteen educators, two police officers and one director of education, all of us a thousand miles from home, leaping out of our chairs, holding hands, hugging and laughing, while others in the hall smiled with pleasure at our unbridled joy.

It was April 1995, and South Simcoe Public School, which three years earlier had suffered the humiliation of having the worst student marks of all the schools in the school district, had just won a national award for Excellence in Business and Education Partnerships from the prestigious Conference Board of Canada. What's more, the travel expenses for the staff members who were attending the ceremony in Saint John, New Brunswick, had been paid for by business partners who believed in us, supported our work, and wanted to provide an opportunity for as many teachers as possible to participate in the celebration.

But I wasn't thinking of that as we all crowded onto the platform to accept the prize and receive the standing ovation from the audience. No Academy Award-winning celebrities could ever have

1

felt a greater thrill of accomplishment than we did at that moment. We had managed to prove something vital about education, first to ourselves, then to our students, their parents, their community, and now to the entire country and beyond.

How far we have come, I thought, watching the staff celebrate that evening in Saint John. We embarked on a journey, where the destination could only be reached by taking one small step at a time.

Becoming principal of my own school was a dream of mine almost from the first day I chose teaching as a career. It's not an unusual ambition, I suspect. Every teacher dedicated to making a positive impact on students, and prepared to challenge the usual way of doing things, thinks from time to time about being appointed principal. In early 1991, the position was offered to me. However, when I discovered that my school would not be a neat and tidy suburban one, furnished with shining facilities and peopled by solidly middle-class students, but a tired, seventy-five-year-old inner-city school that probably faced closure, I admit my heart sank a little.

Built when schools were considered part monument and part institution, the structure was small and dark, its brown brick walls crowned with stone and concrete in a style that reminded me of pictures of Queen Victoria glaring at the camera, stern and foreboding. The location, directly across the street from a strip mall, was a principal's nightmare. The teachers at South Simcoe faced enormous difficulties as a result of these and other factors. The proof was in the test scores. Of all eighty-nine schools in the Durham District School Board, South Simcoe Public School ranked last when it came to measuring student performance levels in reading, writing and mathematics.

Yet, within a short number of years, South Simcoe Public School would rise to the top of all schools in its district. Not just higher, or among the best of its group, or even among the top ten-it would sit at the very summit, *with 100 percent of its students performing at the highest levels in the same subjects in which it had fared poorest.*

This is the story of its journey from Last to First. The journey was not always smooth or swift, and from time to time we encountered a pothole or two along the way. But, oh, how rewarding the trip was for everyone…especially the children!

When I first learned that I would be stepping up to the role of principal of a school within my district, I was naturally pleased and excited. Promotion to a principal's position is more than recognition of your abilities and experience; it represents an opportunity not only to lead educational change, but also to be an agent of social change. The role extends far beyond running a school and ensuring that the curriculum is delivered. It includes opening up the children to their unlimited potential and to new possibilities, in a manner no other profession can offer.

As a parent, you can influence your own children. As a teacher, you affect the lives of perhaps twenty-five or thirty children in your care each day. But as a principal, you have the opportunity to make a positive impact on literally hundreds of children and improve their lives in at least some small way. If you touch their hearts as well as their minds, you can leave them a legacy of life-long success and happiness. Me, a principal? I could hardly wait to get started.

Just tell me where!

To say that I had mixed emotions when the answer came back "South Simcoe Public School" is something of an understatement. In fact, my first reaction was immediately negative. "I don't want to go there", I said to my superintendent, Carol, when she called me at home with the news. For as long as anyone could remember, South Simcoe was located on the "wrong side of the tracks." This is more than a cliché in industrial Oshawa, where economic and social conditions are clearly stratified. "It's an old school, they're going to close it soon, and it's not my kind of place." Those were three pretty good reasons to send somebody else there, I believed.

"Sandra, South Simcoe *is* your kind of place," my superintendent replied. "The children need someone like you. You can make a difference there. Look, I promise if you go there you'll shine." She must have sensed that I remained unconvinced, because she added, "If, in a few months, you still feel you would rather go somewhere else, we'll talk about it."

Naturally, I agreed. I really wanted to be a principal, after all.

One of the things all educators discover is that you never stop learning. There are lessons to be gained from virtually everything you experience as a teacher. Certainly, over my seven and a half years as principal of South Simcoe Public School, I learned many lessons, and the first came from my own family on the very day I was told of my appointment.

"We're so proud of you," my husband, Ishwar, said. My sons, Shiva and Rishi, along with other family members, added their congratulations. But the expression on my face, and my own self-doubts, became immediately apparent.

"I'm not sure I can handle it," was my reply. The truth was, I felt more than doubt; I felt disappointment as well. Like every profession, teaching has its share of prestigious positions, and being principal of a school like South Simcoe didn't seem to be one of them.

"Of course you can," Ishwar said. "You'll make a great principal. You have the training, the experience, and most of all, the attitude to deal with kids who need the extra care, love and attention. It's the best place for you."

"It's kind of dreary," I said. "You know how those older school buildings are. Not much light, dull colours, huge hallways, and"—

"Then we'll help you fix things up," Ishwar said. "The boys and I will pitch in before the school year starts. A little paint and some wallpaper can make a big difference, you know that. Besides," he added in a more serious tone, "it's not the building that needs your talents, it's the children."

This initial lesson, of course, taught me that I wasn't alone. I enjoyed the total support of my family, and the support base grew over the years, to encompass first the school staff, then the parents, local merchants, service clubs, the police department and finally the entire community. Ishwar was absolutely correct. I was not alone, and in no way could I have accomplished as much as I did without the support of this ever-widening circle of people who worked with me to make a difference for the children.

Many of my beliefs and values about raising and educating children are hardly new, such as the idea that children are to be valued and nurtured in order to bring out the best in them. Their precious spirit stems, in my opinion, from their innocence and vulnerability. We all know that these two qualities dissipate with the passage of time and the experiences of living; that's part of the process of maturing into an adult. But too many children lose them too early and in the wrong way, through abuse, neglect and the challenges of their prevailing social environment. I have yet to encounter a troubled child who could not benefit from healthy doses of love and care. For some reason a few members of our society believe that individuals in the two extremes of life, childhood and old age, either don't require or don't deserve our full attention. How can this be? Why can't children enjoy the same degree of dignity and respect that we demand for ourselves? Imagine for a moment that you are no longer as independent as you are today. You can be either a child or an elderly invalid—it works either way—and you are under the control of someone stronger than yourself, someone who seeks to dominate you with threats and punishment. How would you feel?

Control and manipulation of children are ultimately doomed to failure. I saw proof of this during my years of teaching, in my position as vice-principal and, of course, in my experience as a parent. I sincerely believe that the best method of educating children is, first, to love and care for them and, above all, to believe in them; and second, to provide them with ways of increasing their own sense of self, who they are, and who they could become. With this emotional foundation in place, we need to provide them with opportunities where they can experience the joy and deep sense of fulfillment that comes from accomplishing something and doing it well.

You don't teach a child to ice-skate, for example, by threatening punishment if she doesn't learn how to keep her ankles stiff. You demonstrate and encourage. You praise and support. You do not threaten. And when you experience the delight on a child's face as she finally masters such a skill, you share in her pleasure, pride and sense of accomplishment.

Does this mean that *any* behaviour is acceptable from children? Of course not. As adults we recognize the sense of responsibility expected from us as members of society. Physical assaults, theft, disturbances hurting and harming others in any way were simply not acceptable. But, neither, I believe, should they be dealt with simply by punishment.

There are quick and easy consequences that may seem to be a solution but they are not; it isn't that easy. It is *never* that easy, as almost anyone in our justice system will agree. These ideas represented the core of my beliefs which I mulled over as I prepared myself to assume the role of principal at South Simcoe Public School, the first step in a journey that led to all the whooping and excitement in New Brunswick, and beyond.

Looking back on it, I realize that my career could have taken one of two very different routes. The one that I originally longed to travel would have been smooth and paved, across generally flat terrain. I would have followed this route as principal of a bright and shiny school in a wealthy suburb, a school populated by students whose minds were filled as much (or, let's face it, more!) with visions of new fashions and the sounds of new music as with the lessons at hand. Such a journey would require little passion and energy from me.

The other route was uncertain and rocky, traversing new territory and climbing from a deep valley up steep canyon walls, ever upwards, stumbling from time to time, with the ever-present risk of falling to disaster. Finishing the trek would test my abilities as an educator and strengths as a person, and require large reserves of nerve, energy and belief in myself. In addition this was not something I could do by myself, I would need an entire team to work with me. But at the end, if we succeeded, we would all stand higher and prouder than when we began. We would leave a legacy that would benefit others for years to come. That's the route I took when I agreed to become principal of South Simcoe Public School. I did it because I knew I had the support of my family, my friends, my colleagues and my school board.

"Did I do something wrong?" I asked Ruth Lafarga the day after I learned I was assigned to South Simcoe School. Ruth chaired the school board and was the elected trustee of the area that included the school. As much as anyone, she knew the challenges facing South

Simcoe...and me. "No, of course not," she said laughing. "We *want* someone like you there."

That was my second lesson. I wasn't being sent to South Simcoe merely out of convenience. I was being sent there to turn the school around, by people who believed in my abilities. This was a challenge that would put all my professional skills and capabilities as well as my personal values and beliefs to the test. It was a place where I could do a lot of good for many people. Well, I thought, hanging up the telephone, we might as well get started.

LEADER'S REFLECTION

Leaders who have a legacy consciousness lead with Mind, Heart, and Soul and help others to become leaders by unleashing their inner wisdom and harmonizing the Mind, Heart and Soul.

- Do you have a legacy consciousness?
- Have you taken the time to examine your values and beliefs about leadership?
- What is your philosophy of leadership?

CHAPTER 2

The Task I Was Meant To Do

W hen I am asked about the source of the ideas and concepts we used at South Simcoe Public School, I realize that many of them have their roots in my experiences growing up in Trinidad, and most were a part of me by the time I was ten years old. Trinidad is a country similar to Canada in some ways, yet very different in others. The climate and geography of the two countries could not be more different, and the total area of Trinidad and Tobago is much less than that of Prince Edward Island, Canada's smallest province. Perhaps as a result of the sunny and warm climate, people in Trinidad and other Caribbean islands find it natural to be open and extend their hand to others without being asked. I loved living in this environment as a child, and when I became an educator I wanted to recreate the village environment and the extended-family concept for the children in my care.

My clearest childhood memories in Trinidad are of my father, who actively sought out those who were in need and found a way to provide assistance. Instead of waiting to be asked for help, he would travel to villages far beyond our own city, looking for ways he could make people's lives easier. As a young child I often accompanied my father on these journeys, and I was constantly struck by the difference between the lives of those he encountered and my own. Our family was solidly middle class. We enjoyed luxuries and never wanted for food, shelter or security. Meeting people who were desperately in need of support, and watching my father find ways to help solve their problems, made him something of a miracle worker in my eyes.

When I asked my father why some of these people did not have enough to eat or a comfortable place to live, as we did, he explained that they had no money to purchase those things. "Why don't they just go out get a job and make the money they need?" I asked.

"That is not always as easy as it sounds. They need help to be able to do that, that is why I try to help them," my father explained, "so that they can find ways of improving their existence."

It was a simple and honest response, but an important one to me. My father did not believe in simple handouts of food and other items from those, such as our own family, who had resources to share. Gifts to those in need were important of course, but he wanted to help people to learn how to help themselves, to learn how to take responsibility for themselves. He knew that this was the way to help them to create new lives for themselves and their families. This way, along with the material benefits they would also experience a sense of achievement, learn that they were capable and thus become more independent.

I have never met anyone who takes pride in being handed food, money or clothing and then being sent on their way. And I have never failed to notice the pleasure felt by people, especially children, when they achieve something that they and others once believed was beyond their reach. That feeling of accomplishment and success is like a small miracle: it lasts longer than any handout and can literally change people forever. I was impressed by my father's concern for others because it made me realize how privileged our family was in many ways. As the eldest child in our family, I may have been the most privileged of all.

The significance of family ties and the importance of education reigned supreme in our house. Our ancestors had emigrated to Trinidad from India, where wisdom and knowledge were considered among the greatest treasures anyone could possess. They arrived in the mid-nineteenth century after slavery had been abolished on the island and new labour was needed to harvest the sugar crops. Even as fieldworkers, they retained an appreciation for the value of education and a respect for the wisdom gained over a lifetime.

I was continually reminded of the importance of education by my grandmother, who, ironically, never attended school (which I realize now was a lesson in itself). Although her father and brothers were well educated, (her father had arrived from India as a court interpreter), she had never been to school. During her childhood years, education for girls had been considered a waste. Beyond knowing how to sew, cook, clean house and raise children, what other skills did a woman need? That was how most people thought in the early twentieth century. In quiet rebellion, my grandmother taught herself to count, a skill she used when selling vegetables from the small garden she planted and tended, and she expected all her grandchildren, boys and girls alike, to obtain all the education they could absorb. In my grandmother's view, education, living a good life and happiness, were all intertwined. "You have to ask yourself why you were placed on this earth," she would tell us. "You have to choose or make your path, do the task you came here to do, help others, and then you will be happy and fulfilled. We are all here to do something special. It is up to you to discover what it is."

I spent my early school days in a private convent school, where the teaching nuns were kind and caring, creating a sense of family among us. The sisters had high expectations for their students, and firmly instilled a strong sense of self-discipline in us. If something needed to be done by a certain time, at a certain level of skill, we were expected to achieve it. If we did not, we were encouraged to keep trying and not simply give up. We knew that they were always there to support us.

There were times when other students and I at the convent school doubted our ability to do something, whether mastering a new algebra method or completing a reading assignment. But the sisters were always convinced that we were capable of anything we were passionate about and put our minds to, and they managed to pass this belief on to us. I cannot overemphasize the value of this lesson to a child, even a child such as myself who was constantly being told by her parents that I could achieve anything I wanted to if I cared about it enough. It is important for everyone, parents, teachers and the entire community, to believe in the potential of children.

For our twenty-fifth wedding anniversary, Ishwar and I travelled to France. There I met my retired school principal, Sister Marie Joseph, who had taken a special interest in me back at that convent school in Trinidad. I wanted to let her know how much she had influenced me, and how many of my successes owed their beginnings to her interest in me. She had encouraged me to read a wide variety of books, not just for knowledge but for the sheer joy of reading and discovering. She introduced me to the work of Pearl S. Buck, a humanitarian and teacher. After I read her book "The Good Earth", I wanted to be a teacher and write like she did). She had made me feel good about myself as a student and as an individual, and encouraged me to be courageous and take risks. She was kind and caring, and while I don't know if I meant any more to her than anyone else, I knew that she believed in me, valued me as a person and that I was special to her. She had a profound influence on me. That was why, so many years after I left the convent school, I wanted to meet her again. I wanted her to know that I had become a teacher and then a Principal. I wanted her to know how much she had influenced my career and life choices and I wanted to thank her for believing in me. I went to France to do it. I would have travelled much farther if I had to.

I was taught to value education; it is a treasure in your mind that you can never lose. Knowledge enables you to think for yourself, care for yourself and help others. This idea of a treasure you carry in your head is probably why a lot of families in Trinidad aspired to higher education—because it has a value of its own that can never fade.

At home, my parents had high expectations for us, both for academics and behaviour. They never allowed anything to intrude seriously on our education. If we had a school test, or homework or an assignment to complete for the following day, our family would not plan a social event for that evening. School work came first, and that was that.

Family ties in Trinidad are extensive and powerful and we saw our family members every weekend. Socializing is not something you do to pass the time or fulfill an obligation. It is as much a part of your life as the work you perform—perhaps more so.

Socializing began with our immediate family. My mother insisted on all of us eating a nutritious breakfast and enjoying healthy meals during the day. We were always expected to eat together, sharing stories of our day with each other across the dinner table. Naturally, holidays were celebrated with great joy and much tradition. On Christmas Day my father and his four brothers would visit their grandmother with their children, even great-great-grandchildren in later years. These were wonderful times. We shared news and gossip, each of us knowing that we enjoyed the support of one another in times of need, as well as in the good times.

And it wasn't a one-way street between the generations. My grandmother travelled regularly, spending time with each of her children and grandchildren, ensuring everyone was all right. She even visited me in Canada when my son, Rishi, was born. She spent several weeks with me and her newest great grandchild to help me adjust and get settled into a new routine, as much as to let me know she loved and cared about me. It's the kind of thing mothers and grandmothers did in our family. Her journeys reflected the same kind of attitude my father displayed when he reached out to see who needed assistance in a far-off village. You didn't wait for someone to arrive on your doorstep pleading for help; you went looking for ways to help others.

There were other lessons to be learned as well. I remember one year when, as a young girl, I discovered a special fascination for dolls. I wanted not just ordinary dolls but *special* dolls—large and lifelike, dressed in fancy clothing. One Christmas I received just such a doll from my parents, and I thought it was the most fabulous of its kind in all of Trinidad.

That same Christmas, a visitor to our home had brought his brother along to meet us. Friends and family always made a point of visiting during the Christmas season, and tradition held that visitors were always welcome to bring friends or relatives with them to share the joy of the season. The brother was kind enough to bring a gift for me.

When I unwrapped the gift in front of the visitor, I discovered it was a doll. The doll was pleasant enough, but it couldn't compare with the large, elaborate doll my parents had given me. "Oh," I said, "another doll, thank you," and I set it aside.

My mother immediately suggested I come to the kitchen to assist her with the meal preparation. Of course she didn't need my help at all. I was the one in need—of a lesson.

13

"That young man is a guest in our home and you haven't left him with a very good feeling," she said, after setting me down in a chair. "He told me that he took a great deal of time choosing the doll for you because he wanted you to have a special gift. You should accept it with the same amount of love and care he put into selecting it for you and show that you appreciate it. So when you go back into the room, you need to pick up the doll, walk over to him, thank him for it and find something good to say about it."

I think I may have pouted a little. "But it's not as nice as my other dolls," I said. "I don't like it."

"I know you can find something good to say about the doll," she told me. "Look carefully at it until you do. Then you go and thank him for it properly, and give him a hug to show you mean it."

As usual, my mother was pleasant but firm. So I returned to the living room and examined the doll more closely. The hair, I saw, was all curly and shiny and actually quite pretty. So I carried it to our guest and said "Thank you for my doll. I like her curly hair."

His reaction was immediate. His eyes lit up with joy and he reached out to hug me. "I'm so glad you like it," he said. "I took so much time to choose it and I was so afraid that I might choose a gift for you that you would not like."

I have never forgotten the feeling this gave me. Or the lessons it taught me. I learned that all gifts should be received with gratitude and love, that we must avoid hurting the feelings of others; instead we should always leave them with their dignity intact, feeling cared for and respected. I learned that guests in our home should be treated with courtesy and kindness. I also learned that, if you take the time to truly look, you will discover beauty in things that you may at first have thought to be ordinary. With the right mindset, you can "Find the Good" in anything and any situation.

Childhood is filled with such lessons. I was fortunate because virtually all of my lessons were positive ones, and I am often surprised at how many I was able to apply when teaching children. The lessons include the importance of:Giving a gift of love everyday, including doing something to help others. You can bring great joy and happiness to them and to yourself. Believing in yourself, and valuing the unique gifts, talents and capabilities you carry within. Believing in children, as shown by nurturing them, caring for them and, above all, loving them, so that they have a chance to blossom and follow their own unique paths. - Acting with caring, kindness, respect, and love, accepting that everyone has the right to be respected. Knowing that everything you do, every small gesture, every act, the things that you say, all create ripples that affect someone else. Understanding that everyone has value, worth and a role to play in the grand scheme of things. We are all family, like a giant puzzle that needs all the pieces in order to be complete. One person is no more or no less important than another.

For most of my life, I probably did not analyze these lessons in this manner; I simply applied them from instinct. But that's the point: they were so deeply rooted in me that I cannot be separated from these values any more than I can be separated from a part of my body, and this has helped me to help other parents and teachers understand the importance of understanding what your values and beliefs are, how they guide the decisions and choices that you make, and how they define you as an individual.

These lessons would prove just as valid to the children of South Simcoe Public School as they were to me. We used them as a starting point for discussions about how we should go about making change, what we should guard against, what we should aim for, and gradually they formed the basis for our guiding principles which served as a compass for all our efforts. Applying them to all that we did made a remarkable difference for our children.

At age nineteen, my life changed in three significant ways: I graduated from the University of the West Indies with a degree in sociology and political science, Ishwar and I were married, and we emigrated to Canada—all within a few exciting months.

Ishwar was continuing his graduate studies in electronic physics at the University of Western Ontario in London, Ontario. The special atmosphere of a university campus made our transition from Trinidadian to Canadian life a little easier, because so many people we encountered on the university campus were also from somewhere else. We were not looking forward to our first Christmas away from our families. We missed our families very much. Then our new friends George and Acklema Phills welcomed us into their fold and invited us to spend Christmas day with them so that we would still experience a sense of family. Their warmth and kindness, and the beauty of the first heavy snowfall, helped to create a foundation for this new phase of our lives.

The birth of our two sons quickly plunged me into all the activities of motherhood. Things changed, of course, often in ways I did not immediately recognize. Until then, I had little interest in furthering my education. But the sight of my children playing, sleeping, yearning to learn and reacting to life itself, sparked something in me. I realized that I did want to pursue a career and that I wanted to make a difference not just to my children but also to others, in the same manner that many people made a difference to me as a child.

I decided that teaching would offer the best opportunity. I was especially drawn to the idea of teaching young children who were hampered with difficulties of some kind. I knew that the biggest changes were often made during the earliest years, and that children with learning problems needed a special kind of help. I wanted to give them that help.

Incidentally, becoming a teacher after earning a degree in sociology and political science is not as much of a leap as some people may think. My studies had reaffirmed my belief of the need to find a way to engage people and help them to help themselves. In that way, they can develop the capacity to become whoever they choose to be. If you believe that everyone is important and has a role to play in the overall scheme of things, you'll find a way to give people a voice by providing them with opportunities to engage and participate in decision making. In my opinion these concepts are also the basis of an effective approach to leadership.

So, with the enthusiastic support of my husband, I obtained my teaching certificate and began my career by working with children who suffered from mental handicaps. From there I progressed through a series of public schools until, by 1987, I had achieved vice-principal status at a school in an affluent area of Whitby, Ontario, about thirty miles east of Toronto. In 1991, I also began teaching the principal's course at the University of Toronto's Ontario Institute for Studies in Education (OISE), and later at York University.

These leadership sessions, on evenings, on weekends and during the summer months, helped me to maintain a wider view of the challenges of education, especially from the perspective of a principal. This helped me to avoid getting caught up in the day to day challenges at my school, become frustrated and think that everything that went wrong was because of me. It wasn't about me. It also helped me to keep abreast of the on-going research on learning and schooling and I was careful to take all of this into consideration when making changes at South Simcoe.

"You should be a principal." my husband would frequently suggest to me. I would reply that I certainly hoped to be, someday. "Then I'll be able to make a difference for many more children.," I would add. Only when I discovered that my long-dreamed-of appointment was to be principal of South Simcoe Public School did my confidence waver. "Be careful about what you wish for," I recalled having read years earlier, "because it may come true." Well, my wish had come true, in a sense. Now I had to prove I really wanted it—prove it to my family, my staff, the board officials who recommended me, and most of all, to myself.

LEADER'S REFLECTION

When being a leader is a calling of the Heart as well as the Mind, and when leaders use principles as a compass to guide their actions, they lead with a passion and enthusiasm that makes them successful at whatever they undertake.

- Was your call to leadership a calling of the heart as well as the mind?
- What guides your actions as a leader?
- What do you use as your compass?

CHAPTER 3

A Warm And Loving
Place For Learning

As familiar as I was with South Simcoe Public School and the challenges faced by its staff and students, I had never set foot inside the building. When, among the many congratulatory messages I received, one came from the woman I was replacing as principal, I quickly accepted her invitation to visit.

The steady roar of traffic, speeding west to Toronto and east towards Montreal on nearby Highway 401, is a constant reminder of the transient nature of the South Simcoe neighbourhood. And it is not just the traffic that is constantly in motion. About half of the families whose children attended the school moved in or out of the area each year, an astonishing rate of turnover. Whatever the reasons for this steady migration, and there were several, the effect on young children of this repeated coming and going of neighbours and friends was often devastating. Add the familiar problems of other inner-city schools, such as family disintegration, high unemployment, spousal abuse, drug and alcohol abuse and more, and it's no surprise that the local public school was often a maelstrom of rebellion, aggression, vandalism and failed dreams. The building itself seemed to reflect the despair. The square, brown-brick building squatted on a low, bare rise. I remember especially the barren ground and the peeling paint on the window frames. When built in 1916, South Simcoe Public School had sat amid the homes of proud factory workers, many of them recent immigrants employed at the giant General Motors automotive plant. Over the decades since, most of the more stable families abandoned the area in favour of moving up to middle class suburban comfort, and so did businesses, banks and other organizations. As a result, property values nosedived and many homes in the area became stopovers for transient families.

The school became more than a casualty and a symptom of this decline. From the outside, South Simcoe Public School held little promise that anything positive could happen beneath its roof.

I left my car within sight of several bored teenagers who were smoking in the mall directly across the street. Inside, the school maintained its rather dark and sad appearance. Much of it was due, of course, to the old building's basic structure, dating back to a much earlier period of architectural design and educational environment. The school's library was miniscule, and as for the gymnasium—well, there *was* no gymnasium, and that was that. The staffroom was in the basement, a converted coal bunker and just to make things more annoying, the only staff washroom was up three flights of stairs.

My attention was quickly diverted from the building to the students. I developed the habit of always smiling at children in my roles as teacher and vice-principal. It put them at ease and helped dissolve the barriers created between students and staff.

When I smiled at the children I passed on my way to the principal's office, the smiles I received back from them were more spontaneous and intense than I had become accustomed to at my suburban school. Their entire faces seemed to light up, as though they were waiting for me to arrive and express pleasure at seeing them. Naturally, I couldn't help commenting on it when the outgoing principal graciously welcomed me into the school and escorted me into her office. She wasn't surprised at my reaction.

"The kids here are truly wonderful," she told me. "They appreciate every bit of attention you give them, and that's what keeps me going some days."

Of all the discoveries I made that day, her comment about the need of these children for attention and support was the most encouraging. You can't, after all, blame a community for the troubles that occur in and around it. Nor can you blame a teaching staff faced with the challenge of teaching children whose minds may be diverted by empty stomachs, strife between their parents, neglect and abuse.

The fact is, I didn't believe in placing blame at all. Blame would not help me to provide the children with breakfast, resolve their insecurity and fear of failure, or comfort them when the world seemed hostile and unforgiving. It is an essentially useless exercise, a waste of energy and time. I wasn't sent there to do that, I knew. I was there to do the best job I could for the children, and the brilliance of the smiles I received on my way to the principal's office made me more determined than ever to achieve my goal.

During the rest of the day I chatted one-on-one with the teachers at South Simcoe and discovered, to my surprise, that most of them enjoyed their time at the school. Sure, the old building was inefficient, even depressing sometimes. And creating a bond with parents was especially difficult because so many families moved in and out of the neighbourhood so often, and those who remained frequently did not feel confident enough in their own academic skills to help their children with homework and projects.

"Then what is it that gives you so much enjoyment here?" I kept asking, and over and over the answer came back. "The children." I left South Simcoe convinced that working with these people, we could make a difference.

I knew that I had the support of my family and friends, the school board officials who had placed me there, plus my years of training and experience to back me up. The most encouraging thing was that I would be helping the children whose needs were so compelling that I felt I simply *must* apply my very best efforts to make a difference for them.

I was no longer dwelling on the question of whether my appointment to South Simcoe was a good thing or a bad thing. I was no longer hearing those voices. Instead, I was hearing my father's voice. "Don't wait for others to ask for help," I could hear him saying. "Reach out and help them."

And my grandmother's voice echoed as well. *You've got to find the task you were meant to do, and choose a path to take to pursue it. Then you'll find true happiness.*

I realized though that all my training and good intentions would not be enough to change South Simcoe into the kind of school I envisioned. I spent a good deal of time researching reference material on inner-city schools, assisted by Professor Ken Leithwood, a friend and mentor from the Ontario Institute for Studies in Education at the University of Toronto. As we quickly discovered, the problems of inner-city schools in Canada and the impact of family trauma on children were well documented by statistics.

We also uncovered a great deal of general information on education problems experienced by children in these situations, and the impact of poverty and domestic conflict on society as a whole. But there was very little written on what to do to solve the problems that came into the classrooms as a result of these situations, or best practices and Canadian success stories that we could learn from and use as models.

I moved from the general to the specific: what could I discover about South Simcoe from its records? The answer was devastating, and once again my roller-coaster ride of emotions took a nose-dive. Poring over records provided by the previous principal, I discovered that the attendance rates for South Simcoe Public School were disappointing, as were the academic scores of its students—although on two occasions a child from South Simcoe had won Student of the Year recognition. Schoolyard fighting and bullying were a continual problem. Complaints of disrespect to school staff and local residents were ongoing, and the students were responsible for a high incidence of vandalism and shoplifting in the mall across the street.

But I kept remembering the words of the principal and teachers, and the sudden bright smiles on the faces of the boys and girls I encountered on my visit there. If there are problems, I thought, they certainly don't begin with the children.

When summer vacation arrived, I continued to work on the building, making some major changes. I remembered how, as a child, I had looked forward to my hours at school. School was a bright, pleasant place to be, among adults who, despite whatever frustrations they may have experienced, really wanted to be there. That summer with our new paint job as a background, I recruited friends and family to add some finishing touches and turn the school into a bright, cheerful and welcoming setting for the children.

One of my friends, Wendy, volunteered to make curtains for the windows. She needed accurate measurements but could only accompany me to the school during evening hours. The outgoing principal had warned me against visiting the school at night. Not only did we risk returning to our cars to discover the tires slashed or the paint scratched, but incidents of serious violence were not unknown. In fact, someone was stabbed in the neighbouring strip mall the month I assumed my new position at the school.

So we were already a little nervous when we entered the darkened school late one evening. The custodial staff left hours earlier and the old building was strangely quiet, with dark corners that threatened to conceal all sorts of perils and menace.

Wendy was standing on a ladder holding a measuring tape to the window, and I was dutifully writing down the dimensions she called out to me, when I distinctly heard footsteps in the darkened hall beyond the room.

"Listen!" I hissed.

We stood frozen to the spot as the footsteps approached, heavy and threatening.

Did I lock the front door behind us? I wondered. I was sure I did.

The footsteps stopped, and we heard a door open and close down the hall. Wendy and I looked at each other, holding our breath and trembling a little. The traffic moving outside seemed so remote now. No one would hear us if we screamed.

"We have to see who it is," I whispered.

The footsteps resumed. They were definitely coming closer.

"I can't let you go alone," Wendy said. "I'll come with you." She was using a hammer to place small nails in the window frame, and now she seized it like a weapon.

We both crossed the room and opened the door to the hall, Wendy with the hammer raised and me attempting to hide my fear, with little success. Several feet away, a man confronted us.

"What are you doing here?" I said in my sternest principal voice.

"What am *I* doing here?" he said. "What are *you* doing here?"

I couldn't believe his arrogance. "I am here because I am the principal of this school and I am doing some work," I said in my most authoritative voice. "Now explain who you are."

"I'm the head of security for the School District," he said, "and you obviously did not turn off the alarm when you came in."

All three of us burst into laughter, we were so relieved. Nevertheless I did get a rather stern lecture on the importance of disarming the security system correctly when entering the building, especially late at night. Another lesson.

I sensed this would not be the last frightening incident I would encounter at South Simcoe and, of course, it was not.

My appointment to South Simcoe coincided with the school's seventy-fifth anniversary, and some funds were made available to spruce up the old building in recognition of this milestone. The outgoing principal continued to be gracious and welcoming, and we spent a good deal of time talking to staff and visiting other area schools in search of decorating ideas.

Perhaps it's my Caribbean heritage, but I have always appreciated the ability of colour to set a mood. In Trinidad, colours are vibrant and exciting, and it's a joy to wear clothing in rich reds and bright yellows. I felt the school needed some colour, more of an elegant backdrop for the children's artwork and other displays, leaving the more brilliant colours to be applied here and there in the classrooms. The feeling I wanted everyone to experience when first entering South Simcoe was one of welcome and warmth. We narrowed the colours down, then asked the staff to make a final choice. They selected an off-white finish for the walls with country-blue trim, and the result was perfect.

Among other changes I made was to relocate the principal's office, keeping it on the main floor, the same floor as the grade one classroom. This was, I must confess, partly a practical but also an emotional decision on my part. I wanted to be near loving hugs and smiles provided by "my little darlings," as I called the youngest students, and I wanted to hear them singing together. There are few greater joys to a teacher than the voices of a grade one class joined in song, lustily and joyfully. I expected to encounter frequent challenges to my normal optimistic state, days when I would feel weighted down with doubts and decisions. On those days I knew my spirits would be lifted by the sound of young voices singing in a room down the hall, and if I needed an emotional lift I could always drop in to read stories, or give and receive warm hugs.

In the remaining days and weeks before I welcomed the children on the first day of their new school year at South Simcoe, I focused much of my attention on making the school warm and welcoming. The new paint and bright curtains were just the beginning. I wanted more than a physical environment for learning. I wanted an ambience, a climate, that would wrap the staff and the children in positive feelings and make them feel emotionally safe, as though the school represented the very best place they could be. I wanted the children to be faced with reminders of their value and potential everywhere in the school, and evidence of their successes. Displaying photographs showing them interacting respectfully, performing acts of service and being honored and recognized for their achievements would model valued activities. Affirmations stating positive and inspirational thoughts would focus them on the fact that they had within them, the power to make choices that would take their lives in any direction they wished to travel. I wanted them to anticipate Monday mornings, (many children face such disruption in their lives over the weekend, that it leaves them feeling dejected, and abandoned), and rejoice in their return to the school after the weekend. I wanted them to feel physically and emotionally safe and secure within its walls, and in years to come be able to look back on their time at South Simcoe and remember it as exciting, fulfilling and memorable. All of this may make the school sound more like a loving home than a place of learning, but that's the family environment I felt the children needed.

With the principal's office relocated, I moved the kindergarten to a larger room and found some money in the budget for new toys and furniture. We carpeted the floor, added plants and obtained rocking chairs for the teachers to sit in as they read books to the children gathered around to listen. Does a rocking chair help a teacher read better? Probably not. Does it add a sense of warmth and security for the children who are listening to the story? Does the type of atmosphere this generates help to "turn children on" to books and reading? Somehow it does, and that's all that counted.

I didn't neglect the staff either. I wanted them to know that I valued them as people and understood they needed a place where they could take short breaks during a stressful teaching day, spend quiet time planning and preparing or simply putting their feet up for a minute. The staffroom was relocated out of the basement and onto the main floor. Instead of a dingy refuge, it became a bright and cheerful place for sharing ideas, consultation, celebration and laughter, and it was also more accessible to parents.

Through the balance of the summer we transformed South Simcoe Public School into Cinderella prepared for the ball. Over the Labour Day weekend, just hours before the children were to begin their new school year, Ishwar, Shiva, Rishi and I were busy hanging wallpaper in the staff room and adding plants and attractive posters. It was important, I believed, for the renovation to be completed before the students arrived. I wanted them to have a wonderful surprise. Children arrive on the first day of school looking their best, and I wanted the school to reflect all the pride and optimism they were feeling. The involvement of parents, I knew from a very early stage, would be difficult but absolutely critical. No matter how attractive the school became and how dedicated the staff were, none of the goals we envisioned could be reached without the support of parents.

We needed them to share our high expectations for our children's success. We needed total co-operation and collaboration—not just periodic attendance at school events, but on-going involvement in their children's learning. I also wanted to include them in decision-making and problem-solving. Did this mean parents who were not well educated themselves, could take an active role in the teaching and learning process? Of course!

Even if they didn't all graduate from secondary school themselves, this did not mean that they couldn't hold these aspirations for their children and support them so that they could finish school and go on to other stages of learning. I wanted to make parents and visitors feel welcome at South Simcoe.

I was taught from an early age that you always welcome guests with an offer of something to eat or drink, so I suggested during a staff meeting that we add a coffee machine in the staff room, and offer parents and visitors a cup of coffee. Someone asked who would pay for the coffee. "I will," I replied.

Someone else noted that parents might come in just to enjoy a free cup of coffee. I doubted this would always be the case, but if that's what it took to bring parents into the school, I had no problem with the idea. Eventually, we installed not only a coffee machine but a large selection of teas and a cooler dispensing spring water.

We needed the students to recognize that the changes at South Simcoe were not limited to brighter colours and new décor. We wanted to show that changes had taken place beneath the surface as well, so I proposed a few critical ones at my first formal meeting with the teaching staff.

"We are role models in the way we dress, speak, present, and conduct ourselves," I reminded them. The students, I added, needed to see us dressing, speaking and presenting ourselves according to the same standards we expected from them. They agreed unanimously. This led to us developing a series of agreements, that clearly spelled out what this would feel like, look like and sound like. There was some slight concern when the 'looks like' for attire, including one that jeans and track suits would not be worn by teachers and staff during their teaching time. To offset this, we implemented "South Simcoe Days." These were more casual days, usually on Fridays, when everyone on staff wore South Simcoe Public School T-shirts or sweatshirts. What a beautiful sight it was to see everyone--teachers, principal and custodial staff—all decked out in the school colours, with the school motto and logo emblazoned on the front!

We also agreed that we would all greet the children with a smile and a pleasant "Good morning!" or "Good afternoon!" as they arrived to school. Instead of being seated at our desks, as was the custom, we would be positioned on the stairs, landings and in the hallways, so that the children would be cheerfully greeted and welcomed. By the time they got to their classrooms, they would have been greeted at least three times by a smiling adult and a friendly word. What a wonderful way for them to begin their school day. Greeting people cheerfully and politely is a habit that many people grew up with but it seems to have been lost in recent years. In Trinidad, I remembered being expected to greet everyone with a smile and a friendly word, and this seemed like a worthwhile custom to introduce to South Simcoe.

By putting our guiding principle into practice, *Everyone has the right to be respected and the responsibility to respect others,* .we were creating a physical and emotional foundation for learning and accelerating this process by modelling the way we expected the children to behave. We agreed that as role models we would demonstrate that "respect was a two way street." That meant that even if a child was four years old, they deserved the same respect as an adult. We agreed that we would never raise our voices in anger, speak or act disrespectfully to the children, we knew that keeping our voices and tone calm and respectful would not be easy, after all many adults, including teachers, raise their voices to exert authority. To assist in this area, we agreed that if a child got really angry or out of control, and difficult for a teacher to handle without responding angrily or disrupting the rest of the class, the teacher could find support by sending him to 'cool down' in a designated area of my office. This support was vital, if we were to achieve our goals of being role models, and treating our children with the dignity and respect they had a right to. The whole focus on rights and responsibilities provided the children with a sense of dignity, emotional safety, security, and an awareness that they were loved, cared for, and respected. All of this created a wonderful environment for teaching and learning.

Teaching is always more successful when children feel physically emotionally and intellectually safe. Concerns in these areas are distractions from learning.

As educators, we were determined to focus on what we *could* do instead of dwelling on what we could *not do*. We couldn't change the home conditions or the state of the community around the school any more than we could change the underlying causes of many of these problems. Neither, of course, could the children. But we could provide a safe, healthy, warm and caring environment in which the children could learn, grow, and develop a sense of who they were and who they wanted to become.

This I believed, would be the emotional and psychological foundation for creating success and eliminating problems such as bullying, vandalism, poor attendance and unacceptably low achievement rates.

It was not difficult for us to reach agreement on these issues, once the reasons behind them were explored, discussed and clarified. The ideas represented a substantial change from the current mode of dealing with behaviour. We were delving deeper and going to the root cause as opposed to tackling the surface symptoms that negatively affect learning and achievement. We were moving into areas that would test our personal and professional abilities, but it is what we needed to do in order to make the long term sustainable changes that we wanted. We were setting out on a journey that would positively affect not only the education but also the health and well-being of our children. And as the teachers had been telling me since that first day's visit to South Simcoe, *"The children are the reason we are here!"* Another agreement was that the staff room would become a positive welcoming place, an environment where we would share ideas and feel safe enough to take intellectual risks without fear of criticism, and where "badmouthing" children, parents, other staff members or any aspect of our activities would be banned. Instead, we would share stories of our students' accomplishments, resources, ideas that worked and generally encourage one another whenever we felt discouraged or overwhelmed.

Changes are rarely made in any system without generating discomfort, and that was the case during one of my meetings with the school staff early in my first year at the school. When I proposed moving a classroom from the first floor to the second floor, the teacher angrily—and very loudly—objected. "I have been teaching in that classroom for over twenty years," she said. "And now you come in and tell me you're relocating classrooms and putting me upstairs?"

Someone else added: "You seem to think that moving around classrooms and furniture, and adding a fresh coat of paint here and there is going to solve our problems. Well, they are not. Do you realize the kinds of things we have to deal with here?"

I was taken aback by the anger of these two teachers. Things were going well to this point. Later, I realized that adjusting to so many changes in such a short period of time can bring feelings of frustration and bitterness to the surface.

"We have children who come to school hungry because there is no food in the house," said the teacher who had objected to having her classroom moved. Her name was Sharon McLean, and I knew she cared about her job and the children with a deep passion. I liked that, even if it meant that I became the target of her frustration and concern. "Or they'll come to school half asleep because their parents were fighting all night long. Or they'll show up here with cuts and bruises from being beaten. I can understand that you want to create a wonderful atmosphere for the children, and we've all agreed to support you and your ideas. But what you are doing is not enough. How will paint and new classroom locations solve those problems for the kids?"

"They won't," I agreed calmly. "And I'll admit I still have much to learn. But let's think about this for a moment. Children who are facing the kinds of challenges our children are, need many things, and one of them is a place where they feel welcome, safe, secure, where they feel accepted, appreciated, loved and cared for. When they have this, they will be under less emotional stress, they will be ready to learn and we will have a better chance of reaching them. Our long-term goal is not only to educate them but also to prepare them to take their place in society, and live successfully. In order to do this we have to help them to become more resilient, so that they stay strong, face life's challenges and avoid falling into the same kind of life as their parents. If we can all come together to pursue the common goal of breaking this cycle that our children seem to be caught in and help them to envision and work towards a different future for themselves, they will not only improve behaviourally and academically, they will also become stronger, emotionally, more confident and have a greater sense of self.

We have to help them to develop inner and outer strengths. They have to understand and practice self-respect and respect towards others. We all know that this is a whole lot more than the curriculum but it is probably the only way to make sustainable change. The reason that we are spending all this time, effort and energy is because we want to make long term change. Are we all in agreement about this and are we committed to work towards this? This will take everything we have in us and we have to do it together as a team."I can't do this alone," I said. "It can't just be *my* vision. It has to be *our* **vision.** In fact it isn't even just about our vision, it is also about the **legacy** that we all wish to leave. Therefore it's not a question of giving me your support, it is more about all of us working together in a spirit of harmony to make changes that will last long after the children have left us and gone on to other stages in their lives.

We have to brainstorm together, to feel free to voice our concerns, our ideas and opinions, to be frank with each other about what obstacles we may face, what could go wrong and put strategies in place to deal with this. Most of all, we all need to commit to working together to do whatever is necessary to achieve our common goal of making a positive difference in the lives of the children in this community, by preparing them to live successfully in society. Surely with the children as the ultimate beneficiaries of our efforts, we can agree. Can we do that? Please tell me we can."

We were in agreement for the most part, the few that were not, agreed to work towards the goal and although they did not think that it was worth the extra effort it would take in the early stages, they agreed not to sabotage the group effort.

Sharon McLean continued to be my harshest critic as well as one of my strongest supporters. The same care and concern she had expressed for the children when she raised her voice at me provided the energy to do what needed to be done, and I will forever thank her for that.

Things were still far from complete on that day in September 1991, when I welcomed the children for the first time as principal. But I could tell from the expressions on their faces that they realized changes had occurred at South Simcoe. Their eyes widened at the sight of the bright posters, plants and curtains, and at the teachers who were turned out smartly in jackets, skirts and slacks.

With school underway, I began tackling some additional housecleaning and decluttering chores. I have always believed that when you are surrounded by functional furniture that it is easier for you to function and get your job done. To me keeping the broken and badly mended furniture was like a reminder of past failures. Many old school buildings, old buildings in fact, tend to be collection points for discarded materials, and the sight of them carried a message that was exactly the opposite to what I wanted to convey. I decided that any broken article that could not be restored to its original condition would be dispensed with. There would be no broken furniture and no makeshift shelving in South Simcoe. These would become reminders to the staff and students of the past neglect of the system. It is very common to withhold spending money on facilities that are slated for closure. I wanted to emphasize the future. I was determined to find new ways of accessing resources, and I began to lobby hard with board officials on behalf of the school. After all, I reminded myself, when they sent me to South Simcoe, they knew I would rather store books neatly on a clean floor than have them sitting haphazardly on a broken shelf or table.

When we added newly discarded materials to old broken furnishings that had been stored in the basement over the years, there was a gigantic pile, in fact during the first year, I sent twelve truckloads of unwanted objects back to the school board office.

Naturally, this "It's good or it's gone" attitude left a few holes in our classroom facilities. But with the clutter gone, we had more room to move about our classrooms and make them more functional and conducive to learning.

Then, something occurred that convinced me I was meant to be at South Simcoe, and encouraged my determination to find a way to make things better for children.

Several years earlier, while Ishwar and I were living on campus at the University of Western Ontario, I had made friends with a librarian named Lucy Greene. In fact, Lucy hired me to work in the library with her. Lucy left the library and pursued a career in the business world and by the time I arrived at South Simcoe, Lucy was a senior executive with Sun Life, a giant insurance firm in Toronto, and she was among the first people I called in search of furnishings.

I couldn't believe my luck. Lucy's job and mine fitted together like two pieces of a jigsaw puzzle. Each newly appointed vice-president at Lucy's firm was given new furnishings for his or her office. It's a corporate status thing, I suppose. In any case, perfectly good desks, chairs, sofas and computer tables—some only a few years or even a few months old—were constantly being replaced by new furnishings to match each new executive's personal taste. Company policy prevented the old furniture from being distributed among its employees, so it sat in limbo, waiting for someone who could use it. With Lucy's help and her company's generosity, South Simcoe Public School inherited oak credenzas, cozy sofas, comfortable armchairs and a variety of other fine furniture, a far cry from what we moved out. We added sofas to our staff room and to a special parents' meeting room that we created, desks and tables were replaced. Many of the children (and some of the teachers, we jokingly said) had never curled up in a chair or worked at a desk as comfortable and attractive as the ones they encountered inside the walls of South Simcoe Public School.

Did I call it luck? I believe it was much more than that.

The exterior of the school was more challenging. On Monday mornings we often arrived to discover broken beer bottles on the ground and fresh graffiti on the walls. I never did accept the idea that these things "just happen" to inner-city schools, and I involved our older students in coming up with ideas to solve this problem.

Talking with them, I learned that a supposed "cure" can sometimes cause a bigger problem. That was the case, in part, with South Simcoe. In an effort to avoid vandalism, the school sported no lights on its playground at night. The board felt that if there were no lights, no one would want to be there. The open area however, continued to attract older children, but there was no outlet for their energies, and the prevailing darkness just seemed to encourage silly pranks.

Following the suggestion of our students, we installed lights that turned on whenever anyone was present in the back playground, and added basketball hoops and nets. The vandalism ceased. Our local member of provincial parliament, was so impressed by this single idea that he made a point of stopping by the school and commending us on this gesture of generosity to the youth in our school community.

At this point we made one of those decisions that seemed rather small at the time but proved to be significant in the message it carried. When we asked for basketball equipment, someone at the board office offered hoops and backboards that could be removed and stored inside the school building at the end of each day, to thwart vandalism. We were grateful for the offer, we knew that they meant well, but we politely refused. The message would be precisely opposite to the one I wanted conveyed to the children and the community. I didn't want anything on or in the school that suggested we didn't trust the kids, or that we didn't want them on the school grounds after hours. To children who wanted to burn off energy, this would have been a slap in the face. So, we insisted on installing hoops and nets that remained in place for anyone who wanted to use them.

It worked! Over time, the broken bottles and graffiti decreased, and one morning we arrived to discover the basketball court festooned with a hundred colourful balloons. "It's a thank-you note," one parent said, and I agreed with her totally.

We launched a series of informal chats with senior students at the school to involve them as young leaders in the changes being made and to enlist their help in accomplishing them. Traditionally it is the children who excel academically or in other areas. who are seen as leaders. We opened up the definition of leadership to include children who traditionally would not have been seen as having leadership potential. Some of the best ideas that we ever heard came from children we would not have expected to make a contribution like that. During one of our sessions, I casually suggested that it would be nice for the school to have a mascot, that we could identify as ours, it would be an expression of our pride and our identity, something fun and playful for all the children. They loved the idea, and promised to get input from all the students, then put their heads together and select one. I assumed they would choose something warm and friendly to reflect the peaceful nature we were trying to create at South Simcoe. You can imagine my horror when the students suggested...a shark! "Sharks are mean, cold-blooded predators," I reminded them. "They attack and eat people. Who could ever want something as vicious as a shark for a mascot?" "That's the whole idea," said Ryan, one of our more shy students. "We want a mean mascot for sports, one that will scare the other team. But he can be a friendly mascot to the school."

Then he pulled out a pencil and began drawing, with surprising talent, a whole family of friendly sharks, some smiling and winking, and others working. I was so impressed by his talents and his thought process, we would never have thought that Ryan would speak up like this, far less take charge. Empowering the children to choose the mascot unleashed in children like Ryan a level of leadership, creativity and innovative thinking that might not have emerged in the course of regular classroom activities. (How often do children like Ryan get passed over when choosing student leaders?)

Once the shark mascot was agreed upon, one of the teachers, Kim Hutchinson, drafted her mother-in-law, Pauline, to depict it throughout the school. We hired Kim directly out of teachers' college; in addition to being an outstanding teacher, Kim added to the school's success through the sheer power of her enthusiasm.

Pauline was a gifted artist, and within weeks the lower floor of the school had sharks everywhere. Every classroom in the school displayed our shark mascot, and next to it we added the school logo, motto, school and classroom goals, and respectful relationship agreements. This was an anchor point for every classroom.

A shark stood with poised pencil and steno pad on the walls of the school office, and a bespectacled shark, painted on the wall of our library, read a book among shark-infested banners that invited students to "Come take a bite out of a book!" Sharks peeked around corners in the downstairs hall, and we even had a shark in the custodian's room—holding a dustpan, of course.

The children were delighted! For some reason kids are fascinated by fearsome creatures like sharks and dinosaurs. Our sharks were as friendly as you would ever want (or *not* want!) to meet, and their presence were a source of pride for everyone. I later learned that sharks are not predators of people but that they are survivors; an interesting choice, don't you think?

Somewhere along the way the staff began referring to me as Mother Bird. I suppose it was in response to the way I kept talking about nurturing our children until they were prepared to leave the nest and fly off to bigger and better things. "If I'm the Mother Bird," I said jokingly, "then South Simcoe is my nest now." The idea of me watching over my "fledglings" was carried one step further when someone contributed a jar of Gummy Worms to my office, and the staff began stopping by to nibble on them like a flock of hungry baby birds themselves.

The "Mother Bird" nickname launched Pauline on a new round of mural painting. She found some corners of the school that did not sport a shark, and there she displayed nests of baby birds and a mother arriving to feed them. A little room off the library was painted to depict a Victorian English country garden, with blooming flowers and vines climbing up an elaborate trellis. Joan, our librarian, added lace curtains to the window opening and placed large, comfy cushions on the floor against the wall. It became "The South Simcoe Secret Garden." We knew the young children would want to curl up there and read books, and they did. But they soon were joined by older children as well, who were drawn to the beauty of this little corner that sat dark, empty, and unused for so many years.

The shark proved to be a great mascot for the children and their sports teams, but something more was needed. We needed a symbol to represent our hopes and aspirations for the children. To continue creating a sense of identity, a feeling of belonging, we set to work on a motto and a logo, that would show what we stood for, and could use on all official school materials and documents.

We brainstormed with the children, staff, parents and many of our community partners. We began with the Lamp of Learning, the symbol for all schools in the Durham Region. Lamps provide light, and light leads us through darkness. Then we added hands to symbolize people reaching out and joining together in partnership. Then we agreed on a motto to articulate our style and our philosophy of inclusion, *Together We Light the Way.*

The motto was great, everyone loved it , but our symbol needed an artist's touch. One of our students told us about her father's skill as a graphic artist, so I invited the father in to meet with us and discuss making our school symbol more pleasing to the eye. He listened attentively to our ideas, promised to enhance the design, and left.

Weeks passed and we saw nothing of the father nor the symbol. When I asked Sara what had become of her father and his promise to create a symbol for South Simcoe, her response was, unfortunately, not surprising.

"Dad's been drinking again," she said, disappointed. "But I'll see if I can get him back here."

She must have been persuasive, because the father showed up again, promised to create the symbol again…and vanished again.

This went on for a few weeks, until I realized that some drastic action was needed if South Simcoe were to have its own school symbol before I retired. The next time he arrived, at his daughter's request, I closed the door to my office, handed him a pencil, several sheets of paper and some coloured markers, and said, half-jokingly, that he would not be permitted to leave until he finished his assignment. It made me feel like a primary school teacher again—but it worked.

He was such a talented artist that he produced a wonderful symbol for us in purple and yellow, the school colours. I especially like the way the two hands encircled the lamp of learning in a gesture that fit our concept of creating a healthy, safe and caring learning community, protecting the children while they were learning and growing. *Together We Light The Way*, we had our motto and now our symbol, a beautiful one, illustrating that we were all working together to light the path of learning for our children!

At the core of my beliefs about educating children, is the value of helping them to develop relationships based on mutual respect. At the time this seemed to extend beyond the mandate of the education system, but I felt that the importance of relationship building was an area within schools that was underestimated. Creating relationships built on mutual respect was the foundation on which a major part of our success rested.

I remembered a childhood lesson from my grandmother. She showed me a bucket of water, the surface of the water as flat and unmarred as a sheet of glass. "You must always be kind and respectful, to others" she told me, "and everything you do must be done with thought, caring and love." Then she poked her index finger into the water. "This is you, the person you are in your heart." She said, indicating her finger. "And this is what happens whenever you do or saysomething." She pointed with her other hand at the ripples radiating from her finger, disturbing the water. "When you do or say something," she continued, "It affects other people, it affects everything and everyone around you, so you should think good thoughts about people and treat them as you would like to be treated yourself. Always remember that."

I remembered her lesson and later when we created the Circles of Respectful Relationships graphic, we described it in the same way. It all begins with you.

Respect for yourself, was the finger she had poked through the surface of the water. The first circle was you, the self, (later, as the programs were embraced by other cultures some groups made an additional circle inside the self with the label Creator, in some cases God), the circles radiating out from it represented your family, your classroom and school family. Then, as the circles widened, they reached beyond the people and places immediately around us to include the local and global community. Imagine, your one action can affect so many people. Imagine, one person can have all that impact!

As we worked with the children, we explained: when you truly respect people, you treat them with caring, kindness and love. You encourage them. You treat them with the same respect you yourself want to receive. You respect their cultures and traditions, their race and gender, you avoid racism, sexism and ridicule of any kind.

Respect for the local community comes easily when you see them as people, as friends and neighbours, as people with whom you want to have a positive relationship. You respect their property, their goods and services, you respect the fact that they, like others, are trying to earn a living and that destruction or vandalism of their property can cost them their livelihood. The police, the firefighters, and other community groups work hard to keep the community a safe place in which you can live. The senior citizens have all contributed to the community and now it is your turn to contribute to them by helping them to feel safe, cared for and respected.

Respect for the global community goes hand in hand with respect for the environment. You must take the time to think about the impact of your actions on others who, though far away, also have the right to be respected. So when you create less garbage for example, you contribute to the greater good by creating a cleaner world for them, for yourself, as well as for many others..

Understanding and relating to others and developing and sustaining relationships with them is a very important part of life. Let's make sure that every time we interact with another person, we leave them with the great feeling that comes from being treated with kindness and respect, we leave them 'feeling good.'. Our Respectful Relationships program embodied these values and it was the foundation on which all initiatives and activities were created at South Simcoe.

When asked, "How did you people manage to achieve so much in that school?" we always referred the questioner to this foundation of respectful relationships. The answer was there. It all begins with you!

Keeping a school clean and tidy is always a challenge, and in spite of the transformation that was taking place, this remained a concern at South Simcoe. In a meeting I held with Gail and Randy, the custodians, Gail explained that she was allotted only half an hour to clean each classroom. Most of the time, she informed me, was spent on removing pencils, pieces of erasers, crumpled papers and other discarded materials from the floor, where they had been tossed by students.. "That doesn't leave me much time for dusting and cleaning," she said.

I asked if she had any suggestions for solving the problem. Gail noted, that while we were emphasizing teamwork and respect for others in the school, it didn't seem to be applied to helping the custodial staff—and she was right. "If we can just get the kids to see things from my point of view, maybe they would understand how they are making things difficult for me," she said.

I thought this was a great idea and invited her to explain things to the senior classes. It seemed to me that the children should assume some responsibility for their school's cleanliness.

The next day in the classroom, Gail arrived to explain the problem to the children. She entered with a vacuum cleaner and I watched open-mouthed as she dramatically emptied its contents onto the floor in front of the students. "This is what I picked up from your room yesterday," she told them. She could have picked up even more, she explained, but some items kept clogging her vacuum. "I can't clean your classroom as well as I would like to, because I spend so much of my time picking things off the floor, things that you could be putting in the wastebasket or storing away in your cupboards and desks. If you did your share, I could do a much better job, we would be a team."

The children were aghast. They had no idea of the extra work they were creating for Gail. No one ever took the time to explain things this way. Whatever the reason, they immediately began apologizing for the extra work they were creating for an already overworked woman, and began putting their heads together to find a solution.

"How about a fifteen-minute cleanup session at the end of every day?" one child suggested, and the rest agreed. When the children saw how well this solution was working, they wanted to help Gail even more, so they accompanied her from classroom to classroom, explaining the problem and their solution and over the course of a few months, the children's idea of the fifteen-minute cleanup session at the end of the day was adopted by the entire school. Not only did these children solve their own problem, by using the principle of respect for themselves and others, to guide their decision-making, they also demonstrated their leadership and their ability to influence others for the common good.

This improved things for the whole school. The children stepped up without being asked and showed all of us what they were capable of, if given the opportunity.

And it didn't stop there. A week later the two custodians came up with a method of recognizing the children's efforts in the school. Each Friday, Gail and Randy selected the cleanest classroom for that week and presented them with the Golden Dustpan Award to be displayed proudly. The custodians purchased a dustpan, covered it with gold paint and added a drawing of our shark mascot to it. Every classroom in the school vied to win it at least once during the school year. As a result, we not only had a cleaner school, but two smiling custodians as well. We also, I hasten to add, had a smarter principal, who realized she could learn a great deal by listening carefully to the staff and students, involving them in developing effective solutions to problems and inviting others to participate in the leadership process.

One day I received a telephone call from a warm and gracious man name Carl Rimar. Carl, a member of the local Kiwanis Club, heard of our accomplishments from a social worker and liked the inclusive approach that we were adopting. "You're on the right track," he assured us and asked how he and other members of his club could partner with us to assist us. I suggested that Carl could begin by reading to our younger children and spending time chatting with our older ones. He arrived to do this on Monday afternoons. He was so enthusiastic that the children quickly warmed to him. In fact, Mondays became Carl Rimar days at the school, so many children looked forward to his visits. He was warm and loving with a grandfatherly presence and he enthralled the younger children by reading stories aloud in his mellow voice. Older students grew to trust Carl as a mentor, as a "Dutch Uncle," a man to whom they could vent their frustrations and concerns and always receive a sympathetic hearing.

I began referring to Carl as my Guardian Angel, because he arrived in the early days when I desperately needed someone like him—an understanding and compassionate man who said, simply: "How can I help you." Over time, we learned to consult Carl about new ideas. We would brainstorm them with Carl and bounce suggestions off him to help decide which concepts were practical and which needed more planning. We valued his wisdom and opinions, especially because he was guided by the same principles and values that we were, and always kept in mind our guiding question, our covenant, *What's best for our children?*

Carl submitted ideas of his own, and when he proposed holding a weekend bicycle safety rodeo for the children, we agreed it was a good one. He suggested holding the rodeo at the school. We would start early on a Saturday morning and the children would learn the importance of wearing a safety helmet, how to check their bikes for safety and how to negotiate an obstacle course. As icing on the cake, Carl's Kiwanis Club would donate a brand new bicycle to be won in a raffle.

I loved the idea, but I had to agree with some of Sharon McLean's concerns. Friday night was Party Night in the South Simcoe area, and many of the children might have difficulty arriving for an early start on Saturday morning—not to mention the adult volunteers. We never held an event like this in the school, which made the response of the children unpredictable. What if no one showed up? What if it rained? What if…?We ran the gamut of what-ifs and decided to hold the First Annual South Simcoe Bike Safety Rodeo in spite of many misgivings. Even if just twenty people showed up early on Saturday morning, I pointed out, we could consider the event a success; so let's do it. With Sharon's realistic cautions in mind, we went ahead with organizing the event, and I went home on Friday evening looking forward to it.

When I woke up early the next morning and looked out my bedroom window, I saw rain. Steady, depressing, drizzly rain falling from a low grey sky. As I dressed and prepared to drive to the school, I refused to accept the possibility of being defeated by bad weather, and I began willing the rain away. The rain was still falling when I arrived at the school about eight o'clock, and there were several large puddles on the yard. Soon, a half-dozen soggy community partners joined me. "Let's will the sun to arrive!" I announced, which generated some uncertain smiles from Carl and the others.

Wouldn't you know it? Things got better almost immediately. The rain soon became a light mist and ceased completely. The small group grew steadily with the improving weather until, by ten-thirty, about a hundred children, Kiwanis Club members and parent volunteers were on hand. Soon the sun was shining in all its warmth, the puddles were vanishing, the children were learning important safety rules, and the Kiwanis members were fulfilling their mandate of providing important services to the community.

Wow! Did we bring the sun out that day by the sheer force of our will and determination that nothing would spoil the day for our children? Doubt it if you will, but I remain convinced anyway.

Lessons for all of us were learned in various ways at South Simcoe. When we heard from a parent whose mother had attended the school, that South Simcoe once boasted lovely rose gardens along the south wall, we decided to restore the grounds to their original splendour. That spring, Jacki Devolin, one of our teaching assistants, recruited a team of students to canvass the neighbourhood for volunteers, old garden tools and bedding plants.

Many of the people they approached were pleasantly surprised to learn we were not looking for money. We didn't want their money— we wanted their support and involvement as a community. Nor would their contributions benefit the school exclusively. In fact, since the flowers would be planted just prior to the school's closing for summer vacation, the neighbourhood would enjoy their beauty as much as anyone at the school. Sharon proposed planting flowers in front of the nearby Legion Hall as well, as a thank you gesture, for them letting us use their facilities anytime we needed them.

We had another, more subtle motive behind our gardening efforts. We wanted to demonstrate how many things of little or no value to others—including used and often broken garden tools, rejected spindly plants, and even the long-ignored grounds surrounding the school—could be put to good use with a little care, time and effort.

We organized our first Community Celebration Day and not even the heavy rain that day could dampen the enthusiasm of our planting team. Included on the team were Ruth, our school trustee; two local business people; members of community organizations; and a large team of teachers and students. At Ruth's suggestion, we all cut armholes in plastic garbage bags, slid them on as waterproof vests, tied others around our heads as hats, and set to work.

Once again, we discovered we set something in motion that was much larger than anticipated. We all took turns watering the flowers during the summer, but more than our periodic efforts were necessary to keep the flowers blooming. Two employees of the Kmart store (Now Zellers) in the plaza across the street began to eat lunch beneath the trees in our garden. When they noticed the flowers were wilting from the heat, they borrowed a sprinkling can from the store's garden display and watered them thoroughly.

Our second Community Day included a small fun fair on the playground, complete with ponies carrying delighted children on their backs, who were led around the grounds by two staff members. Inside the school, invited guests munched on cookies and sandwiches, and were entertained by songs and presentations from each class.

From then on, Community Celebration Day seemed to acquire a life of its own. In the following years members of our planting team included the mayor, various politicians, school board members, mascots from local businesses, several police officers and firefighters, and so many other volunteers that we were running short of room to plant the flowers. Many Grade eight students, who were on their way to high school, offered to tend the flowers during the summer vacation.

Community Celebration Day activities eventually moved directly into the classrooms. Our community partners were invited to visit the classes and talk to the children about what they were learning and achieving and what in particular helped them to be successful, whether it was a particular educational strategy, or working with a particular community partner, sometimes it was simply knowing that one of our partners cared about them and wanted them to do well. This was such a win-win situation because our partners were able to see the difference they were making to the education and well-being of the children and the children relished the opportunity to show off their achievements to interested and caring adults.

In every classroom, students placed their *Together We Light the Way* portfolios on their desks, prepared to discuss their accomplishments one-on-one with their visitors. These accomplishments were wide-ranging and invariably impressive to the partners—not just because of the way the children described the good choices they made and the goals they achieved, but the manner in which they supported their stories with evidence. They all used some type of graph to trace their progress in Reading, Writing and Mathematics. Other areas depended on the needs of the particular individual.

We learned several lessons from Community Celebration Day. We discovered that everyone likes to be part of a success story, and once word of our success spread, we never again had to go out asking for assistance, we often received more offers than we could handle.

Community Celebration Day also taught a lesson to the small handful of skeptics. "The school planted flowers there before." they said when we first proposed the idea, "and vandals always ripped them out." None of the flowers from CommunityCelebration Day were ripped out. Why? Because "the school" didn't plant them. They were planted by the entire community, including the students, the staff and the mayor, plus police officers, firefighters, business people, mascots and service club members. So many people could say, "this is our garden".

Other lessons were learned from the garden as well, including some we neither wanted nor anticipated. One day, when an overenthusiastic student knocked off a branch from one of the young trees planted on our grounds, he began to use it as a weapon, chasing others across the play area. They in turn ripped more branches from the tree to fight back, and before Cathie, one of the supervising teachers, could bring a halt to the mayhem, ten branches had been torn from the little tree.

Cathie carried them in her arms to my office, her eyes welling up. "Look what they did, Sandra," she said. "Look what the kids did. I can't believe it after all the work we have done teaching them to respect the environment.""No", I couldn't believe it. "Not our kids?" I said.

"Yes," she said, "*our* kids."

"Tell me they're all new to our school," I almost pleaded. South Simcoe kids didn't go around destroying property. They respected their school and the environment, and this kind of thing went against everything we were striving to teach them. These must be new students who weren't yet tuned in to our ways .

"No Sandra, they're not new," she said. "These are students who have been here for a couple of years, they just got carried away."

I rarely became angry, but this one struck a nerve. "I need to see them all," I said to Cathie. It meant removing children from class, something I rarely did, but it was an expression of how seriously we took such a breach of our agreement to respect the environment. I was also disappointed and frustrated.

With all the children gathered in my office, looking sheepish and, I admit, a little anxious, I displayed the branches to them. "How could this happen?" I asked. "How could our children, students of this school, do such a thing? How could children such as you, who take pride in our school and our gardens, do such damage? Please explain this to me."

They blurted out a series of explanations. "We were just fooling around." "We got carried away." "We didn't mean to."

I could see they were truly sorry, but I also saw an opportunity to teach an important lesson. Children, I knew, could seem to be destructive when they were simply being thoughtless.

"Do you realize you severely injured a living thing?" I asked them. They hadn't considered things in that light before. "A tree has life," I said. "A different kind of life from your own, but it's still a life." I held the branches up for them to see. "This is what you did to a living thing." Then I set the branches on a table in my office and sat staring at them, as though I were mourning them, while the children found their way back to their classes.

The next day I carried the branches in my arms from class to class and explained what had happened to them. I didn't name the children responsible for the damage, because that was not our practice. I wanted everyone to understand the seriousness of the matter. I explained how sad it made me and the other teachers, how the torn branches demonstrated a complete lack of respect for a living thing, for the environment, and how this was a dishonouring of our agreement to respect the environment. It was certainly not the kind of behaviour that we expected from our wonderful children at South Simcoe. Then I asked for suggestions to ensure this type of behaviour never happened again.

The students thought very seriously about this. Some even proposed that anyone who went closer than ten feet to a tree should be suspended. We did not go that far, of course. The point was made, and the lesson was learned. The offending children offered to work with the custodian in the garden to make amends for their actions and restore the area around the tree.

Our care for the garden, in many ways reflected our care for the children who attended the school, and the garden generated so much beauty that South Simcoe Public School won the 1995 "Looking Good Award" as the most attractive of all 120 elementary schools within the board's jurisdiction.

Changes to the school's inner and outer appearance were making an impact, no doubt. The children were feeling more connected to their school and their peers. They took great pride in their achievements and in their school, as did the community. They

47

took care to keep it clean and tidy. They loved being surrounded by affirmations and photographs evidencing their success. They were polite and respectful and they truly felt a sense of ownership for all that had occurred, because they helped to create it.

But the major challenge, I knew, lay ahead. We had to do more work with the children. We had to help them make the changes within, believe in themselves and their capabilities, envision a brighter future for themselves, then help them to acquire the skills and strategies that would ensure they improved academically. This involved so much more than exterior appearance, it involved touching their hearts as well as their minds and even deeper.

LEADER'S REFLECTION

Leadership in others is best awakened and nurtured in a healthful, vibrant and inclusive environment.

- What do you do to create an environment that is conducive to others awakening to their own uniqueness, then leading in their own right, regardless of their job desciption?

- How do you nurture leadership in others?

CHAPTER 4

Loss And Renewal

As we grew up many of us were told that the more you give love, the more you receive it in return. But nothing prepares you for the hole left in your heart when you lose someone you love. The unexpected loss I suffered during that first year at South Simcoe was no less painful and searing just because I was learning to love the school, the staff, the children and my work. In some ways, these made it more agonizing.

I came to South Simcoe Public School with many hopes and expectations, but with very few answers. In fact, I learned there is never a single answer or set of answers when dealing with the challenges facing the children of areas such as South Simcoe. Because we did not want to have "band-aid solutions" to the problems our children were facing, we always tried to get to the root cause of problems. This unearthed a complexity of issues that we never imagined. Layer after layer of risk factors accumulated over the years and over the generations. Finding solutions was challenging to say the least.

We didn't have many resources so we worked with what was available. We had to rely heavily on the collective life experience and wisdom of staff, students, parents and community partners. We worked together to create a climate where everyone felt comfortable making suggestions, collaborating on a plan of action and moving forward together.

During September of my first year at South Simcoe, two grade eight boys raced down the hall towards my office, followed by several other worried students. I heard them coming, shouting as they ran: "Where's the principal? Where's the principal?"

"What's the problem?" I asked, "what is going on.?" "A man in a truck tried to take away two of our girls!" they said.

The abduction of a student is a nightmarish fear faced by teachers and parents alike. I asked where the girls were, trying to conceal my apprehension.

"We have them," one boy said, and the other added, "They're only six years old." The girls were walking home through the mall opposite the school when a man drove up in a van and offered them some candy. When they approached to take it from his hand, he tried to pull them inside. The two grade eight boys, witnessing the attempted abduction, rushed to the vehicle and pulled the girls away. The boys also alertly recorded the van's license number, proving that despite—or because of—the challenges confronting many children at South Simcoe, they were very streetwise.

Two detectives arrived in response to my telephone call and interviewed me, the grade eight boys and the little girls who were almost abducted. When they completed the interviews and began to leave, one of the girls tugged at my skirt. "Ask for their badge numbers," she said, indicating the officers.

I was a little confused, and asked why, "In case you need more information," she replied. Even the detectives were impressed. "She's right," one of them said. "You need both an incident number and a badge number. That way, when you need information about the progress of the case, we can quickly find the information and bring you up to date on the progress of things."

After the police left, I looked down at this little waiflike beauty who, just an hour or so before, had narrowly missed being abducted in broad daylight by a repulsive pervert. "Are you all right?" I asked. She smiled as though to reassure me, the adult and professional educator. "Yes, I'm fine," she said. Then she asked if I was all right, and advised me not to worry. With the excitement behind her, and confident I survived the event as well as she had, she skipped down the hall as though she didn't have a worry in the world Me? I remained frazzled for the rest of the day.

We were continually being surprised by the street-smart character and maturity of the students at South Simcoe. One day a member of our staff, a bright young teacher named Doug Beeston, was reading to a kindergarten class. They remained quiet and attentive until Doug came to a passage in the book that referred to babies springing from cabbage patches. Suddenly the entire class shot their hands up in the air. "That's not where they come from!" the children protested, and before Doug could respond, one boy began reciting the process of procreation in exquisite and colourful detail while all the other children nodded soberly in agreement.

The children were calm about the event, but Doug was still flustered when he described the incident to me later that day. "I hope you don't get any complaints from parents about what went on in my classroom today, I just wanted to read them a story," he said. "I didn't want to teach a sex education class to a bunch of five year olds." I assured him we all had much to learn from our street-wise student body.

Other events faced by the staff were not quite as humorous, and often more dramatic. One day early in September, I called in a supply teacher for a teacher who was ill. Unfortunately this was a class in which several children had mental health issues and the supply teacher had no real experience with this type of situation. The children's behaviour was very challenging, and, halfway through her teaching day, she threw up her hands and told me that she was leaving, she had had enough. This left me with no one except Andrea, a new teacher, to supervise the class. Upon entering the classroom, Andrea discovered one of the students, an extremely bright girl with significant mental health issues, sitting in a corner, barking like a dog. The girl had removed her shoes and stockings and placed wads of tissues between her toes, so that her feet were more like paws. While this was happening, another young student was performing somersaults across the desks, risking broken bones or worse, and a third announced that Andrea was not to speak directly to her but only to her stuffed toy mouse.

Andrea said it was like entering a setting for a *Twilight Zone* episode. There was total pandemonium in the class. This was in sharp contrast to other classrooms where children were working and moving about quietly and respectfully. Fortunately, Andrea was able to deal with the situation by making agreements with the children and using some of the behavioural techniques we taught new teachers.

She knew that the girl who was barking like a dog suffered from a multiple personality disorder, and was awaiting placement in a high-care facility. The student who insisted on the teacher talking not to her but to her "pet mouse" was undergoing serious psychological trauma. Andrea remained calm throughout the afternoon, simply redirecting inappropriate behaviour, or giving children "safe places" in which to calm down, or sort themselves out. (A safe place was an agreed-upon, supervised location, such as my office or the library, where a student could withdraw until his or her anger subsided. An older child could even, under special circumstances, and with permission, leave the school and calm down alone on the playground, if that was the agreed upon course of action). Andrea was calm and took charge. Once the children realized this they too became calmer.

Often, it seemed as though each time we solved a problem or overcame an obstacle, another appeared to take its place. How could we possibly keep up with this volume of new (and sometimes reappearing) challenges? For us, the answer was openly discussing the problems at staff meetings and putting our heads together to come up with solutions. I was always amazed at the power of this process. Strategies and techniques were shared and practical, doable and cost-effective solutions were developed.

So instead of the traditional monthly staff meetings, we scheduled meetings every two weeks. With all the problems to deal with, the issues to resolve, and the time this kind of collaborative approach took, a month was too long a period between meetings. We knew if we left things that long, issues would pile up and we would never get through them all in a reasonable time frame. Many of our staff members had young children and couldn't stay for a two hour staff meeting, plus who wants to stay two hours after school attending a meeting when you are tired and have lessons to plan for the next day and families to attend to? After exploring a number of different scenarios, we agreed we would have staff meetings every two weeks and in order to honour and respect the fact that everyone had life commitments beyond the school, we agreed that each meeting would be no more than an hour in length. We did not want our meetings to place any undue stress on anyone, what would be the point?

How did we manage to fit in all of our issues and give so many people time to express their views in just one hour? We looked after personal and professional needs. We structured the meetings in such a way that they elicited conversation and dialogue, we took care of the physical and emotional needs of participants by giving everyone the opportunity to have input into the agenda, we provided snacks and music, and we started and **finished** on time. We all focused on making the meetings informative, productive and fun. We always focused on the positive. We kept asking, "What can we learn from one another, what ideas can we share, what worked well?" and "What can we do to make it even more effective?" Everyone who attended our meetings grew assured that their opinions were valued and their ideas would be given serious consideration. This did more than generate effective ideas—it also gave everyone a true sense of partnership in the running of the school. We became a large, inclusive and cohesive team sharing leadership, and all committed to the goal of making a positive difference in the lives of our children.

During my first year at South Simcoe, it quickly became apparent the most immediate goal, academically, was teaching the children to read. When I taught grade one, my goal was to have my students reading by the end of the school year. Yet, during that first year at South Simcoe, we had large numbers of students unable to read in grade five. This was not acceptable .

This was a reflection of the reality of the South Simcoe community, the transient nature of many families there, and the social and economic difficulties faced by both the parents and children. When students are being distracted by major problems at home—problems ranging from hunger to severe physical and mental abuse—the intense concentration required for learning simply vanishes.

Working with trustee Ruth Lafarga, we started small and set ourselves the realistic goal of every South Simcoe student reading by grade five. We knew that achievement of this goal was impossible without the wholehearted support and assistance of the parents. To involve them, we added a component to our monitoring and measuring system. Goal-setting and achievement booklets were developed and sent home with every student in the 'Wednesday Envelope' to inform parents of the goal set by the teacher and the child, the progress made at the end of every day, strategies the teacher was using that were working well and suggestions as to how the parents could assist. It was like having a customized weekly report card.

All students had weekly booklets, and those needing higher levels of support took their booklets home with them daily. There were always three questions that children were to reflect and comment on at the end of the day.

What have I done well today?

What helped me to succeed?

What do I need to focus on tomorrow?

The booklets served several purposes. First, they were a medium of communication between teachers and parents. Since we asked parents to make comments on them, sign and return them, they were able to use this system to communicate with us about anything, even the smallest thing that might get in the way of a child's success, for example, the child may not have homework completed because the family was out late and there was no time for homework. The children learned that we cared about their parents' opinions, and that the parents cared about what the school was saying, that we both held the same high expectations for them, and were working together to help them to succeed. Finally, they involved the parents in the goal setting and achievement process and prevented surprises at report card time.

Using this system effectively and integrating it into all classrooms took some time. We began by introducing the system in one class, working out the details, working through the problems and refining the system. Then we added three more classes in the second year and by the third year, this strategy was being used throughout the school.

It was Sharon McLean who said; "This system is good but it takes time to learn how to use it properly; please go slowly, and give everyone time to catch their breath." Comments like these would cause me to reassess the pace at which we were moving and usually slow down a little. They also encouraged an honest and open dialogue about the difficulties being encountered with implementation of a new idea however good, how we could refine the system in a way that would benefit everyone, not just those who could adapt to change quickly. This led to everyone embracing the entire monitoring and measuring process, a process which strengthened us as a team and yielded many rewards.

Inevitably, regrettable incidents occurred. Once, when handed a class set of report cards to sign, I reminded a veteran male teacher that we had agreed as a staff to two things about the report cards; one that they would be written in simple language that was easy for the parents to understand, and two, that the opening comment on every report card leaving the school would be a positive one about the child, FIND THE GOOD, after all we were writing to a parent about their child. Some simple adjustments to his report cards were necessary. He had never in all his 28 years of teaching had anyone ask him to adjust his report cards, certainly not a brand new principal; he responded by throwing the report cards on my desk and swearing at me in front of a group of parents and students who happened to be passing in the main hallway. I put on a brave face, but I admit I drove home in tears, I hated being yelled at and I certainly was not used to anyone swearing at me..

The next day, following the advice of the teachers' federation representative, I set up a meeting with this same teacher to figure out how we could solve our problem. I wanted the report cards fixed and he felt he spent enough time working on them, plus he had little time left before the due date. In addition he was tired because he stayed up half the night working on them and thought that they were very good. I agreed to give him extra time to work on them during the school day, since he felt he simply could not find positive things to say without first having another conversation with his children. He appreciated the extra time he was given; I appreciated the advice from the Teachers' Federation; he agreed to redo his report cards and we shook hands, vowing to make every effort to work together to make a positive difference for our children. I learned I could be yelled at and survive, and most of all that flexibility is a part of every successful negotiation.

Many things were falling into place and progress was being made. Our goals, which some once said were overly ambitious and unattainable, were now being achieved. Christmas was coming and we were all looking forward to another term of student success amidst the joy of the holiday season. It would also bring, of course, a much-needed break for all of us.

Then, on the very afternoon that I was handed the rewritten report cards, my brother called to inform me that my father had died. The words came to me through a blur of emotion and gloom. A heart attack. No warning. Sixty-six years old, much too young. Funeral plans. Family gathering.

The death of a parent is traumatic for everyone, and I do not intend to suggest that I suffered any more pain or sadness than someone else in my position. But, everything seemed so *unfair*. Here I was, determined to improve the lives of children, creating a team of wonderfully dedicated professionals, achieving success beyond measure and I was so busy I couldn't remember the last time I told my father I loved him. What did all my achievements mean now?

They meant as much as ever, of course. I knew that in my heart. but as the eldest child in our family I enjoyed a special relationship with my father. When I was a small child, he would rock me gently on his knee and read to me from storybooks. He taught me how to draw flowers and he had a special way of whistling my name as I arrived home from school. He told me I was the most special girl in the world and that I could do anything and become anything I wanted to as long as I remained strong inside, remembered who I was and remembered he believed in me and would always believe in me no matter what! Naturally, I believed him, and that belief kept me strong over the years and through all the tough times in life. It is at the core of who and what I am today.

I know millions of parents express the same kind of love and support to their children each day, and their children are blessed because of it. But, this was *my* father saying these things to *me*, and despite what my mind knew, my heart always believed he would live forever. Now he was gone, without even a goodbye spoken between us. He was the first close relative I lost to death and to say I was devastated as I replaced the receiver after that telephone call…well, there are no words to describe my emotions.

With guidance from the board office, things were quickly put in place for me to go to the funeral. Someone was assigned to oversee the school and assume my duties. Then I set off for my sad journey to Trinidad.

The days I spent there are now a jumble of memories—tears, hugs, stories of my father's kindnesses, and a reaffirmation of all that my family meant to me. I returned to Canada during the Christmas vacation with a strange longing simply to stay at home. As much as I loved the kids and the challenge I accepted at South Simcoe, I was emotionally drained and unable to find the energy to continue dealing with the stress and struggle involved in realizing my vision for the school.

Let's face it, I discovered myself thinking one day, you are an inexperienced principal dealing with some very experienced staff members, and you are trying to make a lot of changes without alienating those around you. You may believe in what you are doing, but until everyone around you believes, shares the same vision with the same passion and commits to undertaking the journey, you aren't going to achieve your goals. Accept that making the changes you envision will be a long, slow and often painful process. I was ready to listen.

Some obstacles at the school that seemed overwhelming had nothing to do with the children or the staff. In spite of assistance from surprising sources, such as my friend at the insurance company, the school still needed essential items like good bulletin boards and carpeting. The delays in obtaining furnishings, materials and resources, and the tight restrictions on expenditures, were doubly frustrating because we were starting to see what we could accomplish with the appropriate resources. I knew that other schools were facing the same challenge of limited funds and restrictions, but it seemed doubly unfair to us at South Simcoe. In my emotional state, I seriously questioned whether I could maintain the confidence I had shown to others—a confidence I felt eroding within me after my father died. I simply did not want to return to South Simcoe. I wanted only to stay at home, where I felt safe, warm and loved. That's when another of those events that others call "luck" occurred. I prefer to think of it as proof of the Eastern proverb: *When the student is ready, the teacher will appear.*

During the holidays, about a week before school resumed, at the very height of my self-doubts, I began to express my uncertainties to a friend, she suggested I speak to a man she knew named Steve Ramsanker. Steve was just awarded the Order of Canada for his work at the Alec Taylor Community School in Edmonton, a school that faced many of the same challenges as South Simcoe. Like me, Steve was from Trinidad, which made it easier for me to talk with him by telephone.

As I spoke to Steve, I felt my doubts begin to fade and my resolve return. Part of it was the familiar island lilt in his voice, and part of it was his enormous energy and infectious sense of humour. "I'm a Rhodes scholar," he says to most people when meeting them for the first time. Then giving them a sly look, he adds: "The railroads." After immigrating to Canada, Steve had paid for his college education by working on the railway in Western Canada. It was Steve's description of his experiences at Alec Taylor Community School, however, that I most wanted to hear. The school is in Edmonton's toughest neighbourhood, set among taverns and cut-rate hotels, where students have to thread their way among prostitutes and drug dealers on their way to and from classes. The annual murder rate in the compact Alec Taylor neighbourhood often equaled the rate in all the neighbourhoods of the rest of the city combined.

Steve's educational philosophy was remarkably similar to mine, but Steve went even farther. To alleviate the hunger of children who often arrived at school without breakfast, Steve served them early-morning meals of moose-meat cakes and fried bannock, as well as more traditional fare, often paid for out of his own pocket. Food wasn't the only need faced by these children. Many wore tattered, dirty clothing, because they had no washing facilities, so Steve actually convinced the board to install showers, a washing machine and a clothes dryer in the school for students to use to keep themselves clean and neat. This made a huge difference to his students and in addition to having food and being clean, they began to improve academically as well.

Steve's dedication to his work and his students was nothing less than awe-inspiring. He wanted the students at Alec Taylor to experience a world that existed beyond their inner-city neighbourhood, so on three occasions, he took students to his native Trinidad so they could experience the warmth of the people and the culture. He once mortgaged his house to cover the travel expenses. During his stint at Alec Taylor, he arranged several trips for over 2,500 students and 400 seniors to travel across Canada, the United States and into the Caribbean. As word of his achievements spread, Steve was often tempted away from Alec Taylor by offers from government and university groups, to come and work with them, but he loved what he was doing and stubbornly chose to remain where he was. "This is what I am meant to do with my life, it is the special mission I was born to do," he would say, sounding very much like my grandmother.

When I expressed the misgivings I was feeling, Steve's response was: "The path you have chosen is not an easy one, you have chosen to tackle the root cause of the problems; this is hard work. You will have to draw on all the strength you have inside, and reach beyond yourself to give the children what they need." I must have expressed at least a little doubt because he added: "You can do it. You *will* do it. I'll be here to support you. Call me anytime you need me."*

Steve's inspiring words were like a tonic to me. I resolved to continue pursuing our goals at South Simcoe, discarding any idea of giving up in favour of reading in a cozy chair at home every day.

Steve entered my life at the right time, with the messages I needed to hear. He was like a life line to me at the time.

I returned to the school after the death of my father, a changed person in many ways. Staff, parents and children were extremely supportive, reaching out to help and comfort me in any way they could. Even the ones who did not support all my changes, supported me as a person in my time of loss. They tell me that I became more patient, more compassionate, more willing to accept that we could not change everything overnight. They told me that I also became more approachable, (Does that mean that I was not before?).

On reflection, I think the passing of my father strengthened his lessons of tolerance and care for others in me; it helped me to gain a deeper appreciation of the people around me and it helped me to mature as a human being.

The team became even more important. I could not change all that needed changing by myself, like some warrior riding alone to do battle with injustice. That was comic-book fantasy. At South Simcoe, we dealt with real-world challenges every day, and I needed a strong team to work with me: a team in which everyone was valued, even those who were resistant to change. I could envision, I could lead, I could encourage and I could participate, I also learned to accept, include and listen carefully to those who resisted. The benefits were beyond measure.

* Later in my first year at South Simcoe, another principal and I arranged for Steve to travel from Edmonton and address the staffs at our two schools. He emphasized the need for all staff members to offer their total support and total involvement, and praised the concept of schools reaching out to the community. The audience was moved by his words. Steve was able to touch them in a way that energized them to continue their work.

An example of a real-world challenge came with the arrival of Desmond Harris*, an angry grade eight student who was constantly bullying other children, including his own younger brother. We worked hard to eliminate bullying in the school and the neighbourhood and now there were very few incidents of bullying, and we were certainly not going to allow Desmond to continue this unacceptable behaviour. We tried a variety of strategies but we knew we needed co-operation from his parents if we were to make a long term change in his behaviour. Our attempts to involve his parents in the process proved fruitless; in their eyes, we were making a fuss over nothing, Desmond was "just being a boy," and they refused to support us.

Desmond's behaviour slowly escalated and became a nightmare during a visit by his class to the Royal Ontario Museum in Toronto, where Desmond stole students' lunches and deliberately damaged an exhibit, then ran off to hide in a washroom. The teachers and museum officials took so long to locate him, that there was no time left for the class tour, so it had to be cancelled, disappointing dozens of students. Museum officials also stated, in no uncertain terms, that Desmond would not be welcomed back.

Back at the school I had just discovered that the previous day Desmond bullied four younger students, he took their lunch money and then locked them up in an old tool shed in a neighbour's yard, taunting them and throwing them pieces of pizza that he purchased with their money. Desmond's parents gave Desmond a good allowance for his lunch so I knew this was not simply a matter of hunger.

He really seemed to enjoy terrorizing others. I made a decision; I suspended him. I did this with some regret, because suspensions were a last resort for us and we knew they were never a solution. Yet the younger children had the right to be safe at school.

The interesting thing about Desmond was that, in spite of his actions, I sensed a goodness within him. That's not the opinion of some idealistic dreamer, by the way. I talked to Desmond and watched him respond to my words. When he was ready to listen and you reasoned with him, he would become the most wonderful child, then he would slide back into his role as an angry, resentful bully.

What I remember most fondly about Desmond was his voice. He sang in the school choir, and frequently performed solos. When he did, the sound of his voice could bring tears to your eyes, and

---

* I have used pseudonyms for students and their families throughout the book.

suddenly he was no longer a bully but a specially gifted child. I need to make this point because it is too easy to measure a child's worth according to only one or two dimensions. Yes, Desmond was aggressive and hostile, but he was as complex as any other human being; and the special qualities within him justified all the time and effort we expended, trying to help him improve his behaviour. Unfortunately, it came to naught, with disturbing consequences for me.

Nothing else had motivated Desmond's parents to become actively involved with the school in any way, but our decision to suspend him generated an immediate and hostile reaction. Desmond's father came to my office the following morning for a meeting to discuss the situation, he was furious with me for suspending his son for what he considered a harmless and playful incident. Mr. Harris was a large man who towered over me, and my staff, his very presence was intimidating.

Desmond's very attractive teacher told me that he always tried to arrange meetings with her after 5 PM, when he knew the custodians had left for the day; she said that once he ogled her as if undressing her with his eyes. She never reported this to me because she wasn't sure if it was all in her head but she quickly filled me in when she heard I was arranging a meeting with him.

Mr. Harris was furious about the suspension. "Who the hell do you think you are lady?" he said pointing his finger in my face. "You take that suspension off now!" "I am sorry but I can't do that but I do want to discuss the situation with you." I replied. He exploded, hurling every scream and threat he could think of, all of them directed at me. I tried to explain but my explanations only seemed to fuel his hostility, so I stood quietly letting him have his say. I refused to lift the suspension and he finally left my office, but not without spewing threats against me, the school, the school board and much of the universe.

The next morning he returned, he stormed past my secretary and some children gathered around her in the office, he walked into my office and slammed the door shut. With his fist raised he started shouting curses and threats. "I am here to deal with you this time, you bitch!" he roared, banging his fist on my desk, "I'm going to teach you a lesson that you will never forget." I sat at my desk, petrified. "I'm fed up with you," he said before I could speak. "I'm sick of you picking on my boy, picking on my family, picking on me!"I managed to remain outwardly calm but I was scared. Then, realizing that I was dealing with a classic bully, I decided to take action. I stood up slowly and deliberately, looking him straight in the eye. He stood between me and the door. "Get out of my way now!" I said in my loudest and most authoritative voice. My no nonsense manner obviously caught him off guard, because he reacted by stepping aside. I quickly walked out of my office into the open where a small crowd of children and staff had gathered. They had heard Desmond's father ranting and raving, thumping the desk and shouting abuse at me, acting in the same manner that we were telling students was unacceptable from them. How then, could it be acceptable from this adult?

"Call the police," I said to Joan when I opened the door. "This man is bullying and threatening me. I want him arrested" Wide-eyed, she reached for the telephone. Children who overheard the man's angry shouts stared at me with concern, and one six-year-old girl burst into tears, running to me and hugging me, asking if I was all right.

I assured her I was fine just as the man strode out of my office, subdued a little by my instruction to call the police. "Don't think this is the end of this," he said, pointing his finger at me. "You just wait!"

I found out later that Desmond's father had lost his job a week earlier, and whether this was the cause of his rage, or as a result of his rage, it was unclear. It didn't matter. His fury grew white-hot, all of it aimed at me. He even visited the director at the board office, sweeping documents from her desk onto the floor in an explosion of rage before leaving. He, then, contacted the minister of education, but I held firm.

Unable to find support from official sources, he launched into an even more bitter personal attack on me. Soon, letters began arriving, calling me a bitch, a tyrant, and using other unspeakable words to express his opinion of me. He placed copies of his letters under the windshields of cars in our parking lot, those in the mall across the street and others in the neighbourhood. The day that happened, I drove home in tears. Once again I began questioning my decisions, my resolve, my ability to do the job I had to do at South Simcoe. One parent, familiar with Desmond's father and his actions, advised me to back down. "He's a bully," she said. "He won't give you a moment's peace. He terrorizes us in the neighbourhood until we give in to him. Why not just drop the whole thing and get on with your life? It's not the end of the world." Perhaps she was right. I could back down and give in to his threats. After all, I expected hurdles when I accepted the position, but not character assassination or the threat of physical violence. Besides, I didn't suspend Desmond in a moment of spite or weakness. It was a carefully considered decision, made after going through the pages and pages of documented evidence of his bullying and extortion, after repeated interventions to stop or at least curb his inappropriate behaviour, it was a last resort to demonstrate that we could not accept him bullying other children and also to assure the other students that South Simcoe was a safe haven for them.

My husband, Ishwar, provided a solid foundation of support, as usual. "Do what you know is right," he advised. "Spend some time alone, think through it, then do what your heart tells you. The boys and I will support you regardless of what decision you make."

For a very long time, I sat quietly reassessing everything I had done, and all the difficulties it created. The truth is, I seriously considered backing away from the issue. Was the parent justified in his anger at me? Had I done the correct thing after all? Should I back down and resolve the matter or continue to fight, making things more difficult for everyone on my staff and at the board office?

I went back and forth with these questions all evening, and one thing was clear. The man was a bully, no more and no less. We taught our children that bullying was not acceptable, we taught them to stand up and say "No," to bullies, as one way of dealing with them, how then could I give into this bully myself because I was scared? How could I simply walk away from this bully just because it affected me directly? What kind of message would that deliver to

64

the children? What kind of role model would I be for my students, my staff and my own children? I finally went to bed, knowing what I wanted to do.

A few days later I invited the staff to a meeting at my home to discuss the situation and let them know what I was thinking. I did not hold this meeting at the school, because I felt it was my personal issue that I wanted to discuss with them in my personal setting, one human being to another. I realized that with all my abilities, I needed their psychological and emotional support, if I were to continue to take a stand against this bully. Was I that different from the children? The staff was already aware of most of the details, then I explained that I did not want to back down and give in to this bully's threats and abuse, but at the same time I realized if I stood firm, it could have negative repercussions on anyone associated with me and there was a possibility of them becoming targets of his abuse as well. I didn't want to put them under more stress because of the situation. I asked for their opinions and advice.

"He may say things about me directly to you," I explained, "and if you defend me in any way, he could turn his anger on you. So this is a decision that will affect everyone in this room, and I cannot make it unless I know that you are aware of the consequences and support me in doing this. If you feel that there is a better way, please tell me because I honestly don't know if this is the best course of action. But I feel that I have to take a stand against this bully. I feel it is the right thing to do and I feel that in my position I must model what we teach about dealing with bullies.

Without hesitation, they all said "do not back down, be a role model for us, for our children and for our community. Show them that bullies can be faced and dealt with.

Bless their hearts, they supported me one hundred percent, even those who didn't always agree with me professionally. At the end of the meeting we all felt closer and more united than ever. This was the first time I spoke to them so openly about my personal feelings, and I realized how comfortable I was becoming with them, how much like a family we were.

The harassment continued, just because I stood up to him, this did not make him go away. In fact he grew even more irate. He started waiting for me in the parking lot, at the end of the day to scream abuse at me in front of all the passers-by. When he began to threaten me and my family physically, staff and parents began escorting me to and from my car.

When property trespass letters were ignored, I complained to the police and obtained a court order warning him to stay away from me, this had no effect. He continued to lurk, sometimes hanging around the schoolyard, just outside the boundary, sometimes boldly entering the building and walking out again just to prove that we were unable to banish him. And so it went on, through the rest of the school year. It was a horrible situation.

Something good came of this. Parents began thanking me for taking a stand against him. Many of them were the man's neighbours and were victims of his bullying tactics but had been too afraid to stand up to him. Now they too were telling him boldly to leave them alone. Their support for me extended to offering stronger support for the school. By standing up for myself, I 'walked the talk' as it were and demonstrated how to stand up to a Bully. This taught a lesson to the children and earned the respect and appreciation of their parents. We emerged from this a stronger and more tightly knit group, who gave each other personal support, even though at times we disagreed professionally. We were more determined than ever to do whatever was necessary to make South Simcoe the kind of school we all wanted it to be. That's the ironic result of this entire episode, as painful and disturbing as it was.

At year's end, when Desmond completed grade eight and went on to high school, his father finally left me alone, even though his younger son continued to attend the school. A twinge of sadness runs through my memory when I recall this whole situation because as I mentioned earlier, at heart Desmond seemed to be a decent boy. But, without his parents' support and assistance, we were unable to help him to change his bullying habits.

Yes, we built a stronger team at the school as a result of his father's outrageous actions, yes parents appreciated the stand that we took and this generated more support for the school, and although there appears to have been no alternative to our actions, I feel that somehow we failed Desmond. He didn't get the help that he needed, which meant he would more than likely bully again.

The younger a child is when bullying behaviour is addressed, the greater the chance of turning the situation around. We all missed the chance. And I still hear his sweet voice singing in the choir. My dreadful experience with Desmond and his father was balanced by several smaller, less dramatic but no less important episodes. All of them taught us things about the children and their needs. Many involved children like Janice, whose need was so basic we almost overlooked it.

Janice was a grade seven student with learning problems. She came to South Simcoe after failing earlier grades. She was well behind her friends, who would be advancing to high school the following year while Janice remained in elementary school. Peer status, of course, is important to children in their early teens, and Janice's was about to suffer a blow she did not feel capable of handling. Her social worker, who was trying to guide and encourage Janice, alerted us that Janice was planning to drop out of school at the end of the school year. "I want to go to high school with my friends," Janice tearfully confessed to her. "If I can't go to high school, I'll quit. I'm too old to be hanging around with the kids at South Simcoe for another year. Look at me, I am a woman." (She was indeed). Thanks to the extra attention and academic assistance she was receiving at South Simcoe, Janice was making great progress. None of us wanted to see her toss away her best chance to obtain an education, even though we understood her frustration and her embarrassment at past failures.

Refusing to write Janice off—you never write children off, in my opinion—I invited her to my office for a chat and asked Jacki, who was especially fond of Janice, to sit in. "Is it true you're thinking of leaving school?" I asked Janice when we were settled. She nodded glumly, avoiding my eyes. "I don't understand why, can you help me to understand?" I asked. "You seem to be doing so well now, and we are so proud of what you are doing. Aren't you pleased with your progress?"

"I guess so," Janice said. She looked so forlorn and confused. Her eyes began to fill with tears. "I just want to be with my friends more than I want to be here."

"Everyone wants to be with friends," I said. "But your education is important too. You have been working so hard, and your teachers have worked hard to help you, Janice. You're beginning to make great strides. We understand how you feel but we know that you will get up to your grade level if you continue with the program we have put in place for you. We care about you so much Janice; we want you to do well."

She looked directly at me for the first time, with an expression of hope and maybe surprise. "You care about me?" "We do, Janice," I assured her. "We care about you. All of us." Then I added: "And we love you, Janice. We care about you and love you. Can't you see that?"

"You never said that before," she said. "You never said that you cared about me or loved me, nobody did."

"Janice, you know I love you," Jacki said. "You know that you are special to me." I never saw such relief and gratitude in a child's eyes as I saw when Janice heard those words. "We all do, and we want what's best for you. We want you to stay in school."

No one has ever said that to me before," Janice said. Then she smiled, her eyes glistening with tears. "OK," she said. "I'll stay." Jacki and I were stunned. That was all it took? All we had to do was tell Janice that we cared about her and loved her?

It was true. Janice stayed, completed grade seven, excelled in grade eight and went on to high school and college. We made no threats or pleas, and we painted no glum pictures of a life ruined without an education. That wasn't what Janice needed. She simply needed to hear that we cared, and that we loved her. Once again, a student had taught the teachers. It wasn't enough for us to provide academic instruction; we also needed to provide a psychological and emotional foundation of love, caring and support.

After the meeting with Janice, I began to apply the lesson over and over again. In fact, just a few days later, one of the teachers began describing her troubles with a particular student who just didn't seem to care about school, about life, about anything.

"He needs to know you care about him," I advised the teacher.

"But I do," she replied.

"Then tell him," I said. "Let him hear the words. Believe me, I've seen it work. And I think it's a good idea to tell as many children as you can that you care about them. If you're not comfortable about saying it to the entire class, then say it to one child a day. But *say* it."

It never failed to work with children who craved the comfort of knowing that someone cared about them. They had to hear it spoken aloud. "We care about you and we love you." We all need to hear it in our lives; the children of South Simcoe simply needed to hear it more often.

Sometimes the anger and frustration within the children would suddenly ignite and the situation could become dangerous, without warning. When this occurred, our teachers had to draw upon their experience, their own good judgment and basic common sense to defuse the situation.

Nothing in the background of Kim Kelly, who taught grade seven, could have prepared her for the day when Paul, in anger, withdrew a rusty razor from his pocket, stared her in the eyes and said, "I have a razor; I'm going to get you."

Kim was having an end of the day chat with Paul about his behaviour in class. Although the classroom door was open, she was alone with him, what was she to do? He was standing between her and the door so she couldn't run from the room, or reach the intercom to call for help. Instead, Kim had to think on her feet. She stood her ground while the boy waved the razor at her. She remained outwardly calm, and she said, "Please stop and think Paul, we have talked about making good choices. Think about the choice that you are making right now. You can make a better choice Paul. You did misbehave in class, that's why we are here talking, that's a small problem and we will deal with it, you know we always do. Let's keep the problem small, put down the razor and let's work this out together."

Fortunately for Kim, the time that she was taking to build a good relationship with Paul, (such an important and often overlooked strategy when dealing with behaviourally challenged children), paid off. He was beginning to trust her, so she kept talking to him quietly and finally, her message began to sink in. Gradually Paul lowered his hand, then put the razor away, Kim alerted the office, then she quietly resumed her chat while waiting for me to arrive. Later, when we reviewed the situation and discussed her response and alternate responses, Kim admitted that she thought that he was going to kill her. We informed his parents and the authorities and invited the police to talk to us about how to effectively handle this type of occurrence in the future.

Years later, when we were reminiscing together about our time at South Simcoe, Kim said that she learned so much from this incident that no student could ever intimidate her again. She went on, "What I liked most about my years at South Simcoe, was our team, how we were all leaders each in our own individual way, and we were all so determined to help the children. We shared resources, we exchanged ideas, we laughed together, we cried together, we always ate, and we found the smallest things to celebrate and that kept us going. I am so glad I had that experience, I know we made a difference."

I was continuously impressed by the staff's creative thinking and their practical solutions to problems. Sally Roberts, for example, was an enormously gifted and dedicated teacher with a knack for encouraging her grade three students to discover the joys of writing. When Greg appeared to have a deep-seated fear of putting anything down on paper, (his hands would literally shake), Sally decided a bit of fun might work, she made a game out of the writing process. They took turns speaking words out aloud, then seeing who could write them down first. Greg would start with a single word, perhaps "The," and they would write it down. Then Sally would say a second word, maybe "cat," and they would write it down, next it was his turn again, and so it went on until they had a complete sentence written on paper, then they would work this way to create another sentence, and then another, until they had constructed an entire story. Greg won most of the time, of course. The boy blossomed under Sally's warmth and guidance. By the end of the year he was able to write a complete eight-paragraph essay on a tropical rain forest, a topic that fascinated him during his social studies class. Individual attention paired with the determination to 'find a way,' and Sally's warmth and humour, all made such a difference.

Tom was a difficult student in Kim Kelly's grade seven class. Along with his disruptive behaviour, he demonstrated serious reading problems. Were the two situations connected? I have no doubt they were. Tom's struggles to read at the same level as his classmates made him feel insecure and a failure, and soon he refused to even attempt reading. Nothing seemed to work until one day Kim overheard Tom speaking with great enthusiasm about fishing. The next day Kim arrived in class with some fishing magazines. She read a short article to Tom, then had him read it with her. Tom was so interested in the information that he forgot all his reluctance about reading. She stood back and watched as he devoured the magazine, absorbing everything he could about fishing. She struck gold; Tom was motivated to read because she took the time, and made the effort to look for an entry point. To Tom, fishing was one of the greatest experiences he ever had. Although he only went fishing once in his short life, he was successful. He caught fish after fish, while many of the adults on the boat didn't catch any. He loved the feeling of success. Reading magazines in class, especially fishing magazines, wasn't work, it was fun, so he made an extra effort to figure out unfamiliar words, ask for help when he needed it, and even use a dictionary. Tom's initial fishing experience gave him a taste of success: he knew what it was like to be in that emotional state. Sally was able to use the fishing magazines to link him back to those great feelings and help him to become a successful reader.

Jacki had a knack for winning kids to her side. She would use pet names when addressing them—David would become "Davey," for example. It may seem like a small, silly thing among all the other teaching methods available, but the children appreciated her nicknames for what they were: terms of endearment, a kind of shorthand that said, "I like you. You matter to me. You are a good kid."

Few of us tire of being told we are loved, that we matter, that someone cares about us. To children who might rarely, if ever, receive those messages at home, Jacki's simple use of pet names was a tonic, and another reason to value and enjoy every hour spent at South Simcoe.

We were more than the usual teaching staff. We were a vibrant and highly functioning team and the difference between the two is much more than just semantics. We were all personally and professionally committed in a deep and heartfelt way to making a difference to the children at South Simcoe, and we all cared about each other, personally and professionally. We felt responsible for everyone's well-being and functioned in a way that only the most fortunate and successful teams do. "The South Simcoe Smile" was a manifestation of our caring. We had a smile for everyone, for each other, for parents and visitors, and most importantly, for the children. It made us feel better, it also made us more approachable to everyone.

We began to be known as "The school where everyone is always smiling," and the description included both the children and the staff members. Our smiles were never forced, we felt good about what we were doing, we knew that our efforts were paying off, and we knew that our children and the community were benefitting. There was a real family atmosphere at the school.

At the end of one school day a student burst into my office to announce that the Prime Minister had arrived and was sitting in his limousine right outside the front door. The Prime Minister of Canada? Had our fame spread so far and so fast? I followed the boy down the hall to the door and, sure enough, a white stretch limousine was parked at the curb, the motor idling and a uniformed driver behind the wheel. The children could barely contain their excitement, climbing on the hood and trunk, stroking and sniffing the finish—one child even licked it! They had never seen such an impressive vehicle. If the Prime Minister was not inside, it was some celebrity, maybe even an entire rock band—the car was that big!

I knocked on the window to see who was inside. When the window rolled down, I was surprised to see not the Prime Minister, but the boyfriend of one of our teachers, grinning at me from the back seat. He had a special surprise for her, and I had a good idea what it might be. When the teacher finally emerged and climbed into the limo, the children all cheered as they drove away to a special dinner, where her boyfriend proposed to her.

We all joined in the preparations for the marriage, planning teas and choosing gifts as though it were our own sister and not just a member of our staff who was being wed. Later, when the teacher was hospitalized for over three months while pregnant with her first child, at least one staff member visited her or called at least once, every day of the week. We took the same personal interest in other teachers as their own children were born, the children became 'South Simcoe Babies,' and we shared in the joy of their arrival. Our family was growing.

As time passed, we discovered the impact our approach was making on the students—Sometimes with touching results. One day in the middle of an otherwise uneventful afternoon, Sally walked into my office. Her face was white, her hands were trembling, and she looked as though she were about to burst into tears. "Oh Sandra, I've done something terrible," she said. Sally was a wonderful, caring teacher, one of the strongest supporters of our initiatives at South Simcoe. I urged her to sit down, handed her some tissues and asked her to tell me why she was so upset.

"I told a student to shut up," she confessed. "I said 'Please shut up! But still it was 'Shut up!' and I feel so badly about it. I can't believe I said it." Shut up had become the 's' words at South Simcoe, so telling anyone to shut up meant dishonouring an important respectful relationship agreement. Children did not use it in conversation, they agreed not to say it to teachers, and teachers agreed not to say it to children. It violated our basic principle of maintaining mutual respect on all sides. Sally knew this and nothing I said would make her feel any better—or any worse. Once the words were out of her mouth, Sally immediately realized that she was frustrated and spoke before thinking. So she did the same thing she would have asked a student to do. She took a deep breath and asked for some time to calm down. She announced to the class that she needed a 'time out' to calm down. She then left the room, to regain her composure. I reminded Sally that she was a wonderful teacher; she simply lost her cool and made a mistake. "We all make mistakes," I assured her. "Stay here until you feel ready, then go back to the classroom and explain it to the students, tell them exactly what you told me. They are going to make mistakes too and this will be an opportunity for you to model how to deal with this type of situation."

And Sally did. She explained she made a mistake by using the "S words," and even though she was frustrated, this did not give her the right to speak disrespectfully to others. She then asked the class to help her decide how to make amends to them. When she finished speaking, one of the eight year olds in her class approached her and said, "It's all right, Miss Roberts. You made a mistake. We'll work with you to help you manage your frustration better so it doesn't happen again." She said to Sally exactly what Sally would have said to her, if she was the one to use the words shut up in frustration. Sally, as she explained to me later, didn't know whether to laugh or cry. When the student begins to teach what they are learning, you know they understand.

I cannot overemphasize the importance of the psychological and emotional support we all needed to keep us focusing on the positives. Creating a warm and caring environment helped to provide some of this support. Physical manifestations of this were our new large windows that allowed lots of sunlight into the rooms, our plants and flowers and our *Bouquet Board*. This board, was a simple chalkboard, on which staff members took the time to show they cared by writing notes to one another. Notes of congratulations and best wishes, thank you notes to recognize achievements with students, events in their lives and little favours performed. We also had a series of stars hung over our bouquet board, they highlighted the many successes we achieved as individuals and as a team within the school and the community.

We all loved coming into the staffroom to read the positive comments. and to share in the successes of our team. All these demonstrations of caring energized us to continue our work, made us a stronger team, and were essentially the glue that held us together in the tough times. Like all families, we encountered crises. And like all supportive and caring families, we helped each other through them.

When Michelle arrived at South Simcoe to teach, she was a great addition to our team. The children loved her bubbly and bright personality every bit as much as the rest of the staff. Within a few months, however, Michelle began to have difficulties. First, she started forgetting things. Most of us would laugh off these incidents, saying we were all simply becoming too busy, or it was due to stress and overload. But in discussions with Michelle, I found out her father was diagnosed with Alzheimer's and she spent most evenings and weekends caring for him.

This certainly heightened her awareness and understanding of his condition, but caring for him as well as her preschooler while looking after family obligations, placed intense pressure on her. Michelle's energy was drained and this was having a negative effect on her ability to handle her teaching workload. Then, just when it seemed she couldn't possibly handle another source of stress, her marriage began to collapse. Her work was obviously affected, how could it not be? Eventually, I had to have a serious discussion with her about the situation. She told me she felt her only solution was to leave teaching and get a job that was less emotionally draining. I refused to accept that. "We certainly have highs and lows here. The lows are tough, but the highs are wonderful, aren't they? And you know that staff as well as children can always count on everyone's love and support here. Then I added: "Remember what Sharon always says?"

She smiled and nodded. Sharon McLean often said, "We may crash from time to time, but we never burn." She meant we often encountered challenges that put us off the track or leave us feeling helpless and that we couldn't go on. But we always recovered, because we always looked out for one another. When someone needed an emotional boost, they could count on receiving it from another staff member, or sometimes the entire staff. We took responsibility for one another's welfare; we were a family. I shook my head. "I can't let you give up," I said, "I'll help you to get through this. How can I help?"

Michelle was a fighter, she decided to take charge of the situation. With the assistance of personnel from Public Health, she began to access the help she needed. We all gave Michelle our support. I would stop by her classroom twice each day to remind her how much she was valued and how many people cared about her. When passing her in the hall, I would give her a thumbs-up signal to lift her spirits and remind her that we were all there for her.

Experiences like Michelle's continued to strengthen the team and remind us not to give up on anyone, child or adult. Years later Michelle said, "I'll never give up on these children. People didn't give up on me and I made it, so will they!" Michelle felt her experiences made her a better teacher and a better human being.

Caring for someone with Alzheimer's takes a toll on the caregiver, and can negatively affect their home life as well as their work life. Adults who are caregivers need support every bit as much as our children did.

The staff needed this emotional support as well and I took every opportunity I could to provide it. I ended our staff meetings on an uplifting note by reading passages from inspirational books or essays. After an hour of discussion and solution finding, we were usually exhausted but energized at the same time, it seemed appropriate to end these powerful sessions with a thought that recognized and reinforced the importance of lighting the way for the children in our care, and how spiritually uplifting this work could be Due to an overwhelmingly positive response to these readings and a request for more, we expanded this idea into what became known as our Wonderful Wednesday sessions. Every Wednesday at lunch, a group would gather together in an area in the staff room to think and talk about ourselves as people, as individuals who needed emotional support to do our work. Sometimes someone would bring a book with an uplifting passage; we would read and discuss it, talking about how it made us feel, the significance of the words, the ideas and how we could apply them to improve our lives and the lives of the children entrusted to our care. Sometimes we would sit and share strategies to help us get through stressful times, personal traumas, or day to day crises. Sometimes, we simply talked about how emotionally draining our work was and how we could do little things for one another to show we were all there as a support system. We realized, as time went on, we were all undergoing a personal transformation, the work actually got less emotionally draining and more spiritually fulfilling.

We gained a great deal of strength from these personal transformation sessions. They helped us create a more positive environment in which to live, learn and grow as professionals, yes, and also as people. Now and then, we would invite other people to share their personal stories and strategies with us. We didn't stop there. We began assembling a library of books on uplifting topics. We displayed affirmations in the staff room and around the school. These kept us focused on the positives and the difference we were making in the lives of the children. At the beginning of a new school year, one teacher remarked that she really missed these sessions over the summer and was really looking forward to the new school year and our Wonderful Wednesdays.

We even created small rituals to strengthen the team and anchor our positive experiences. I must admit that many of our rituals involved food and eating together as a school family and sharing each others company. We sought every opportunity we could to celebrate. For example, we held end-of-the-term breakfasts for the staff, on the last morning of every school term. We would arrive at 7 a.m. rain or shine, all decked out in our school colours, to eat breakfast together and celebrate our personal and professional successes. As we sat down to 'break bread' as one researcher termed it later on, we all took part in an activity that helped to demonstrate how far we had come as individuals and as a team over the past term.

We each took turns sharing our personal and professional successes, which we documented in our portfolios. (Our portfolios paralleled those of the students). We never focused on what we did not accomplish except to say we would continue to work on it. In keeping with our asset-based philosophy of 'finding the good, and focusing on the good,' we shared our accomplishments, our strengths, and celebrated the good, this left us on a 'high' at the end of each term. It gave us the strength to continue, knowing we were making a difference in the lives of our students, and growing stronger as a team of professionals, while at the same time developing as individuals, growing more grounded as human beings and through our work life, giving back in a way that warmed our very souls. The celebrations were unforgettable events.

The word "team" sounds almost inadequate to describe the strength and support we gave and received from one another as a result of these activities. These were deeply emotional experiences and, I believe, they were responsible for much of our success at South Simcoe.

The staff were all unique individuals. They brought a variety of backgrounds, experiences and strengths to their work and their responses to many of my suggestions were just as varied. My experiences in dealing with staff too were varied and my experiences with Jacki, Randy and Frank are three very different examples.

Jacki Devolin was a classroom assistant and at first this made her reluctant to participate as a team member in many of the initiatives we launched. Since she did not hold a teacher's certificate, she often backed away from speaking her mind at staff meetings or volunteering for certain projects. But I encouraged her, pointing out that everyone was an important part of the team. As long as we all kept our focus on our common goal to do what was best for the children, we each had a right to comment and make suggestions. It took time to help Jacki overcome her inhibitions, say what she felt, and even disagree with a solution being presented, instead of just sticking to her job description. When Jacki began to participate as an equal player in the process of change, the transformation was astonishing. Almost overnight Jacki became the person everyone went to for advice; she became everyone's big sister. We all, staff and students, felt comfortable confiding in her—including me, by the way—knowing she would listen and offer a wise suggestion. She also began to show her wonderful knack for planning and organizing, and no event at South Simcoe was launched without

Jacki's meticulous eye going over all the details. What an amazing woman!

In sharp contrast to Jacki, Randy Weekes needed a mere invitation to become an active member of the team. Randy was the chief custodian at South Simcoe and quickly warmed to the idea of attending staff meetings, enthusiastically adding his ideas and suggestions. He and Gail, of course, were the original inspiration behind our successful Golden Dustpan Award. A dedicated environmentalist, Randy began doing small projects with the children to teach them about respect and responsibility for the environment. He would work with them to build birdhouses and bat houses using recycled wood, and he created a small area in the garden with plants specially chosen to attract butterflies. Eventually, he formed an Environmental Club with the children, teaching them about environmental issues and setting up a program for them to recycle paper, plastic, glass and other items (this was long before the idea became mainstream).

Randy made an impact across the city. When he saw the positive results of our gardening efforts at South Simcoe, he contacted all the other school custodians along Simcoe Street and suggested they plant gardens in front of their schools, using flowers that repeated their school colours. A few years later, Mayor Nancy Diamond reminded me that, thanks to the leadership of our school custodian, the entire city of Oshawa grew more beautiful.

Jacki was a classroom assistant, afraid at first to "act like a teacher." Randy was a custodian who could hardly wait to add his contribution to the children's education. And then there was Frank. From the first time he heard me talk about a turnaround for the school, a focus on achievement and success, he made no effort to hide his skepticism. "It can't be done," he would say, reminding me of the extra years of experience he had, as well as his deeper understanding of the community. "You just don't understand these people," he would say. "Not like I do. You have to be firm with the kids. Start suspending more of them. And start supporting teachers like me, who expect them to toe the line, because we know things about this neighbourhood that you can never begin to know."

I suppose I realized from the start Frank was never going to see things my way. I was unable to hide my resentment at his attitude and Frank could not conceal his animosity toward me. The result was neither of us handled our disputes as well as we might have, and Frank chose to transfer to another school at the end of the first year.

He wasn't the only one to leave in disagreement with me. Three other members of the teaching staff chose to leave at the end of my first year, so I spent a good deal of time interviewing and hiring candidates to replace them. I wanted bright, energetic and enthusiastic people, of course, but more than that, I wanted people who cared as passionately about the children, their education, their well-being and above all, making a positive difference in their lives, as Sharon McLean did. I wanted people who would help to create a stronger and better functioning team, not just within the school, but also with parents and members of the community.

I finally selected three new teachers, and I am proud to say they all strengthened and enhanced our focus on turning the school and community around; they all contributed enthusiastically to the respectful and inclusive climate we were seeking to create at the school. They joined with others to focus on "creating small miracles" every day, by celebrating things like the thrill of discovery on a child's face when he or she mastered a new skill, like reading a difficult passage, understanding some mathematical process, or simply learning how to tie a shoelace. They all saw teaching as a calling of the heart as well as a profession, or calling of the mind.

Still, other teachers would leave over the years, and in some cases the losses hurt me. I wished I had the skills to inspire them and encourage them to embrace a new way of teaching and learning. Colleagues and friends had warned this would happen; you cannot, after all, reach everyone or expect them to agree with you when you are introducing significant change. And I make no apologies for having high expectations for the children and being determined to do everything I could to help them to succeed in school. Still, I regret losing the valuable experience Frank and others might have contributed to our journey. Over the years as I developed more experience as a leader, I would reflect on this and say, "I would like to think that if only I knew then what I know now, I would have been able to redirect their efforts towards a different outcome.

LEADER'S REFLECTION

Leaders who lead consciously from the inside out are grateful for, and understand the power of the team's collective wisdom.

- How do you tap the collective wisdom of your team including the resistors, when designing workplace systems, and when making decisions about the change process?

CHAPTER 5

Parenting Voices

With the school building spruced up and looking more attractive and welcoming, entry/dismissal and other necessary routines in place and working well, more students showing up regularly and on time for school, we were all encouraged. These early successes were motivating and spurred us on to take the next steps. It was time to turn my attention to another critical element, parental engagement. I saw parental engagement as essential to student success. I knew from all the research I read as well as from all my years of teaching experience, that when parents are engaged in the education of their children, and have high expectations for them, their children are more likely to succeed. I wanted what I experienced before at my previous school, parents who supported their child's learning in the home, who supported and encouraged their child's aspirations and dreams, parents who worked with the school to help us to better understand their children, to understand our teaching strategies but who also offered us their support and encouragement. I wanted deep, caring and positive relationships based on mutual respect and trust so we could have honest and open conversations about their children and work together to help them to achieve academically, and to grow and develop socially and emotionally. Once again, as principal, I received a harsh lesson in reality. The outgoing principal told me it was not easy to involve the parents in the neighbourhood, far less engage them deeply. Many families were transient and did not stay long enough to develop strong relationships, some had such poor school experiences as children, they had absolutely no interest in becoming involved with the school.

At every other school in my experience, I was able to develop good relationships with parents, and even with the most reluctant groups, there were always some who responded enthusiastically whenever called upon by teachers or the principal to come to the school.

Thus far at South Simcoe, parental attendance at school meetings to discuss their child's progress was much lower than I anticipated. Even the meetings that were more social in nature were not well attended. When we tried to make personal invitations over the phone, a technique that worked well for me in the past, many parents simply refused to answer telephone calls from the school. This seemed strange until I discovered that call display was carefully scrutinized before the receiver was lifted. If the school or any other unwanted caller was displayed, parents would not answer the phone. My immediate reaction was irritation; why would they not answer a call from the school, what if we needed to get in touch with them in an emergency? This was not acceptable.

I was determined to change this so I took the time to ask why? Eventually, I found out many of the parents who would not answer the telephone were single mothers who used call display to avoid speaking to bill collectors and threatening or abusive ex-husbands or former boyfriends, who they felt wanted to harm or hurt them or their children. Call display was a defence mechanism. South Simcoe School fell into the category of unwanted callers. When a parent saw that the School was calling, she simply assumed that it was bad news about her child, which she could do without.

There is a perception that built up over the years which is extremely difficult to disspell: schools only phone parents if there is a problem. In many cases, the parents who refused to answer the phone calls did not want to hear about problems the teachers were having with their children. They felt if their child was misbehaving or not doing her work, this was the school's problem not theirs, after all it was during school hours, and it was the school's job during school hours to deal with all of this, not theirs.

No one wanted to be asked to come to the school and pick up his/her child. They had enough of their own problems to deal with. Even when parents did answer the telephone, many failed to respond in a courteous and respectful manner. Since they expected bad news, they would be non-communicative and reluctant to discuss any aspect of their child's schooling. Others were defensive right from the beginning, some even abusive, actually shouting and cursing before hanging up.

This had to change, we needed better one-on-one communication between the school and the home. I refused to be discouraged. I saw how capable and promising many of our students were, given the right emotional and academic support. I knew without the participation of their parents, these children would never realize all their potential during their time at South Simcoe. I was determined not to give up; I needed the parents to work with me to help and support me, and the children needed them, too.

To deal with the phone call issue, we implemented a strategy I implemented at other schools; making "Sunshine Calls" to parents. A Sunshine Call was a "happy" call, largely social in nature; it was a call from the school to the home to convey good news about a child. It could be about the child's progress, about the results of a test, the completion of an assignment, it could be about something the child did, or it could simply be about how wonderful it was to have the privilege of teaching the child. I encouraged the teachers to make Sunshine Calls. Remembering my mother's lecture about the unexpected Christmas doll, FIND THE GOOD, we brainstormed ideas about how to find something positive to say about children who were being extremely difficult. In the case of a child who was always shouting out questions in class, his teacher decided to praise him for always asking good questions, in other cases teachers praised children for being pleasant to other students, or for always smiling. Sunshine calls focused on something good about the child. Trust started to build and relationships became stronger. Teachers were seen as people who cared and so teachers were able to phone to discuss a child's progress or bring up an issue, without having the phone slammed down or the call go unanswered. Good news was always the conversation-opener, before going on to further discussion.

The first few Sunshine Calls incurred suspicion, and even disbelief teachers would take time to phone parents simply to share good news about their children. Little by little, word of our Sunshine Calls spread among parents in the neighbourhood. One parent would tell another that their child's teacher called home, not to complain about Sammy or Emma, but to say how much they enjoyed teaching him or her. How about that? They might comment. Isn't that different? They didn't call to complain.

More and more parents with call display began to risk answering the phone when the school called. Calls from the school became ones that were welcomed. Parents loved to hear teachers say things like, "I just want you to know that I'm delighted to be teaching your child this year," or a similar statement. Sunshine calls became such a hit that in the following years the teachers decided that they would make at least two sunshine calls for every child. One would be by the end of the first month of school, the other during the school year. This may sound easy but it took a great deal of time and effort. Teaching, especially at a school like South Simcoe, can be an intense and emotionally draining process, one that usually extends the teachers' work hours well into the evenings and weekends. Many teachers made their Sunshine Calls, from their own homes during the evening. I'm sure they would have preferred to spend the time with their spouses and families, reading a book, or just relaxing. But because they knew it made such a huge difference to the children, they took the time to make these calls. This high level of commitment dedication and caring, laid the foundation for creating deeper and more meaningful relationships with the parents. This was key to so much of what we accomplished at South Simcoe, and I am honoured to have been a part of this group.

Building on the foundation laid by the Sunshine Calls, I began to gently but firmly insist every family attend the first report card interview at the end of the first term, usually in December. Attendance at these interviews was extremely important because it showed the children their parents were interested in what they were learning at school. They also helped parents to better understand what the child was learning, how she was doing in school, what the teacher's expectations were, and how they could better reinforce these efforts at home. These end of term interviews also gave teachers the opportunity to speak to parents face –to- face and better understand the expectations the parents held for their child's education, their beliefs about education and to clarify any misunderstandings. They could find out if communications from the school were being received and understood. The biggest thing for me was the children had the opportunity to show their work in their portfolios and share their successes.

Making Sunshine Calls, (or was it the commitment from the teachers to make them regularly?) was a strategy that far exceeded our expectations. They created a major shift in relationships and a level of parental and community involvement that still astounds many people, and frankly, continues to surprise me a little as well. We were on our way, but I wanted and needed more. I needed a deeper level of engagement, I needed the parents to be more engaged in the teaching and learning process and to provide more support for education in the home. I needed to hear their ideas about what would work for their children, after all they had parents' understanding of their children, their input could help us to design more effective instruction for individual children. I wanted to have parents brainstorming ideas and discussing issues of concern. I envisioned dynamic meetings where they felt emotionally and intellectually safe enough to speak their minds. I wanted them to work with me to come up with solutions to problems rather than complaining about what we did not do.

I needed to rethink what I meant by parental engagement and the traditional ways that parents get involved with schools. I wanted to understand and acknowledge their needs and concerns, their issues and their desires, figure out what the obstacles were to their involvement and start the journey from where they were, not where I was.

Timing was an issue, evening meetings were difficult, since many parents had young children. Fundraising was another one; they didn't want to have to sell chocolate bars. In any case, fundraising from an already economically stressed community simply did not make sense to me. Does selling chocolate bars whilst advocating a healthful lifestyle make sense to anyone? I decided to find a more convenient time, a daytime meeting. I sent every child home with an invitation to their parents to gather at the school for an informal meeting with me, in a few days' time. We made flyers advertising the event, announcing we would have conversation, coffee and cookies. I hoped for a turnout of perhaps twenty parents; this would make a good-sized group for discussion.

On the day of the meeting I arrived early to make lots of coffee and set out plates of food, in anticipation of a large turnout. At my previous school, chat sessions like these were always well attended, some parents even invited friends along as company. The time for our chat came…and passed. No one arrived. They may just be late, I thought, and I stood at the window looking this way and that, up and down the street but not a parent appeared. I asked Joan if she had any messages for me from parents. Didn't anyone at least call and send their regrets? Not one…. I sat and drank three cups of coffee alone, reflecting on what had gone wrong, what should I have done differently?…. I knew the parents were beginning to trust us, did they think that it was better to leave well enough alone? Was it simply they didn't want to be bothered during their private time? Did they need more notice? What was it? I had to get to the bottom of this.

After asking a lot of questions, I discovered another obstacle. Parents in the South Simcoe neighbourhood, in fact more parents than schools would like to admit, looked upon an invitation to a chat with the principal as a sign their child was in trouble, they were being "Called to the office". This was never a good thing, another one of those negative perceptions built up over time. It's no wonder they chose not to respond. Who wants to spend time in a school hearing bad news about their kids, or being "told off" for something? I was disheartened by this because I thought our Sunshine Calls dealt with the bad news issue. Obviously, trusting us enough to answer the phone did not carry over to coming to have a chat with the principal.

I decided to persevere; it was too important an issue to let it go. One morning I went out into the school yard and spoke to parents as they were dropping off their children. I wanted to explain to as many as I could, that coming to meet me and chat with me did not mean they or their children were in trouble. I also invited them in to have coffee and chat with me. I approached one mother and invited her in, and she agreed. I was encouraged. So this was all it took, I thought, a personal face to face invitation. I went up to another and her response was frankly rude. "Why should I talk to you?" she said. "I've got better things to do with my time." The next woman was just as brusque. "Leave me alone," she said. "I don't want to see you. I'm not in trouble." Another woman told me that she didn't want to talk to me because she didn't have a problem. "But when I do," she warned, "you'll be hearing from me!" Some parents, thank goodness, heard me out, and out of perhaps two dozen I approached, three agreed to come inside for coffee and a chat. But even they were suspicious of my motives. "Why are we really here?" one parent asked as soon as we sat down. I began by asking them to get more involved with the school, reminding them of our motto, "Together We Light The Way". I explained that we put a great deal of effort into sprucing up the school, so it would be a warm and welcoming place to learn. I explained the school's goals and expectations for our children. I explained why we needed to focus on developing social and emotional skills as well as sound academic skills, increasing academic achievement, as well as overall success in school.

Seeing the interest on their faces, I kept going, explaining that in terms of behaviour, we wanted class rooms and a playground where children felt safe, we didn't want fighting and bullying, we wanted everyone to get along in the school, learn how to develop respectful relationships and to work as one large team that respected and cared for one another. I continued to explain that we saw each child as an individual with unique gifts, talents and capabilities and we wanted to nurture and strengthen those. We also wanted everyone involved in the teaching and learning process to have a voice, not just the school staff and the board but also parents, other caregivers and above all the students themselves. If we were to make the changes we wanted and needed, we could not do all of this on our own, we would have to join together and move forward. This meant the parents couldn't simply rely on me or on the teachers to make all the necessary changes. We had to share leadership and take joint responsibility for the education and well-being of "our children," all doing our part, not a part assigned by anyone but simply just doing what needed to be done. We saw everyone as having a role to play in this process of change.

"How are you going to do all this?" They asked. We aren't teachers, and we don't know how to help you. I, then, explained that we were already getting lots of training on different types of teaching strategies, ways of differentiating and personalizing instruction to help children learn. We now had a daily goal setting process in every classroom and we were measuring the achievement of every student's goals. They were particularly interested when I explained even the most difficult goals can be achieved if we break them down into small achievable steps and use the right strategy that matches the student's learning style. I opened a student's portfolio, pulled out a graph and showed them how we measured each child's progress and how we were teaching the children to understand and interpret the graphs themselves so they could analyze their results and take more responsibility for their own learning and achievement.

I stopped to catch my breath and asked, "How do you feel about all this? Do you have any suggestions for us, any ideas about how to better help your children? You are their parents, you know them best. I know that if we share the same expectations for their success they will achieve all that we want them to". Please feel free to speak your minds. There was a long silence before one woman said, in genuine surprise, "You mean you want our opinion?" I told her I certainly did. "Okay then, I have a lot of things that I can talk about." She began with a list of all the things she did not like. She did not like the way children in some classes were free to walk around the room, she did not like the idea of children working in groups and coming up with the answer together, and maybe copying from one another. She preferred if they sat in rows and concentrated on getting their work done. This was the way she had been taught, and she didn't do too badly.

I patiently explained that children learn and demonstrate their intelligence in multiple ways, and that as educators we were learning different ways of presenting instruction and providing our students with different ways of demonstrating their learning. We used a variety of teaching strategies and techniques, so we could help every child to learn. "When children seem to be 'wandering' around the classroom, they aren't doing this willy-nilly; they are learning in a different way.

Learning co-operatively was one of these ways. Working in groups allowed the students to learn and practice academic as well as social skills. They learned how to work together as a team, how to listen to and respect the ideas of others, how to disagree in an agreeable manner, how to present their own ideas, and how to put all the good ideas together to come up with the best solution. I kept the explanations simple, and saw how keen the parents were to learn about all this. I was relieved: they were, after all, interested in what went on at the school.

I suggested that we meet on a regular basis, so that they could ask more of these kinds of questions and share their ideas with me. "How often?" one parent asked. I asked how often the group felt would be necessary, convenient and realistic. We agreed on once a month for one hour. Another parent suggested that we should find a name for the group, and someone said, "How about Parent Rap?" Parent Rap it was. We agreed that this gathering would be a forum for discussing and exchanging ideas about raising and educating all the children in the school, an opportunity for everyone to become involved in decision-making and a chance to solve problems that affected the school as a whole. Half of the hour would be devoted to their personal concerns as parents, and the other half to educational issues I needed to make them aware of. It would not be a forum for discussing teachers and individual students. If some one wanted to talk about their own child, this would be handled by making an appointment with the teacher or with me.

Half an hour had passed and no one seemed in a hurry to leave, so I invited them to remain and chat, explaining I put aside the morning to spend all the time they needed, since this was so important. They stayed two hours, sipping coffee, discussing the challenges of raising and educating children, and gradually warming to the idea of becoming more involved in helping to make decisions regarding the school's activities.

Although I recruited only three parents to this point, I was elated at the kind of discussion that took place during that first session. I made the Parent Rap meetings a top priority. In all the eight years I was at the school, I only missed one due to illness.

At one early session a mother who was joining the group for the first time arrived upset with me, and quickly began explaining why. "My daughter did not want to eat her food," she said, "and when I ordered her to finish what was on her #%@$ plate," she said, bristling, do you know what she said? She told me that I had no right to swear at her like that. She said I was being disrespectful to her and that SHE had the right to be respected. Can you imagine? My own child! I am her mother! When I asked her who the hell had given her that idea, she said it was you, Mrs Dean! She said that you," pointing her finger in my face, "said that everyone has the right to be respected regardless of their age, and furthermore that no one has the right to yell, swear at them or be abusive in any way. I am her mother; I have the right to tell her what to do. Explain yourself lady!"

The mother narrowed her eyes. "Is that the kind of crap you're teaching here, telling kids not to listen to their parents?" she demanded. I was taken aback at her anger but I remained calm and said, "As a matter of fact, it is. Let me explain." To my great relief and delight, other parents began explaining to her that respectful speech and behaviour were very important at South Simcoe. They explained that one of our guiding principles was "Everyone has the right to be respected and the responsibility to respect others." Furthermore, all the students signed respectful relationship agreements and set personal management goals, saying that rather than fighting or bullying others, they would be respectful and caring. Creating healthful, safe, caring and inclusive relationships based on mutual trust was a key thing at South Simcoe. If you respect children, they will begin to respect you, they told her. It felt so good to hear them say those words, this was a wonderful measure of the positive change that was taking place in our school.

Despite all the good things, by the end of the school year at South Simcoe I began questioning if Parent Rap was worth the time and effort we were putting into it. Our Sunshine Calls and personal invitations were helping to increase the numbers of parents who responded to our calls and came to report card interviews, and they were also helping to build positive relationships with parents and helping them to trust that the school was a place in which their children could succeed.

Although the discussions and the input given by parents was great, Parent Rap was not so far successful in actually bringing large numbers of moms, dads and caregivers into the school. I wanted to reach more people. I knew that teaching and learning would be enhanced so much more if we could just generate a wider base of support and a deeper level of engagement from the parents. "Do you really think we should continue with these meetings?" I asked at the last Parent Rap session in June. "I do a great deal of planning and preparation for them; this takes a great deal of my time, yet we still have only the three of you here for the sessions." "Of course, they answered, you can't give up yet," one parent responded. "We love the time we spend here and the way we can talk so openly to you, we learn so much and we have a better understanding of how the school works and how we can help our children to learn. We now expect so much more for our children because we see that they can do more.

You must admit, now we speak our minds and help to make decisions, we also complain a lot less." Another suggested that we set a goal of doubling the attendance at Parent Rap by Christmas of the coming school year. The parents agreed to take responsibility for spreading the word about our parent rap sessions and recruiting people to attend. They began actively advertising throughout the neighbourhood. Parent Rap was fun, they told everyone. You get to enjoy coffee and snacks, and the principal is always there to talk to you and listen to you. You learn a lot too about your child's education. The big thing is you get to tell the principal what you like and don't like and you get to help to make decisions about what goes on. Wasn't that worth an hour a month?

By Christmas we had exceeded our goal: for every month of the school year thus far, we had over fifteen parents: at the December session we had twenty five. Talk about dramatic increase! I certainly learned that parents listened to parents, more than to the principal. The group continued to grow rapidly with every session. Over the years we consistently had numbers of forty and more.

I wanted the discussions at Parent Rap to be open and lively, with a healthy airing of different opinions and different points of view. I wanted us to be able to confront bothersome issues and deal with them. This naturally led to a few tense moments in the early sessions. To keep the "Feel free to speak your mind" atmosphere whilst still focusing on creating healthy and respectful relationships and avoiding negative and disrespectful speech and behaviour, we developed a series of agreements (ground rules) for successful interaction:

- *We share leadership in the teaching and learning process.*
  We have high expectations for our children and we work together to discuss issues, solve problems and reach decisions, in order to improve their education and well-being.

- *We respect.*
  We recognize that everyone has the right to be respected, and we accept that with that right comes the responsibility to treat others in a respectful and caring manner.

- *We love and we care.*
  We work together in a loving and caring manner to provide a supportive and nurturing environment for our children.

- *We value and include everyone.*
  We realize that everyone has a role to play in raising and educating children, therefore we accept, appreciate and include everyone's opinions and ideas.

We made it as easy and convenient as possible for parents to attend. Some parents, for example, were able to attend only when they brought their preschool children to the Parent Rap sessions. Carl Reimer, a member of the Kiwanis, suggested that we invite St. John's Ambulance members to train a group of students to babysit the children.(this organization was licensed to train babysitters). The Kiwanis group paid for the workbooks and students were trained. This was beneficial to both students and parents, since it provided these students with a much needed skill; many of them babysat their younger siblings and family members anyway. Some even did babysitting in the neighbourhood, with no training and preparation. This also provided the parents with time to concentrate on learning about parenting and educating their children.

In order to maintain the trustful relationships we were building, we always tried to respond to the needs and wants of the parents. A strategy that worked well for this, was to ask at the end of every session: What did you like best about this session? What would you like to learn more about? How will this help you to help your child learn and grow?

When the parents asked for help in street-proofing their children, we invited a police officer to discuss the issue and give them some practical and doable strategies. When they said they didn't really understand what the report cards were saying, even after they attended an interview, we reviewed our report cards thoroughly, dropped the academic jargon and made the language simple and easy to understand. Report cards always began with a positive comment about the child. Interestingly enough some of our business partners who were very well educated told us that they too found school report cards difficult to understand. I guess we all get so caught up in our own fields of work that we forget to simplify the terms we use when communicating to others.

We began inviting speakers from a number of organizations to attend the Parent Rap sessions to discuss and give parents strategies for dealing with situations like, what to do in a medical emergency, handling bedtime routines, temper tantrums, siblings fighting, bullying and so much more. Parents began to see the sense in being more connected to the school since they always left with practical and useful strategies they could implement right away at home. The range of speakers that arrived at Parent Rap, and their topics would have done Oprah proud. A public health professional explained the connection between good nutrition and learning. She told us that if we expected our children to do well we would have to do our best to ensure they were being given healthy and nutritious meals. This seemed to be an insurmountable challenge since most families were on a limited budget. How could they plan and prepare healthy, low-cost family meals with so little to spend on food? To figure out how to best do this, the mother of one of our teachers, a retired bank manager, arrived to explain how to prepare and manage a home budget. Another speaker demonstrated how to shop wisely and read food labels in order to obtain top value for every dollar spent. We went one step further and held a few hands-on sessions where the parents actually went on a shopping trip, bought the ingredients, reading the labels carefully of course, then prepared some sample meals. Later, the teachers said they learned as much as the parents from these sessions.

When we found out that many of the students were not doing well in mathematics and science and parents were not really encouraging them in these areas since they did not see the importance of these subjects, we invited Pamela Anderson, a banker, to speak to the group. She spoke to parents and students about the importance of entrepreneurship and employability skills, and she explained it was important for their children to do well in mathematics and science as well as reading and writing since so many of the jobs today involved these subjects. She also talked about the importance of children practising leadership skills and taking responsibility for their own learning, so that they would be valuable team members in the school and in the workplace. She described how technology was changing the workplace and the skills needed. She received an overwhelming response when she invited the parents to visit her in a gleaming downtown Toronto bank tower to experience what she was talking about first-hand. Parents returned from this visit determined to help their children do better in math and science.

We didn't always go outside the group for speakers. In keeping with our focus on shared leadership, we explored the strengths and talents of our group and found that some of our own Parent Rap members had skills and knowledge of their own to share, and they did, with enthusiasm and great personal satisfaction. They, too, were capable of playing a lead role.

When the government slashed social assistance payments, it was the members of Parent Rap, with the help of our social worker, Theresa, who prepared a community directory of social services in the area. This directory could be used when someone needed help the school could not provide, or when there was an issue outside of the school's mandate or jurisdiction. Later, the directory was used in a number of other schools in the neighbourhood. The South Simcoe parents began to be invited to other schools to explain how the directory could be used. They were so helpful to the other parent groups, they began to receive invitations to talk to parents about parents and educators working together as a team in the raising and educating of children, how parents could and should get involved in decision-making, how to share parental information and understandings about children that would help the school to design more effective instruction. Veronica Lacey, Director of the North York School District (a very large and thriving school district) invited them to speak to her principals at the board's annual principals' conference. Joan Green, Director of EQAO, the standardized testing unit of the Ontario Ministry of Education, invited them to give her their input into the reporting of the standardized testing process, Louise Brown the education reporter for The Toronto Star, a large Toronto newspaper featured them in a front page story.... What a tribute to their talents!

To demonstrate that I appreciated just how stressful parenting can be, we held special sessions to address questions of personal health and well-being, an area of life that parents, teachers and other caregivers so very often neglect. We had sessions on dealing with stress and taking time to nurture yourself, so you were better prepared to look after your children. For these sessions, I began gathering small door prizes, from staff, friends and family; little trinkets, perfume and cosmetic samples, aromatherapy soaps and tea and coffee mugs, things that could be used for self-care. We distributed them and participants loved it. These health and well-being sessions were extremely popular. Parents were really moved by the fact that we cared about them as individuals not only as parents who could help us to help their children. Some said that they became motivated to begin taking better care of themselves. Some said they felt more prepared to accept the great responsibilities that come with having children.

It was at one of these sessions that I had a huge awakening. Here I was focusing on the numbers, getting more and more people involved and I realized that parental involvement was so much more than numbers. When parents didn't "show up" it didn't mean they were not involved. There were so many ways of being involved that were not really being acknowledged even though they were valued. A parent who made sure that her child had nutritious meals, a good night's sleep, time and a place to do homework, all of this was involvement. In fact even if this was all the involvement parents had, what a huge difference this made.

Parent Rap grew into more than a way of involving and engaging parents in understanding the requirements of the curriculum, more than a way of creating positive, healthy and caring relationships between the school and the home, more than a way of parents supporting their children's learning by what they said and what they did. It grew into a powerful phenomenon. It was a catalyst for educational as well as social change in the school community. It helped to raise the parents' expectations about their children's success, what they were capable of, what they could aspire to, how different their futures could be and how important a role they as parents could play in this whole process. Eventually Parent Rap participants gained the confidence to become involved in other community groups so they could have more of a voice in what went on in their neighbourhood around their children.

They wanted to see improvements in the quality of life throughout the South Simcoe neighbourhood. Parent Rap participants became such strong advocates for their school and community, they were cited in the Royal Commission on Learning as a "Success Story and model for others to follow." They broke through social and educational barriers that many parents from low income neighbourhoods face. Over the years, they became engaged. they became leaders amongst their peers.

I began to wonder who was learning more from this experience— me or the parents? In spite of my beliefs about equality, I had to admit I arrived at South Simcoe with some preconceived ideas about the parents of the students. Among them was the possibility the parents did not care enough about their children to become involved with the school. They weren't taking enough responsibility for their children and placed too little value on education. My underlying feeling was: *Why can't they just get up and do something to improve their lives? Then they can help their children. Don't they understand the value of education? Don't they love their children enough to do this?.*

This attitude is not, I'm sorry to say, rare among middle-class people who have never found themselves in situations of severe economic stress, or who have never been deprived of the basics in life, or of emotional support…it is very common for them to look at residents of neighbourhoods like South Simcoe and ask the same questions.

Let me tell you about my encounter with Sylvia. Sylvia's son Mark, a grade four student, suffered from severe learning problems. Mark could neither read nor write and, what's more, he didn't seem to care. Mark's teacher and I discussed his needs and agreed we would recommend placement in one of our "special needs" classes, in order for him to receive the extra assistance and specialized programming he so desperately needed. We needed to have parental permission for this, but try as we might, Sylvia refused to sign the documents we needed to put this in place.

I persuaded Sylvia to visit me in my office, so we could discuss the issue. I planned to carefully explain the opportunity for more personalized programming in a smaller classroom and suggest that it was the best solution we could offer for Mark's difficulties. But no matter how clearly and carefully I spelled out the benefits for Mark, I could not persuade Sylvia to see our point of view. Sylvia grew more and more adamant about her refusal to permit Mark to go to a special class and, I must admit, I became more and more impatient with her. I simply could not understand why she did not want her son to benefit from this approach. In response to my plea, "please help me to understand why you are refusing this opportunity," Sylvia finally opened up with a tragic story that explained her reluctance and forced me to reassess my perception of her. Sylvia told me that her sister, while still a very young child, had been diagnosed as mentally handicapped. "She threw a lot of temper tantrums," Sylvia said, "and she was hard for my parents to control. The doctors couldn't do anything to help her, they thought she was crazy, so they recommended that my parents lock her up. She was just a little child, and they took her away to a home with other people who they thought were crazy too."Recalling her sister's story after all these years was painful, Sylvia's eyes filled with tears, but she kept going. "When she was an adult," Sylvia said, trying to maintain her composure, "after she spent all her childhood years in this home for the mentally handicapped, one teacher realized she was more capable than she appeared to be and asked the doctors to take another look at her case." Tears now began streaming down Sylvia's face. "And do you know what they found out? They found out that my sister was not mentally handicapped. In fact she was close to normal intelligence. She just had some hearing problems. She never should have been put away like that. But by then it was too late." I listened to her tale with growing horror. As a result of all the years confined in the company of truly handicapped people, Sylvia's sister had acquired so many strange mannerisms and made such strange noises, that people, even family were uncomfortable in her presence. Sylvia's sister was not mentally handicapped when admitted, and she was not mentally handicapped as an adult. But she appeared as though she were, and her appearance was so disturbing that she was never considered as a candidate for release. "This cost my sister her childhood," Sylvia said through her tears, "and her freedom. And why? Because somebody looked at her as a little child and decided she should be put away in a special place to receive the help she needed. Now do you see why I don't want my son placed in a special class to receive the help you say he needs?" Of course I did. I didn't agree with her decision, but I now understood her strong opposition to the idea. Sylvia wasn't refusing to agree to give her permission out of stubbornness, ignorance or lack of care, she was doing it out of love. She wanted to protect her son from risking the same horrible treatment her sister received, because she could no longer trust the system to do the correct thing.

Sylvia's story brought me to tears as well, and we cried together there in my office. I placed my arm around her shoulders. "Do you know what? I thought you were being stubborn for no reason and that you didn't care about your child's learning. *Now* I see that I was wrong", I said. "I see a mother who loves her child very much and wants to protect him. I'm sorry I misjudged you." My words took Sylvia by surprise, she told me after. The principal was saying that she was wrong and apologizing to her. This generated an unexpected response. Sylvia realized we had Mark's best interests at heart and asked me what she could do to work with us to improve Mark's situation. We reached a compromise. We agreed we could at least "identify" Mark as a student in need of special assistance, an important technicality. This allowed us to provide Mark with some of the extra assistance he needed without placing him in a special classroom.

I think of Sylvia and her sister whenever I hear people discuss the problems of handicapped or disadvantaged people as though the solutions to their problems are easy to implement and require nothing more than the courage to change, a one size fits all kind of approach. They don't relate to the idea that disadvantaged people, like everyone else, need to experience belonging, validation and love, but the obstacles and challenges they face get in the way of these experiences. We should not be too quick to reject, write off and give deficit diagnoses. Let's take the time to empathize, mentally "walk in their shoes" and treat them with more dignity and respect. The encounter with Sylvia helped me to gain a greater understanding of the school community. More and more I began to appreciate the complexity of the issues they were dealing with, the layers of hurt and long-term neglect and the impact of these on their dealings with me, with the teachers and with the school system as a whole. As a society, we applaud alcoholics who seek support from organizations like AA, drug addicts who go looking for assistance from physicians, and smokers who rely on their families or stop-smoking groups to break the nicotine habit. Isn't it time for us to work together to ensure effective support systems are put in place for broken and disadvantaged families?

LEADER'S REFLECTION

Sometimes it is difficult to reach those who are resistant, those who have had previous negative experiences with the leader and the organization. Successful leaders always "Find A Way," to include all voices.

- How do you facilitate communication with those who are resistant?

- Do you focus on finding a way to include everyone's voice?

CHAPTER 6

"Not My Kids, Our Kids!"

My childhood in Trinidad was influenced, one way or another, by everyone in our community. The African proverb "It takes a village to raise a child" has become something of a cliché, but like most clichés, it happens to be true. In Trinidad, we could always count on neighbours for support when we needed it, just as our neighbours knew they could count on us. Children everywhere need this kind of support from their communities. Life has become too complex for any single group to raise, care for, educate children, and address all their needs.

Yet, I sensed a reluctance among people to reach out to their neighbours in the South Simcoe neighbourhood. Some of this, of course, was due to the transient nature of the people who lived there. It takes time to build relationships among adults (children seem to do it so quickly and naturally!), and some families simply didn't remain in one place long enough to even get to know their neighbours, much less rely on them.

I was determined, naturally, that South Simcoe Public School would become the centre of its community, a place where everyone could put their heads together and make decisions that were in the best interests of the children. I drew on my personal feelings about asking for help, starting with our lack of a proper meeting room. During the first several months the only place we could meet within the school was in the hallway; it was the only space large enough to accommodate the entire group of students and teachers, and it simply would not do. In order to foster a team spirit, we needed a place where we could meet as one, where the entire school could assemble, hold concerts, other presentations, and, most of all, celebrate our successes.

The nearby Legion Hall had been used by the school a few times in the past for graduation exercises. Why not ask if we could use it on a regular basis, I wondered? The manager's own child attended South Simcoe Public School years before, when the area was a thriving community, a place where children felt safe, protected and loved. So he had a special appreciation for our efforts to revive that environment for the children.

He agreed to let us use the hall, reserving the right to review the situation each month, and asking that we leave the room as clean as we found it. Of course we would—and did. This was the critical first step in our partnership efforts, which forged an amazing bond between the school and the surrounding community.

Once we had a place where we could meet as a team, gather to listen to speakers, and generally to feel togetherness, as a school, we grew even closer. Meanwhile, the manager began spreading news of the school's achievements among the Legion members. With time, the members saw South Simcoe children not as ones who might wreck their hall, but as basically decent children who simply needed support and attention. Once that idea was firmly planted, the Legion members began reaching out to us. What did we think of some war veterans visiting the school on Remembrance Day to talk to our students and tell them personal stories of World War II, the Korean War and other conflicts? Naturally, we thought it would be wonderful. There could be no better way for children to appreciate the sacrifices these men and others of their generation made. It would bring history to life, by associating real live faces with events from long ago. It would be like a living library that would bring the generations together.

Their visits were followed by other offers from the Legion members, who donated stacks of *National Geographic* magazines and supported a wide range of school events throughout the year. Soon, four Kiwanis Club members who formed a band called The

Three Harmony Cats and One Dog Drummer began performing for our children, who sang along and accompanied the musicians with percussion instruments. The music from our intergenerational band may not have been concert-hall quality, unless you measure harmony and rhythm according to the level of joy it creates, but these performances were great fun for everyone involved, and the mutual joy created between people separated by several decades is something to behold.

As we began to acknowledge all the assistance available to us from the surrounding community, we agreed on some guidelines about the kind of help and support we wanted. For example, we did not want either the school or the children to be considered "charity cases." We sought people and organizations who would abide by our guiding principles, share our beliefs, and who were prepared to go the extra mile if needed to reach a goal. We wanted support from those who believed in our children, and who would help us awaken all the energy and potential within them, so they could grow and develop and take their place in the community.

We wanted long-term partnerships with these people. Too many of the children had already suffered abandonment of one kind or another in their short lives, and we didn't want to risk the effect of having new people, however well meaning, move into their lives, only to vanish quickly and leave them feeling abandoned once more. We wanted help from people who agreed to be there for the long haul.

The Legion Hall was just to the north of the school. In the opposite direction, and directly across the street, sat a strip mall, and I remembered how my heart sank at the first sight of it. Malls represent tempting opportunities for adolescents, ranging from loitering to outright vandalism and theft. Even though we continued to make steady progress with our children, the mall presented as big a problem to us as many of the children did to the mall merchants.

Shoplifting by South Simcoe students and other children in the community was a major headache for the store owners. Things grew complicated when the owners were both unable to contact the parents and reluctant to call the police. Invariably, they turned to us. Or more precisely, to me.

"We caught another one of your kids shoplifting over here," the store manager might say to me over the telephone. "Why can't the school do something about them?"

The first few times I heard this, I naturally felt distressed, and perhaps a little guilty because I didn't solve the problem. As time went on, I grew more and more frustrated, until one day when yet another merchant called to complain about "your kids." Slipping into my coat, I marched across the street to the mall and entered his store. I try to remain even-tempered at all times, but I must admit I was close to losing it on this occasion.

"Look," I said to the store manager, "I'm tired of being called to come over and pick up *my* kids. These are not just *my* kids. They are *our* kids. They live around here. Their parents shop here. They are every bit as much a part of this community as you are. So instead of expecting me to solve the problem on my own, why don't you offer to help me?"

"OK," the manager said calmly. "I'll help you, what do you want me to do?"

His cool and helpful response was unexpected, and I was taken aback for a moment. The man was offering to help me solve a major problem. " Well.. I'm not quite sure, let me think about it," I said, "and I'll get back to you."

Returning to my office, I gave the idea some thought. If the Legion could become partners and actively involved in our activities, why not the store owners? The first thing to do, I decided, was not to take the children over to the mall—that was hardly necessary, after all—but to invite the merchants into the school, where we could put our heads together and come up with some sort of plan.

I approached the manager of the Swiss Chalet restaurant in the mall, a man named Phil Lawson. He would be, I feared, a hard sell. The kids often amused themselves by loosening lids on his salt and pepper shakers, and similar stunts that created constant headaches for him and his staff. But Phil surprised me by quickly agreeing that we needed to put our collective heads together and find a way to deal with our problem.

At our first meeting, Phil suggested that if he and other mall merchants would cross the street, enter the school and speak to the children in their own environment, perhaps the children would be more respectful. They would begin to see the merchants as friends and neighbours. Phil's biggest concern was that the children might ask him some tough questions.

"If they do," I assured him, "I'll be there to help you answer them, assuming they're not too tough for me as well."He was a hit! During his talk to our grade eight students, Phil talked about what had inspired him to become an entrepreneur, he spoke about employability skills and what he expected in a great employee. He even suggested some of the students might run a restaurant like his one day or be a boss to other restaurant owners. "And if you do," he said, "I know you'll want everyone to treat you with respect. It would also be important for you to treat them with respect and kindness," When he finished, the children swamped him with all sorts of questions, some amusing, some provocative and some rather profound. Phil treated them all seriously, listening carefully and answering in as much detail as the children could understand. When the presentation concluded and the children returned to their class, buzzing with excitement about all they had learned, I posed a question of my own. What would he think, I asked Phil, about pairs of grade eight students actually visiting behind the scenes at his restaurant for short periods of time during the school day, to observe the kinds of activities he had just described?

"Why not?" he said. "We can at least try it."

It became much more than an experiment; it grew into one of the most rewarding programs we launched at South Simcoe. Suddenly, the children realized that concepts such as relationships, teamwork and leadership were not just ideas cooked up by the teachers to keep everyone organized and respectful in the classroom. They were considered important skills and qualities by society in general. Even something as simple as assembling and serving a salad meant accepting responsibility and trusting others to do their job correctly. The person assembling the salad, expected that the person preparing the radishes would wash and cut them properly, the same for the tomatoes and all the other items that went into the salad. Each person depended on the others in the team, especially when the salad was to be served to several dozen people. They also recognized the intangible rewards meaningful work can bring. I asked Samuel, one of the first students to visit the restaurant, what he enjoyed most. "It was fun making the food and then watching people eat it," he said. "They liked the food, and I wanted to go up and say, 'I'm glad you like it…because I made it!'"

Before each visit to Phil's restaurant the students were prepared by their teachers to observe how the lessons taught in the classroom about Respect, Teamwork and Leadership were applied outside the school setting. Phil took the time to reinforce the concepts and explain the work, why it was important, and how everyone on the restaurant staff counted on each other—this brought to life everything we were teaching.

Very quickly we saw positive changes take place on both sides of the fence. The small acts of vandalism at Swiss Chalet virtually disappeared, because the manager and staff were now the children's friends. Phil developed a special kinship with the children. It was no longer *your* kids, but *our* kids. "How are our kids doing?" he might say when we met. He also saw them as individuals, with special personalities and skills. "How 's that little Sammy doing?" he would ask. "Boy he asks a lot of questions! And how about Charmaine? She says she wants to be a waitress, but I told her she's bright enough to run this place." Whenever Phil entered the school, children ran up to shake his hands and say, "Hi, Mr. Lawson! How's business?"

Later, Phil arranged for the Swiss Chalet chicken mascot to participate in several events at the school. Whether it was the unusual sight of an adult-sized costumed chicken or the goodwill generated from Phil's support for the school, the Swiss Chalet chicken brought more than excitement and popularity with him. Whenever the chicken planted a flower in our garden, for instance, it was remembered by the children as "one of the Chicken's flowers," and received extra care and attention.

From this rather uncertain beginning, these visits evolved into a partnering program, later called Connections: Classroom and Community. This program had a powerful impact on our senior students and really inspired them to improve academically. Later, we extended our reach and began to include not only businesses in the neighbouring mall, but major corporations as well, or more specifically, individuals in these organizations.

Participation by these concerned and caring individuals varied widely, according to their situations. Some visited the school, working with our students, on a regular weekly basis. Others arrived less frequently, every few months perhaps, while many chose to work with us in a continuous advisory capacity, helping us in our strategic planning and program operations.

People analyzing the success of this program thought that its strength and impact came from the fact that instead of imposing a task on our partners, we always brought up an issue we needed assistance with and asked "How can we work together to deal with this situation?" We always discussed the issue in the larger context of the goals of the school and its community and worked collaboratively to develop and implement a plan of action. The result was being able to draw on an amazing collection of skills, each adding its own unique dimension to our solutions.

Rob Pitfield, for example, an executive vice-president with Scotiabank, arrived to read stories to our younger children. Soon, his visits included relating tales of his successes and achievements with grade seven students. The bonding between Rob and both groups of students was remarkable. When Rob invited the grade one children to visit him at his office, they enthusiastically agreed and, on the scheduled day, were so excited that they burst in on an important meeting he was chairing with shouts of "Hi Rob!" and began describing him to the startled onlookers as "Our Rob. He's our Rob!" Rob, to his credit, accepted the interruption with his usual good grace and humour.

Another bank executive, Linda Sinclair, grew so impressed with our programs that she also invited students to visit her in her Royal Bank of Canada office. Later, I was invited to speak to a group of

Royal Bank's Ontario managers about setting and achieving goals. Terry Morgan, manager at the nearby Toronto-Dominion Bank, helped our senior classes learn how to open a bank account, write cheques, balance a chequebook, establish and maintain a budget. Canada Trust, through their Friends of the Environment program, assisted the school in planting and maintaining the lovely flower gardens that gave so many people so much pleasure.

Tom McNown, who was with the marketing division of General Motors of Canada, invited our grade eight class to GM'sheadquarters, where he showed how the same mathematical skills they were learning in class were being applied every day by GM employees. And when one of the science classes at our school was having difficulty grasping the concept of fuel, propulsion and energy, Tom arrived in person to explain the principles. I'm told the children talked about his lesson for weeks afterward and, I suspect, will never forget it.

Barry Kuntz, with General Motors, arranged for his staff to provide a large tent at the school during our Community Celebration Days, where members of GM's Ontario zone arrived to read stories aloud to large groups of children who, of course, enjoyed it immensely.

Still with GM, Ann Nurse, owner of a local Saturn autodealership, volunteered to speak on the importance of teamwork and the role it played in helping her firm provide satisfactory customer service. Ann also became a regular guest at our Circles of Love reading events.

It's important to note the value of these partnerships and their positive impact on the children. These were busy senior executives, often with responsibilities far beyond the South Simcoe community, who believed it was important to contribute their time in this manner. Logic told the children that, if these partners felt it was important to spend time with them, then they themselves must be important, and the boost it provided to their sense of self was obvious and immeasurable.

On a more practical note, the children began to understand the skills, strategies and knowledge they were acquiring at school had very practical applications in the world of work and life. The employees at GM and in the banks were using graphs each day, the same kinds of graphs as the students were learning about. Now it made more sense to learn about them. This encouraged the students to strive to do better. They could now understand that seemingly abstract concepts such as teamwork, self-respect and respect for others, as well as leadership, were important to learn and practice in school, because they were needed and valued, not just at school by their teachers, but also out of school by society in general.

Due to their visits to large organizations, corporate offices, universities and colleges, the students could now envision themselves in a variety of career and life situations. I still find it interesting that people expect children or even adults for that matter to envision and aspire to a different life for themselves if they have no idea what that life could look like.

There was very little talk any more about dropping out of school, and in the workplace or out of it, the children realized they would need to collaborate, make decisions, relate to the needs of others, build and maintain relationships, and appreciate and accept differences between individuals. Working with partners, these concepts were modeled, assimilated and brought to life with amazing clarity, impact and conviction.

I'm the first to admit that the idea of partnering with others in this way, did not spring fully conceived from my mind. Frankly, it grew out of a practical need to reach beyond the school itself in search of assistance in helping the children to learn. No one, including me, could foresee the degree of its success and the way it generated innumerable benefits for everyone concerned. Most important of all, partnerships demonstrated the benefits to be gained when schools, businesses and the community at large all work together to help children learn.

I wish I could say that partnerships were responsible for totally eliminating all the problems our neighbours were having with South Simcoe students, but things are rarely that simple. They did make a significant difference in increasing the children's awareness of their responsibilities as citizens. They also changed the attitude of mall merchants towards the children. They moved from suspicion and near outright hostility to understanding and co-operation. Yet problems lingered.

One Monday morning I arrived at school to discover two grade eight boys were caught shoplifting some items from one of the mall stores on the weekend. I called one of them, a cocky but, darn it, likeable boy named Jacques, into my office.

"Jacques," I said with great disappointment, "how could you do such a thing? You know these people now. They are our friends and our neighbours. They came into the school here and talked to us. They work with us here. They help us. How could you treat them like that?"

Jacques looked bewildered. "Why are you so upset, Mrs. Dean?" he said. "Heck, it happened on a Saturday. School was closed."

I couldn't help myself. I burst out laughing, even as part of me wanted to cry. After all we did, after all the progress we made, Jacques and his friends still thought it was all right to shoplift as long as the school was closed for the weekend. Talk about situation specific behaviour.

When we dealt with one problematic aspect in the children's behaviour, another seemed to pop up to replace it. In spite of Jacques's transgression, shoplifting incidents decreased significantly. Then, we heard reports of other unacceptable behaviour. Among the many businesses at the mall was a weight-loss clinic. The clinic's patrons, who were already conscious of their appearance and the need to reduce their weight, began complaining to the clinic owner about remarks being directed at them from some of our students. "Pig!" and "Fat cow!" were just two of the comments made by the children as the customers arrived. This was so upsetting to the patrons, and so damaging to the clinic operator, that she began circulating a petition to have all South Simcoe students banished from the entire mall.

The incidents in front of the weight-loss clinic were not the only ones of their kind. Some South Simcoe children were also verbally abusing visitors to the blood donor clinic in the mall. We needed to do something quickly. One solution was to put an added focus on 'respect for the local community,' in our lessons. Developing respectful and caring relationships was working well within the school; why couldn't it improve things beyond the school as well? If the children clearly understood that as respectful, compassionate and caring individuals, they were expected to be more sensitive to the feelings of others, I knew they would see hurling insults at innocent strangers was hurtful, unkind and disrespectful. But that would be a long-term goal. For the moment we needed to patch things up with the merchants, and save our promising partnership initiative.

Once again, I turned to Phil Lawson of Swiss Chalet and Peter Jefferson, the Zellers manager, for help. They quickly organized a meeting at the restaurant, inviting the mall merchants, our staff and several parents as well. We needed Phil's natural diplomacy and his ability to see both sides of the debate because many of the merchants arrived visibly angered. "Something has to be done about those kids," the manager of the weight-loss clinic almost shouted, thumping her fist on the table, "Something drastic. We cannot have them coming over here when they feel like it and shouting horrible things at our customers, scaring them away. They're stealing merchandise when our backs are turned, and generally acting as though they own the place.

Phil explained how his involvement with the school had changed things at Swiss Chalet. "Since I started working with the kids, I don't have problems anymore," he said. Then, his voice softened, he added: "They're just kids. We have to get together and help them." Phil's words were spoken with deep sincerity, and as he began to relate examples of the positive results he observed, he began to win others over to his side.

"Maybe we can all find some way of working together to do something special for the kids, then they'll see us in a more favourable light," one of the merchants offered. "If we can all work with the school, the kids will know we care about them and will be more respectful to us," another suggested. "I mean the entire mall and the whole school."

"How about the Santa Claus parade?" It was the owner of the weight-loss clinic, the same woman who had earlier been so demanding of tougher discipline. The City of Oshawa sponsored an annual Santa Claus parade through the city to officially launch the holiday season. "Maybe we can enter a float in the parade, representing both the school and the mall," they suggested.

Almost everyone began nodding their heads at the idea. Everyone, that is, except me. I loved the enthusiasm being generated, and the fact they wanted to do so much for the children thrilled me. But I always emphasized the concept of balance to my staff. Christmas was a stressful time for many, and the staff would be facing demands on their attention at home. I was afraid they were assuming too much responsibility—the parade was less than three weeks away, report cards were due, there was so much planning to be done...

Before I could voice my concerns, the idea took on a life of its own. With everyone contributing ideas, it was agreed the South Simcoe float in the city's Santa Claus parade would be a joint

production by the school and the mall. Everyone seemed enthusiastic and confident. "We can handle the workload," Kim and Tamara two teachers attending the meeting assured me when the meeting ended. "We really want to do it!"

For months, I was telling staff and students alike they must have dreams and set goals, then be determined to make them real. How could I suggest they were taking on too much responsibility now? But I had serious reservations. They were soon dispelled. Rob, Kim's husband, an enthusiastic amateur pilot, managed to obtain some hangar space, where the float could be constructed, at the local airport. Every evening for two weeks the staff, mall merchants and members of the local Kiwanis Club pitched in to design and build a South Simcoe float, working in the unheated airplane hangar. That year, the Oshawa Santa Claus parade featured a joint presentation from the mall and the school, with students waving and cheering from the back of a large flatbed truck—decorated with a giant banner declaring "Community Partnerships." The meeting, which was called to find ways of splitting the mall and school apart, actually produced a method of bringing them closer together than ever before, working in partnership for the education and well-being of the children.

As the number of our community partners grew, I was careful to involve only those dedicated to giving openly and lovingly of their time. Actions that demonstrated this attitude meant so much more to the children than a simple expenditure of money. I wanted partners motivated not by a need to assuage their conscience or enhance their corporate image, but by a sense of social responsibility to help educate the children. People who wanted to work with us agreed to abide by our guiding principles; they were much more important to us than those who simply offered to write us a cheque.

Whenever we discussed working with a potential new community partner, our first question was: "What's in it for the children?" If the benefits to them were minimal, we either proposed a different kind of contribution or politely declined the offer.

Partners who contributed their time to help the children discovered wonderful, often unexpected, rewards. The children at South Simcoe were not too "cool" to hide their appreciation for the partners' efforts. Their openly expressed joy made the partners feel needed and important, which in turn encouraged them to spend more time with the children and explore more ways of lending assistance. "The smiles on the faces of those children when they see me," one man told me, "is something I have never experienced before. It keeps bringing me back."

Our remarkable success in inspiring our students to do better academically, by reaching out beyond the school walls, encouraged me to explore new ways to enhance the curriculum. We began involving partners in a different way. At the beginning we sought out successful people who triumphed over difficult childhood experiences, similar to those faced by many South Simcoe children. We invited these people to the school to share their personal stories with the children. "Don't exaggerate and don't try to whitewash the things you went through," we advised the speakers. We explained these were streetwise children with realistic views of the world. "Talk about the choices you faced, good and bad, the ones you made, however small and the ones that moved you forward.," we suggested, adding: "Just be totally honest and upfront with the children.

They won't accept lies, and they don't need horror stories. They do need however, to know you experienced hardship along the way, that everyone has the power to make choices that can change the course of their lives, and they need the assurance they have the

115

strength and capability within to change their lives for the better as well."

Simply put, our children needed inspiration from people to whom they could relate, people who were proof that personal choices make a difference, people who refused to let problems defeat them, people who could help them understand that alternatives really did exist. People who could bring home the point that, while adversity is not what we wish for, often our greatest growth occurs as a result of our trials. It was, I had to admit to myself, a lesson I too was learning.

"The Choice is Yours, —that was the lesson"."The Choice is Yours", yes we had a name, demonstrated the various opportunities in life that are available to everyone, including those who suffer serious family or personal problems. The seeds of our success are within all of us, if we search deeply; that was the basic message.

One of the most popular "The Choice is Yours" speakers was Zanana Akande, minister of social services with the Ontario provincial government at the time. While the students may not have fully realized all of Zanana's responsibilities, they recognized she played a vital role in managing many important affairs, so they were taken aback when she asked: "How many of you have to study in the bathroom because there is no other private place to read or do your school work?" Most students in the audience raised their hands. "Well, so did I," she said. "But I did not let it get me down or stand in my way, and you should not either."

They immediately warmed to Zanana and began to pepper her with all sorts of questions, even asking her age. When she told them, they gasped. Of course all children in their early teens assume that anyone over thirty is a dinosaur. In fact the next question was, "What kind of cream do you use on your face to keep your skin looking so young?" which sent the province's minister of social services erupting into gales of laughter.

She was still chuckling when she bid me goodbye at the end of her visit. "Here I was, ready to answer all kinds of questions about my work and the government and such," she giggled, "and some kid wants to know what kind of face cream I use. It just made my day!"

Zanana was so taken by the students, and they with her, that she invited them to visit her at her office in the provincial legislature a few weeks later.

Somehow, everyone seemed a little more casual and relaxed in the new atmosphere at South Simcoe. Later in our "The Choice is Yours" program, Richard Irish, a business partner from Investors Group, made it possible for Robert Esmie, the Olympic gold medallist, to visit our school. He came bouncing down the hall as though strolling on the beach and, spotting me standing near a doorway, sashayed up, gave me his broadest grin and said, "How you doin'? You smell sweet, girl."

"Thank you, and welcome to South Simcoe Public School," I replied. "You must be Robert Esmie. Allow me to introduce myself. "I," I said in my mock-stern voice, "am the principal." Robert quickly grew sober and apologetic, like one of our grade six boys who was caught being naughty, until I convulsed in laughter.

His message to the students was similar to other speakers' in the program. Flashing his gold medal, won at the 1996 Atlanta Olympics, he told them that winning the medal was the fulfillment of a dream he had when he was their age, growing up in the rough Northern Ontario mining city of Sudbury. Robert and his friends all had dreams, and they shared them with each other. One boy wanted to become a doctor, another a teacher, and still another dreamed of becoming a karate master, opening his own school and maybe appearing in movies. Robert, of course, wanted to win a medal at the Olympics.

Here was the core of his story: *No one laughed at the others' dreams.* In fact they all promised to help one another achieve their dreams as they grew older, and they actually did. Even when some moved far from the city, the boys kept in touch, reminding each other of their dreams and how important they were. "And you know what?" Robert said. "We all made our dreams come true. We all became who we wanted to be. We never gave up."

The children sat enthralled. Here was an honest-to-goodness hero, describing all the hardships he suffered as a young child, first growing up in Jamaica, where he shared a bed with his two brothers, and later training steadily for days on end, often alone and with no promise of success, just to make his dream come true.

"You can become anything you want to be," Robert said, "from a sports hero to an A-average student. The important thing is to have a dream, treasure it, and do the things that will help make it real someday." People may scoff at your dream, he warned them. That doesn't matter. They were to keep believing in it, and believing in themselves. "Your biggest supporter," he said, "has to be you."

From others it might have sounded like just another pep talk, but Robert himself had put up with laughter from others about his dream. When he graduated from high school, Robert was a scrawny 115-pound kid who slept with a relay baton in his hand every night so it would become as much a part of him as his own hand, and so he could fall asleep dreaming of running the perfect relay race. "I began working out to build my muscles," he told the children, "and kept finding ways to run faster. And here I am today." Then he displayed the same baton his relay team carried to win the Olympic gold medal.

"And here is the baton I used." Nobody, of course, was laughing at Robert now.

He didn't sugar-coat life for the South Simcoe kids. He knew some of the hurdles these kids would face, because he encountered some himself. They were bound to face temptations, like drugs, that would pull them away from their dreams. They had to recognize these temptations for what they were: barriers to making their dreams come true. They had to use all the problems they encountered, and overcame, to make themselves stronger. "Don't ever forget where you are coming from," he advised them, "and always know where you are going."

Later he let every child hold his precious Olympic gold medal. "Make a wish when you touch it," he suggested, and I will never forget the expressions on their faces as they closed their eyes, made their wish and imagined their dream coming true in the presence of a real-life hero.

Another speaker demonstrated the need for awareness of major Environmental issues in the world beyond their own community.

Roland Hosein, a vice-president of General Electric Canada whose responsibilities included managing the company's environmental health and safety initiatives, made several valuable contributions to our school and, naturally, I invited him to take part in a session of "The Choice is Yours". As soon as the children learned he dealt with environmental issues, they began grilling him about his company's commitment to recycling materials and reducing pollution. They talked to him about what we did as a school to be respectful to the environment. They were intrigued by the technological advances he mentioned in the environmental area and they so surprised and impressed the GE executive with their desire for more information, that he invited them to the G. E. plant in Peterborough so they could see for themselves. GE became another valued community partner and the GE Fund made its largest philanthropic contribution to an educational program, when they later funded our efforts to help others to implement these programs in their own schools and communities, under the leadership of Bob Weese and Roland Hosein.

My friend Lucy Greene, whose company provided us with new furnishings when we so desperately needed them, also arrived as part of "The Choice is Yours" program. Born into an immigrant Ukranian family and now the mother of six children, Lucy earned her MBA while in her mid-forties and rose to a top executive position, Vice-President, with Sun Life, a giant corporation. "And you know what?" she told the children who were suitably impressed, "I couldn't even speak English when I started school. Not a word!" Like many immigrant families, Lucy's emphasized over the over again the importance of obtaining an education, and Lucy took it to heart.

"You can do what I have done. It's not just a matter of working to improve your math or your reading scores," Lucy advised them. "You also have to focus on making the choice to get better and better. Just keep trying to improve. Never, settle for less and most of all, never, never give up. You can do it, but you have to really want to, then make the choices step by step to achieve your goal."

Some of the senior students were so taken by Lucy they accepted her invitation to visit her at her office, high in a gleaming skyscraper in downtown Toronto. For many of them, this was their first visit to the big city, and I'm sure they were quietly amazed that this warm woman, who achieved so much success in her career, knew not a word of English as a young schoolgirl.

Many more participants in our program arrived at South Simcoe Public School. Some were not as colourful or mesmerizing as Lucy, Robert and Zanana, but each provided the children with a sense of the world beyond their neighbourhood, and the realization others dealt effectively with moral and ethical dilemmas, overcame hardships similar to those they endured, and that they could too.

LEADER'S REFLECTION

What happens in an organization has a ripple effect on the community. Organizations have a social responsibility to ensure that their communities thrive and prosper, as their organizations thrive and prosper.

- How do you demonstrate social responsibility for your community?

- How do you encourage organizational and community partnerships?

CHAPTER 7

The Limits Of Love

Many people who ask me about South Simcoe seem to focus on the challenge of supervising the students and managing their behaviour. This was, in fact, a major concern for us at the beginning, and naturally a primary responsibility for me as principal. Many of the behavioural challenges were directly linked to problems of vandalism, schoolyard bullying, temper tantrums, aggression and anger. "But these are not the causes of problems," I always said to my questioners. "They are the *results* of deeply rooted problems." I never believed in merely dealing with problems at the surface level, I prefer to intervene, deal with the situation at hand, then get to the root of the problem and take steps to prevent it from recurring.

More to the point: the headaches caused by the many "problem children" we encountered over the years were offset by their response to our efforts to meet their need for respect, affection, attention and, yes, love. Sometimes the reaction of the children set us laughing in unbridled joy. And sometimes the tragedy of their lives sent us off into a dark corner to weep in despair.

Here are just a few of the many children in need of love and care, we encountered at South Simcoe—the ones that still flood our memory with joy, sadness, hope, and sometimes a twinge of regret. We all suffer setbacks, injustice and pain in our lives. As adults we learn to accept and deal with it. But children are not equipped to handle adverse circumstances without severe emotional scarring and distress, and no one was more injured in this way than Maria.

Maria had so many strikes against her it seemed difficult, at first, to imagine her life could become even more tragic. But it did. Her life was a nightmare. Besides watching her family struggle through unemployment and poverty, Maria endured the dual challenge of dealing with both a learning problem and being hearing impaired. She was given a hearing aid to wear at one school, but it embarrassed her, and whenever she moved schools she would remove the device. As a result, she would get through classes without fully understanding all that was being explained to her. By the time teachers figured out what she was doing, she was on the move again.

All children are beautiful in their own special way, but Maria was even challenged in this respect. Her brown hair was long and stringy, and her eyes bore constant dark circles and a perpetually lost look. On the rare occasions when she smiled, it was a bittersweet expression, like an attempt to conceal some hidden adversity. She also dressed in baggy, hand-me-down clothes that added to the image of destitution.

There was more. Although she advanced to grade nine, Maria's progress was so poor that, at her own request after consulting with a social worker and her high school principal, she was readmitted to grade eight and placed at South Simcoe. It all made good sense, because Maria would receive the special attention she needed at our smaller school. But the blow to her already crippled self-esteem must have been devastating.

My first sight of Maria, looking so lost and forlorn, made me determined to help her succeed. We accommodated her hearing impairment in various ways, and assured her we would do all we could to help her return to high school the following year. With luck and hard work she would taste success after all, and we were pleased when she began to respond with better grades.

Then we discovered she was pregnant. As a result of a rape. Her attacker, Maria told us, crept up behind her when she wasn't wearing her hearing aid. She did not hear him coming and, when it was over, she was too embarrassed to tell anyone about it. For months she hid her condition beneath her baggy clothing until it became too obvious.

I managed to avoid crying about Maria until I arrived home that evening, and then I let the floodgates open. Maria was barely into her teens, bedevilled by problems many adults would have difficulty coping with, and now this: a child was having a baby. What more could happen to her? I discovered the answer a few days later.

One of Maria's friends, seeking to raise her spirits, loaned her a necklace to wear. During the lunch hour Maria was in the shopping mall across the street from the school, when she encountered her friend's mother, a woman who knew of Maria's troubles and condition. Unfairly, the woman assumed Maria stole the necklace from her daughter and she attacked Maria, physically and verbally, in front of other students and several mall shoppers.

"You thieving little bitch!" she screamed, as Maria cowered against a wall. The mother demanded the necklace back, in spite of Maria's tearful explanation. "The only thing that's any good about you is what you have between your legs!" the mother shouted with unspeakable cruelty. "At least you can trade it for favours. Otherwise, there's nothing good about you, and there never will be, you little tramp!" Strangers stopped and stared, some with contempt, others with disapproval, all of it directed at Maria.

Maria returned to school in near hysteria, feeling more shame than anyone should be asked to bear. She poured her little heart out in my office between sobs. She had done nothing wrong. She was not a bad girl. Why, then, was all this happening to her? I comforted her as much as I could, explaining she had no control over what the woman said but she could choose how she reacted to it. Her friends chimed in unison, "Don't let her get to you, she wants you to feel bad, don't let her take your power away, she is wrong, you are a wonderful human being." There was nothing more to add. I did promise her I would ask the woman for an explanation, and said maybe she might offer an apology.

I was wrong! Even when the mother learned the truth, she refused to offer an apology for her bullying and abusive behaviour.

"She shouldn't have been wearing my daughter's necklace," was her best explanation.

After she left, I sat wondering about a woman who would value a piece of cheap jewellery over the feelings of another human being. What kinds of values was she teaching her own children? What kinds of scars would they bear through life as a result?

Maria had her child in May. The following month she came back to school, determined to write her final exams. On the morning of the first exam, Maria appeared with her month-old baby daughter in her arms. She explained her mother was very ill and unable to babysit the child that day but she wanted to write the exam and she knew she could come to us for help. This posed a major dilemma for me. The presence of a month-old baby in the examination room was certain to be at least distracting to the other students. But I was impressed with Maria's resolve to write her exam. Maria obviously sensed my concern. "Don't worry," she assured me. "I can just leave her near my desk; she's just been fed, so she'll be all right for an hour or so."

We could hardly refuse her. "I knew you guys would help me!" Maria grinned when we agreed to the idea. We kept the baby in my office, while Maria wrote her grade eight final examination, and when some of the children finished their exams early, they volunteered to stay at school to help take care of the baby until Maria was finished. If I had any doubts about our success at creating a true family atmosphere at South Simcoe, they were surely dispelled.

As educators, we accept that marriage breakdowns, economic disasters, parental addiction problems and a host of other factors seem to counterbalance our efforts in the classroom. Even though these kinds of situations threaten to overwhelm everything we're trying to achieve with the children, we can continue to succeed, by helping them to tap into their inner strength and confidence and provide them with strategies to help them learn to become more resilient and thus better prepare them to face the various challenges of life.

Leonard arrived at South Simcoe from Edmonton, enrolling in grade six during mid-term. An attractive, fair-haired boy with pleasant manners, Leonard seemed to fit in quickly. He made friends easily and his school work was adequate, if not spectacular. Rather quickly, however, the staff and I noticed his strange, unpredictable behaviour. "Sometimes when I'm talking to Leonard," his teacher told me, "he just isn't here. He's off somewhere, in a world of his own, and he doesn't hear a word you say." I suggested to her daydreaming was hardly unheard of among children of Leonard's age.

"This is more than daydreaming," she replied. "When I finally get his attention, sometimes he gets right to work and other times he explodes in anger. He'll swear and shout, or throw a book across the room. He becomes very frightening, and then settles down almost as fast. It's as though he has two personalities, one sweet and the other scary."

It sounded as if Leonard was suffering from a serious psychological problem, so we made inquiries at his previous school in Edmonton. Did they have any record of similar behaviour during Leonard's years there? No, the answer came back, he was considered a pleasant, well-behaved youngster. I grew curious and concerned. Something happened to change this boy's personality. Relocation is almost always difficult for an eleven-year-old, but Leonard's reaction seemed extreme. I dug deeper and discovered Leonard was living with his maternal grandparents in Oshawa, and I contacted them to chat about Leonard and his problem. Bit by bit, the causes of Leonard's behaviour became clear.

Leonard arrived at South Simcoe in a state of shock. Back in Edmonton, his mother, a single parent, died suddenly. This was traumatic enough for any young boy, but the death was not accidental. She was murdered. As if that weren't enough, Leonard learned through extensive media coverage of his mother's death, she was a prostitute, slain on the street where she worked. Leonard loved his mother deeply and did not know her evening "job" consisted of meeting strange men and letting them take her to hotel rooms for sex.

It wasn't just Leonard who discovered the truth about his mother, of course. His Edmonton schoolmates learned it as well and, as children will, began to tease him about it. When the pain became too much for Leonard to bear, a decision was made to send him east to live with his still-grieving grandparents. Leonard may have left the taunts of his school mates back in Edmonton, but he carried all his agony to South Simcoe with him. Knowing the cause of his suffering helped us to understand Leonard's extreme behaviour. Nevertheless, there was worse to come.

One Monday morning, two boys about Leonard's age approached me in the hall. "Can we talk to you about Leonard?" they asked me. They appeared concerned, almost frightened. Curious, I invited them into my office, where they stumbled over themselves to describe what took place over the weekend.

Leonard, it seemed, invited the boys to his grandparents' house for a visit. "Do you want to meet my mom?" Leonard asked them at one point. Before they could reply, Leonard removed a ceramic urn from the shelf, carried it to them and lifted the lid. Inside were the ashes of Leonard's cremated mother. "Here," Leonard said handing one of the boys the urn. "That's my mother. Say hello to her."

When the boys pulled away in shock and horror, the urn almost slipped from Leonard's hands. But it was his friend's words that sent Leonard over the edge. "Man, you're weird," the boy said. "you're totally nuts! What's wrong with you anyway?" "Are you going to say hello to her?" Leonard demanded. "Are you going to say hello to my mother or not?""No I'm not!" the boy replied. He and Leonard's other friend looked disgusted. Leonard set the urn aside, left the room and quickly returned carrying his grandfather's shotgun. "You say hello to my mother, or you get out of my house," Leonard screamed, aiming the weapon at them. Naturally, they fled in terror.

"You have to do something about him," one of the boys said to me. "He's crazy!

I was glad I took the time to discover something of Leonard's background. Leonard was not crazy. Under severe mental and emotional stress, hurt, confused, angry and unloved perhaps; but not crazy. Of course, once the boys spread the story about Leonard's threat with the shotgun among other students, Leonard was in danger of becoming more alone than ever. This experience provided us with a "teachable moment," an opportunity to help our children to empathize with Leonard, to understand his emotional pain and act compassionately towards him, without condoning his behaviour. That was only part of the solution. In addition to being as understanding as we could, we sought mental health counseling for Leonard. Leonard became entangled in a custody battle between maternal and fraternal grandparents and returned to Edmonton shortly after the episode with the shotgun. We provided his new school with as much background information about Leonard as we could, in order for him to continue to receive the assistance he so desperately needed. Leonard is out there somewhere, trying to deal with all his pain and anger. We just hope for the sake of his mental health, that he is not dealing with it alone.

Cathy's case was similar to Leonard's in some ways. Cathy was the picture of innocence: large, bright blue eyes, silky shoulder-length hair, and an expressive face that could change from deep, serious thought into a mischievous grin at the speed of light. I enjoyed speaking to her and seeing the glow of her smile appear, like rays of sunshine breaking through a cloudy sky. I loved hearing her read aloud in class, watching her beam with pride at her accomplishments, which were well above the level of most of her classmates.

One morning when Cathy failed to appear for her grade one class, we followed normal procedures for our "Safe Arrival" system and called home to confirm the mother's knowledge of her absence. The woman's response sent waves of fear rolling through everyone. "What do you mean she's not at school?" she said, her voice already shaking. "I took her there myself this morning. I watched her walk into the schoolyard and we waved goodbye to each other. *What do you mean she's not there now??!!*"

While waiting for Cathy's mother to arrive at the school, we began to investigate, we asked other students in her class if they had seen Cathy arrive. One had, and her story was chilling. According to this little girl's account, Cathy was on the playground before entering the school building when a man appeared out of nowhere and carried her off. Fearing the worst, we quickly began interviewing students in their classrooms, asking if anyone had witnessed Cathy's abduction. Two grade eight students had and were already on their way to notify me, streetwise as they were, they provided a detailed description of the man.

"He didn't look so strange," one of them said. "I mean, he had tattoos and long hair and he was wearing a black leather jacket." "He called her name, and she ran up to him and they hugged each other," the other student added. "Then he picked her up and carried her off. She wasn't kicking or screaming or anything."

"If she had been," his friend said, "we would have said something or stopped him ourselves. We just thought he was her dad."

The teachers on yard supervision that morning did not notice anything unusual. My fear, of course, was that the tattooed man may have taken time to learn Cathy's name and build her trust, so he could abduct her without causing a scene. I immediately called the police to report the incident and was still talking to one of the officers when a woman we understood to be Cathy's mother arrived, near hysterics.

When she heard the students' description of the man seen with Cathy, and the police added they received reports of a suspicious man in the neighbourhood, the mother held her head in her hands. "It's Phil," she said. "Oh my god, it must be Phil!"

The police asked who Phil was. "Her father," she replied. "He must have gotten out of jail."

When I asked the woman who had custody and what rights she had regarding Cathy's care, she sobbed, "I don't have any rights."

Slowly, the full story emerged.

When Arlene, the woman who called herself Cathy's mother, first met Phil, he was caring for Cathy, who was just six months old at the time. Cathy's mother was sent to prison on serious criminal charges, and Arlene and Phil soon began a common-law relationship. But Phil became involved in serious trouble with the law as well. During one of his infrequent times out of jail, Phil assaulted Arlene, frightening her so much that she moved out of the home they shared, taking Cathy with her. She had to; without Arlene, Cathy had nowhere else to go. Besides, Cathy considered Arlene to be her actual mother, and Arlene loved Cathy as though the girl were her own flesh and blood. By all reports, Arlene was a caring mother, doing as well as she could under the circumstances.

Convicted of trafficking in cocaine, Phil spent much of the past four years in prison. Now it appeared he reclaimed his daughter and carried her away, for reasons we did not understand, to a place we did not know.

"Would he hurt the child?" a police officer asked Arlene.

She shook her head. She didn't think so. In fact, she suggested, Phil probably took Cathy because, as her parent, he thought he would qualify to receive welfare payments.

The police were naturally concerned, but they were a little confused as well. The father had not actually kidnapped the child; he had legal custody, after all. They were just about to leave the school, promising to look for Phil and Cathy, when my telephone rang. It was Phil. I waved the police back into my office while demanding to know if Phil still had Cathy with him. He assured me he did, and she was fine.

I could barely restrain my anger. "You could have had the courtesy to come into the school and explain who you were and what you were doing," I told him. "The police are here. We were looking for Cathy, assuming she was kidnapped."

His lame explanation was he doubted the school would have released Cathy into his care. In that respect he may have been correct, of course. Some custody issues are not as clearly defined as we would like them to be.

I handed the telephone to the police, who took down all the details of Phil and Cathy's whereabouts, and his plans for her. Phil planned to return home to Toronto, taking Cathy with him. She would be out of the school, out of our lives and, tragically, out of the life of Arlene, who unselfishly loved and cared for the little girl for much of her life.

It didn't end there. Arlene remained in my office, where she spent much of the day grieving for Cathy, spinning us stories of Cathy as she grew into a trusting and loving child. I suggested Arlene might be able to obtain legal advice based on her role as Cathy's surrogate mother, and I asked her to stay in touch with the school and keep us informed. When I called Arlene a few days later, she told me in a still-tearful voice that a legal-aid lawyer thought she had only a slim chance of winning custody, and in any event it would require a long and probably bitter court battle. I assured her we were there if she needed us.

Later, when I realized we had not heard from Arlene for some time, I dialled the telephone number she left with us. The woman who answered explained that Arlene had moved away. No, Arlene had left no forwarding address and the woman had no idea where Arlene was. We never heard from Arlene again.

But we did hear from Cathy. One day I received a telephone call from the principal of a public school in one of the western provinces. Cathy, the principal said, was a difficult child. She refused to speak a word to anyone—not to other students, not to the teachers. She was very withdrawn. It took quite a while to track us down, and the principal was looking for some guidance in helping her come out of her shell. Cathy's father, Phil, the principal informed me, was back in jail, and the little girl was in the care of a new girlfriend.

My heart almost shattered at the news. Was this really our bright, precocious Cathy, the little girl who giggled at funny stories during reading time and sometimes skipped hand in hand across the playground with her friends? I quickly outlined her situation to the principal, then suggested she hand the receiver to Cathy. Perhaps she would speak to me.

When I heard her small voice say hello, I answered, "Hi Cathy. This is Mrs. Dean from South Simcoe. Do you remember me?" Indeed she did. "Mrs. Dean," she pleaded. "Will you come and get me please?" She began to cry.

My eyes filled with tears. Summoning all my training to keep my voice calm, I told Cathy that we all missed, her and we wanted to know how she was doing. Through her tears Cathy assured me she was doing fine.

I just spoke with your principal," I said. "She seems like a very nice lady, and she likes you very much. So will you show her your very best work? And will you read to her from your book, the way you used to read to me?

Across all the miles of telephone wires, I heard her small voice promise, "Yes."

"Your principal will let you call here if you need to talk to us," I said, and we talked for a little while longer before saying goodbye. Hanging up the phone, I sat for several minutes reflecting on all the trust that children place in adults, and consoling myself that Cathy was in the hands of a caring colleague.

Every teacher's experience is a microcosm of life. But events of joy and sadness, triumph and tragedy, victory and loss just seemed to be drawn with sharper edges—literally, in one terrifying case—at South Simcoe.

Where children such as Cathy could melt your heart with one unexpected smile, Tom could harden your resolve with a single angry glance. Tom, a grade eight student, practically snarled his way through every day at school, terrifying the children and insulting the teachers. The various strategies we tried were not very effective, and when he made a particularly vicious comment to his teacher, Anne, in class one day, I called him into my office for a one-on-one session.

I began by referring to his classroom agreements about speaking respectfully "Let's be honest here," I said firmly. "Was that a respectful way to speak to your teacher?" Tom claimed that he had done nothing wrong, "Why should I be respectful to her? She hates me, that's disrespectful. She's a teacher: she is supposed to like all her students!"

"She doesn't hate you, she loves her class, she cares about all her students, including you."

"Yeah?" Tom sneered. "That's what you think. She may like the other children, but she definitely hates me. That's why I bug the hell out of her.""Well Tom, I am sorry that you feel that way. In any case your behaviour is totally unacceptable and we have to find a way to sort out this situation."

I called Anne and asked her to join us. "Tom is convinced that you hate him," I told her, meeting her alone outside my office. " He says that's why he is so obnoxious in the classroom."

Anne sighed, and shook her head. "You know what, Sandra?" she said. "I hadn't thought about it before, but I really do dislike that kid. I try not to show it , but his behaviour is driving me crazy. Maybe my dislike does comes through to him."

Anne was a dedicated and caring teacher and although she tried to conceal her feelings towards Tom, he was able to sense them. "I have tried to reach him in so many ways," she said, "but nothing I've tried seems to work." Perhaps, I suggested, we could work together to find something about Tom that she could relate to, some aspect of his personality she could find appealing. Then we could build on that. (I was, of course, harking back to my mother's lesson to me about the Christmas doll: find something good.) What if we invited Tom's mother to the school to talk to us and help us? We could discuss the problem, and perhaps she could help us to come up with a solution. Anne was skeptical, fearing Tom would continue his rude behaviour, but I persuaded her to get together for a meeting in my office. "Meanwhile," I suggested, "try to find things to compliment Tom about: maybe he'll begin to change his attitude towards you."

Tom's mother arrived the following week. She was a pleasant woman, but somewhat guarded at first. The most remarkable thing I noticed was the change that his mother's presence made in Tom's personality. The tyrant of South Simcoe Public School was transformed into a submissive little angel, sitting silently next to his mother gazing at her adoringly and beaming with joy whenever she gave him a smile. Anne and I were both amazed; he obviously loved his mother deeply and appreciated her attention.

Anne revealed all the ways in which she had tried to reach out to Tom and engage him in learning. "Tom thinks that I don't care about him, but I care about all my students. I honestly want him to do well. But he can be very frustrating. He simply does not respond to me."

"He gives everybody a hard time at first," Tom's mother said. "It's his way of testing you, to see if you really like him or not. The trouble is," she admitted, "he usually gives people such a hard time that they're turned off him."

I was amazed that the mother would admit this so openly. To her credit, the mother promised to work with us and try to change Tom's belligerent attitude. I couldn't persuade her to join us at Parent Rap, where I felt we might make real progress, but both Anne and I noticed a change in Tom once his mother became seriously involved and began to take an interest, as evidenced by signing his goal setting and achievement booklet, returning phone calls and coming to meetings and school functions. Eventually, Tom and Anne began to get along very well together, demonstrating a growing respect for each other.

Tom remained one of the toughest kids in school, which made a subsequent incident with Ted all the more frightening. If Tom could be frightened by something or someone, it had to be serious. And it was. It was Ted.

Ted was at South Simcoe barely a month. We knew he would be a handful; Ted brought a history of violence with him and, as a matter of fact, he was previously arrested and charged with assault. We also knew Ted's home life was somewhat chaotic. Ted transferred to our school after he moved out of his father's home and into a home shared by his mother and new stepfather. Large for his age, he had long dark hair and narrow eyes that seemed always to be filled with suspicion. He would glare at other children as though to intimidate them. He dressed in heavy flannel shirts, worn jeans and heavy work boots, he dragged heavily when walking. He looked more like a construction worker than a grade eight student.

One day, just before afternoon classes began, Tom arrived at my office door, clearly frightened. This in itself was disturbing; nothing seemed to scare Tom, or so he wanted everyone to believe. But Ted threatened Tom with a knife during the lunch hour, a threat serious enough for Tom to report it. Sending Tom back to his class, I called Ted to my office, sat him down in a chair, then quietly asked my secretary to call Ted's home and request his parents to come to the school.

Ted was sprawled across the chair, his entire body a sneer.

"You're new here, Ted," I began, "and we haven't had time to get to know each other yet." I seated myself across from him. "I have a problem I need you to help me with."

No response.

"Is it true you have a knife?" I asked. "There are reports that you brought a knife to school."

Ted mumbled he didn't have a knife.

"Tell me the truth Ted, do you have a knife?" I asked.

"Maybe I have a knife," he said with a slight smile. "Maybe it's in my locker and maybe it's in my pocket."

"Ted you know you are not allowed to have a knife in the school. Besides, you are threatening some of the children with it. That is simply unacceptable. I want you to tell me where the knife is."

Ted sank into the chair his smile became a sneer. "Maybe it's in my locker," he said. His hands were in his pockets. "Or maybe it's right here in my hand." I realized then this was not childish bravado and I was dealing with a very disturbed young man. I made a quick decision, I called to my secretary, Joan. "We have a situation here," I said. That was her cue to call the police. Then I turned back to Ted.

"Ted," I said firmly, "you can give the knife to me now or you can give it to the police."

Ted sat up and pulled out the knife as though to give it to me. He withdrew one of the ugliest, most fearsome knives I ever saw from his pocket, holding it not like he was about to hand it to me, but as though he was prepared to use it as a weapon. When I was finally able to take my eyes from the knife, I looked at Ted. He was staring at me in the strange hooded way he had, his mouth set in an expression somewhere between anger and determination. Too late, I realized I should have waited for the police to handle the matter, instead of demanding the knife from him myself. In one quick motion, I knew, Ted could easily overpower me and thrust the blade into my body from where he sat.

"That's some knife," I said, trying to keep my voice calm.

"Yeah," he answered in a voice that sounded like it belonged to someone ten years older. "It's to kill anybody that bothers me," he said. "And I'm keeping it." Then he slowly curled back into his chair, one hand still pointing the knife in my direction, the other hand a clenched fist, the knuckles white. His eyes began darting here and there and his body continued to fold into a more fetal position, like a coiled spring under tension. I had no way of handling the situation except through my words, and I continued speaking, keeping my voice low and calm and my words gentle, while reassuring Ted I would not try to take the knife away from him.

To my great relief, Ted's stepfather arrived, a tall, casually dressed man who also happened to be an ex-police officer, the stepfather took in the situation at a glance but made no comment as he sat down on the other side of the boy. He and I introduced ourselves as though everything were normal, and I explained that Ted did not want to give up his knife. Meanwhile, Ted remained curled in the same position, the knife still clutched in his hand, with a new hint of fear in his eyes.

"I asked if he had a knife," I said to the stepfather. "Since you're here now, perhaps you can explain the problem to Ted. Ted says he needs it for protection, but it's against the rules to have a knife in school." Thankfully, Ted's stepfather had the training to deal with this type of situation, he kept his voice as low and controlled as my own. "Ted," he said, "hand me the knife. You've heard Mrs. Dean say that you're not supposed to have it at School. You've already said you don't intend to use it on anyone. So why not give me the knife?"

Ted's response was to curl even tighter into his coiled-spring posture. I was afraid things might actually become worse until the stepfather added, "You won't be in any more trouble if you give me the knife." He turned to me. "Is that right, Mrs. Dean?"

I assured him he was correct, "Perhaps Ted wasn't aware of the rule against bringing knives to school," I added. The tension slowly began to ease. The stepfather continued speaking in a calm, soothing voice until Ted finally handed the knife over to him. I breathed a long sigh of relief, and the stepfather suggested he and Ted should go home and have a serious talk together. By that time the police arrived to take over the situation.

We suspended Ted over this incident, and I later found out he was already facing two criminal charges. He needed more specialized help than we could provide; he needed mental health assistance. Children like Ted are as much a danger to themselves as they are to others. Situations like Ted's were very frustrating because they forced us to accept the fact that, even though we wanted to, we could never solve all the problems that arose within the walls of the school alone, no matter how hard we tried.

In some ways Ted was fortunate, I suppose. His stepfather not only cared about the boy but was a sensible and compassionate man with the ability to deal with Ted in a calm and effective manner. It is ironic that other children, who were more likeable and promising than Ted, often coped with parents lacking in those qualities. What's more, these same children often became protective of their parents to a surprising degree, as though they were saying, "I know they have their faults; I know they sometimes hurt me; but they are my parents and I love them anyway."

Nothing illustrated this better than my experience with nine-year-old Bobby during one of our periodic attacks on head lice. This, by the way, is not strictly an inner-city school phenomenon. Head-lice infestations in children can, and do, occur in the most respectable of suburban schools.

In any case, parents of children with head lice were shown by the public health department how to treat the problem with special shampoo and to remove the eggs by combing the child's hair thoroughly with a special comb, before sending him or her back to school. Some children returned with their heads still infested with eggs. In those cases, we contacted the parents and when many said they lacked the money to purchase the special shampoo. Joan and I arranged to purchase some, at wholesale cost, from the neighbouring Kmart store.

In addition to asking parents to perform regular checks at home, we followed the prevention practice of many other schools and began to inspect for lice each term. This angered some parents enough that they phoned the school to complain, stating their children were clean and well groomed, and we had no right to inspect their hair. We discussed this at a Parent Rap session, explaining that head lice were not a sign of uncleanliness, just an unfortunate fact of life. Gradually we won all the parents over by inviting those who protested most vigorously to volunteer their assistance during scheduled head-lice inspections. Soon the inspections became another accepted part of our routine at South Simcoe, and another demonstration of the importance of parental involvement in decisions such as this.

Bobby was among the ones sent home for the shampoo treatment. He returned with lice still literally crawling through his hair. At first he assured us that his mother had performed the treatment. Later he admitted that he had lied. Once again we sent the boy home, this time with some shampoo to be used on his hair. We also called his mother to explain we could not admit her son back into the classroom until the lice were treated.

Bobby was back at school the following day. Unfortunately, so were the lice. We repeated the procedure of handing Bobby the shampoo, calling his mother and informing her of the need to treat Bobby's hair before he could be readmitted to class. She gave her assurance, Bobby went home, and he returned the next day with his hair as badly infested as ever.

I could not understand what was happening. Bobby knew the rules and his mother acknowledged the need, yet nothing was being done to treat the problem. Just to compound my confusion, Bobby's younger sister, Jennifer, who naturally shared the same lice problem, returned with her hair shampooed, combed out and shiny from the very first day. How could one sibling's problem have been solved and another's ignored?

I called Bobby into my office, determined to get to the bottom of the mystery. After several gentle questions from me, Bobby began to cry. I asked him what was wrong. Through his sobs he explained his mother was often drunk when he asked her to shampoo his hair.

"She doesn't like to do it," he said. "She just yanks at my hair and hurts me, and then she gives up." This was coming from one of the sweetest, most adorable and conscientious children in the school, and again I felt my heart break a little.

"Wait a moment," I said as he calmed down. "What about your sister Jennie? Her hair was done right the first time. Didn't your mother wash Jennie's hair?" "No," Bobby said, shaking his head. "I did."

You might almost expect a child like this to grow resentful of his mother, angry she could not fulfill this simple task for her son. But Bobby did not. During the session in my office, Bobby admitted he helped plan and prepare the family meals, sounding more like a concerned father and husband than a nine-year-old boy. Over and over he tried to convince me his mother was wonderful in many ways, except she had a drinking problem. "When she's drinking," he said, "she just can't do some things for us, and I don't know how to do them by myself." In spite of it all, Bobby still loved his mother. I had to understand that, and in a small way I did.

"Listen," I said. "What if I shampooed your hair myself, here in the school? Do you think your mother would mind?" Bobby thought it would be fine with her, so I fetched the shampoo, walked with Bobby to the sink, rolled up my sleeves and went to work.

A few days later Jacki asked if I had noticed Bobby's hair.

"Don't tell me he has lice again," I said. It wasn't lice. Bobby's hair was falling out. He already had a bald spot. An examination by the nurse indicated Bobby was probably losing his hair as a result of stress, all of it based on his home life. One morning, Bobby's five-year-old sister arrived at school looking forlorn and wearing a heavy parka with the hood covering her head. Inside the school, she refused to remove the parka or even lower the hood. When her teacher finally persuaded her to, she was horrified to discover that her head was bald. The mother's boyfriend and one of his buddies, hearing about the head-lice problem suffered by the children, decided to shave the little girl's hair off. She was now completely bald and embarrassed. We, of course, were furious. I felt compelled to report the situation to the Children's Aid Society, who were monitoring the family for some time, and they began arranging to place Bobby and his sister with a foster family. Bobby was devastated. When he discovered the news, he came running to me, convinced I was responsible for breaking up his family. In a way I was, I suppose, but I felt as though I betrayed a confidence with him.

"We all have a duty," I tried to explain, "and my duty is to make sure all the children in the school are cared for." His mother loved him, I was certain, but at the moment she was unable to provide all the care Bobby and his sister needed. Until she could provide it, Bobby and Jennifer needed help. "There is something else," I added. "The law tells us we have to report things like this to the right people, who will find some way to help. If we don't do it, we would be breaking the law."

I think the idea of a school principal being in trouble with the law impressed Bobby, because he nodded glumly and said he understood. But he still wasn't happy. Neither, of course, were we.

Bobby and Jennie were assigned to a foster family in what seemed to be an ideal situation. They lived in a large, comfortable farmhouse with plenty to eat, animals to feed and care for, and adults who treated them with love and respect. But the parental bond is strong, so strong both children constantly mourned the separation from their mother. And their mother too, when she was sober, grieved for them, calling them on the telephone and crying together with her children.

After a year the mother was persuasive enough to win Bobby and Jennie back to her home. Her drinking problem, she promised, was under control, and the children would be enrolled in South Simcoe once again. Soon after Bobby and Jennie returned to school, looking healthier and happier than I ever saw them, I met with the mother in my office. My biggest fear, of course, was the children would find themselves in the same intolerable situation as before, and I suppose my concern was visible to the mother.

"I know what you're thinking," she said. "You're thinking I won't take care of them the way I'm supposed to. Everybody is thinking that way. But they don't understand how much I missed those kids. I missed them a lot, and I'm trying my best to be a good mother."

I grew to like this woman. She was brusque and a little rough around the edges, but so were many people in the South Simcoe neighbourhood. The most important thing, I kept telling myself, was she loved her children and they undoubtedly loved her, regardless of her failings. They were all going to try to make things better, and who was I to judge her?

But I began to suspect the mother was sliding back into her old ways. There was nothing specific, just the feeling that the children were enduring the same old problems at home, but with a difference. In the past the children confided in us, and we could assure them we understood and cared. Now they were secretive about their home life, afraid once again the Children's Aid would become involved and the family would be separated if the truth about their lives was revealed. In spite of her faults, the children preferred to be with their mother in their small house rather than on a large farm among caring strangers. Our attempt to improve their situation came at the price of losing their willingness to confide in us. In attempting to save them we lost their trust.

Time and again, during those years at South Simcoe, we discovered the enormity of the problems faced by many of our children. As adults, we learn to cope with these complications, and most of us have the ability to address them in one way or another. Children lack both the ability and the power to change their environment in a similar manner. They remain at the mercy of adult decisions, made in adult situations, and they are expected to accept them, often paying a high price in happiness and emotional stability. Nothing demonstrated this to us with greater impact or poignancy than Stephanie's rebellion, just prior to Christmas.

Stephanie was transferred from a suburban Toronto school into grade eight in late October. She always dressed in expensive clothes, which made her conspicuous among most of the other students. During her first two or three months with us she appeared quiet and withdrawn, but otherwise co-operative.

One day in mid-December, I entered my office to find Stephanie, visibly angry and sullen. All the students knew that my office was a refuge, a safe place, they could use, when they were angry and frustrated and needed to cool off and calm down. Stephanie, I learned, exploded in an outburst of anger, and directed her rage at her teacher, Doug. This surprised me, because Doug was noted for his patience and gentle manner. The cause of her outburst? A Christmas decorating activity, something the children usually looked forward to. Stephanie, however, called the work stupid and flatly refused to do it.

When Stephanie came to my office to discuss the situation with me, she was tight lipped. I pretended to busy myself with work to give her time. Finally, I asked how she was doing. "Not so good," she replied.

Stephanie seemed in no hurry to return to class, and I filed that away as I encouraged her to talk with me. Why, I asked, was she so rude to her teacher, who was a caring person trying to help her? "He wants me to do some stupid Christmas thing for us to take home to our parents," she spat out. "And I don't want to do it. I don't want to have anything to do with Christmas, and I tried to tell him, but he didn't get it, he kept pushing and pushing…"

I realized immediately Stephanie's anger had nothing to do with the art activity. "You don't like Christmas?" I asked. She hated it. "All you people keep talking about is Christmas, Christmas, Christmas. I'm sick of it. Don't you guys understand this will be the worst Christmas of my life?"

I told her no, I didn't understand. Then I came around from my desk and settled next to her. "Help me understand, Stephanie," I said. It was like opening a door to a storehouse of anger, sadness and tragedy. She began by asking if I knew how much it cost to celebrate Christmas. The gifts, the food, the decorations—you couldn't buy them without money, she reminded me. "I don't know what I'll even eat at Christmas," Stephanie said. "Maybe a sandwich, if I'm lucky. There'll be no presents, no tree, no turkey, nothing. My mother can't afford to do anything this year. Don't you realize what happened to me and my family?" she demanded. "We don't know what's going to happen to us, and you guys are running around the school singing and laughing and making decorations, and nobody knows what it's like in my home."

That's when the flood began. I put my arms around her while she sobbed and sobbed. "You know what, Mrs. Dean?" Stephanie said between sobs. "I might be dead this Christmas. I can't take this anymore. I can't!"

Her words sent a chill through me. The threat of a potential suicide from an adolescent cannot be ignored. At the very least, it is a cry for help.

"I'm puzzled," I said to her. "You're always so well dressed, and your mother has a job. Maybe you're not rich, but I'm still confused over your concern about Christmas and money.

Then I listened. Stephanie explained she was well dressed because the clothes she wore were purchased when she lived in a comfortable area of Toronto. Back then, both of Stephanie's parents had professional careers, earning good salaries. The family owned two cars, lived well and took vacations, and life was stable and solidly middle class—until her father lost his job. There must have been some underlying financial or other problems, because when the father's search for work extended into weeks, and eventually months, the family was plunged into financial crisis. First they lost their cars, then they lost their house, and finally Stephanie's father lost hope. He abandoned the family, a broken man unable to cope. Stephanie heard he became a street person. She neither knew nor seemed to care where he was. She saw him as the source of the family's problems.

Unable to afford housing in Toronto, Stephanie's mother moved to the South Simcoe area of Oshawa, where rents were lower and from where she could commute with a colleague to her job. But their financial situation remained desperate. There would be no Christmas tree, no Christmas feast and no Christmas gifts for Stephanie, as there was in other years. There would be only sadness, and perhaps bewilderment that so many bad things could occur so quickly and with so little logic.

As Stephanie saw it, someone unseen and powerful, probably a man, made a decision that cost her father his job. Her father, in turn, decided that his own family was either expendable or not worth fighting for, and he was gone. Now Doug, who in Stephanie's eyes was just another man with power, was in her words, practically haranguing her to be joyful, make decorations for her parents and get into the spirit of Christmas. Stephanie had no Christmas spirit; she simply had a reservoir of rage against people who turned her world upside down, dumped her onto the cold ground and expected her to smile as though nothing happened.

Stephanie's ordeal opened our eyes to similar problems facing other children in our school. We began to recognize and understand the unusual reaction of some students when facing Christmas, March break and summer vacation. Many children reacted by growing sullen, withdrawn and hostile. We discussed this with our behavioural consultant, Debbie, and our social worker, Teresa. They both explained our children craved structure and stability in their lives. Any break in school routine, while for others might mean looking forward to a joyous and happy time, for them it more than likely meant upheaval, untold stress, and possibly even danger beyond their control. Perhaps they would be shuttled between one parent's home and another like a piece of baggage, or they would lose a vital source of love and security when school was interrupted. Meanwhile, they were being encouraged to take part in what should be a joyous celebration, in total disregard of their inner pain. Was it any wonder Stephanie finally exploded in anger and frustration?

We could not eliminate holidays and celebrations. We could, however, as a school handle them differently and avoid raising expectations of things that might not occur. We changed the way we dealt with celebration times. We moved away from the material and social aspects, gifts, families getting together, festive tables laden with food and goodies and instead concentrated on opportunities for community and sharing. None of this solved the core problems of Stephanie and other children in similar positions, but we knew that it would lessen the ache.

Many of the children at South Simcoe were more mature and wise to the ways of the world than other children their age in more affluent and prosperous areas of the city. They dealt for years with social agencies, charities and perhaps the police as well, and they knew both the power and the limitations of these organizations. They also accepted their role in the family structure, as damaged as it might be, could include being a victim, defender, negotiator and more. Yet, despite their problems at home, children remained loyal to their parents and suspicious of outsiders.

Combine that with remarkable maturity and deep sensitivity, and you encounter someone like Melanie. Slim, dark and obviously a budding beauty, Melanie was a twelve-year-old grade six student who carried herself with great poise, and was threatening to starve herself to death. "That's what she is telling the other kids," one of the teachers confided in me. "We know she's having problems at home, and she seems to have lost quite a bit of weight recently."

I agreed to have a chat with her. Melanie entered my office as though walking into a theatre. She chose a chair, sat down, folded her arms and stared straight ahead, looking for all the world like someone waiting for the movie to begin. My efforts to engage her in conversation produced nothing more than monosyllabic answers, until she finally tilted her head and smiled at me knowingly. "I know why you have me here, Mrs. Dean," she said. "Some people have told you that I'm not eating and you want to talk to me about it. Well, I don't want to talk about it. So you can stop beating around the bush. I'm used to dealing with people like you—"

I interrupted her there, asking what she meant by "people like you." "Counsellors," she said. "People who try to get me to talk so they can help me." She straightened her back and lifted her chin. "I can help myself."

She was very impressive, and almost intimidating—or as intimidating as a twelve year old can be while sitting in a principal's office. "You're quite right," I said. "I do want to talk to you about not eating. I want to help you because I care about you and I'm concerned about you. We are all concerned about you. Now, tell me why you are not eating anymore." "It's my body, Mrs. Dean," she said with total politeness. "I'm entitled not to eat if I don't want to eat."

I felt I was no longer chatting with a child, but debating with an adept adult. It may be her own body, I agreed, but I was her principal and it was my job to look after her. Again I asked her to explain why she was threatening to starve herself to death.

Still as polite as ever, she said "Mrs. Dean, I respect you and what you are trying to do here but frankly it is none of your business." It was time for me to become firm. "Look," I said. "You don't know me very well, and I don't know you very well. All you know about me is that I'm the principal in this school, and all I know about you is you are a student here and not eating, and you are threatening to harm yourself. I can't ignore that, because my job is to watch over the children entrusted to my care. I'm worried about you, Melanie, and I want to help you. Why don't we at least get to know each other a little?"

This didn't work either. In fact, she told me she wanted to leave the office. "I can't let you go," I said "without having some assurance from you." Melanie threw me a knowing smile. "Sure," she said. "What do you want to hear?"

I told her I needed her to promise she would abandon her threat of starvation and resume eating. If she could not agree to that, she would leave me no choice but to call her mother. I might even have to call upon an agency for assistance. This seemed to strike a nerve. "Why call my mother?" she said. "What about?"

I replied her mother had a right to know about her condition. "Sure, my mother would be worried," Melanie said. "But she has enough to worry about already, so don't you dare call her and give her more to deal with." She was angry, but I could detect a pleading tone in her voice as well. "Then why can't you help us solve this situation yourself?" I said, exploiting an opening. "If your mother is already having problems, why add more to her burden?"

It took some time, but Melanie began at last to discuss her feelings. She was not just trying to lose weight, she explained. She was not anorexic. But she was worried. What about? "Everything, just everything." School didn't interest her and life didn't interest her. Then she said in a chilling and serious voice "I just want to die."

I heard children say this before, but in fits of temper, anger or dramatic despair. Hearing this intelligent and composed girl say it as calmly as if she were asking to borrow a pencil was alarming. Thankfully, she knew the impact of the words as well, because she began quietly to sob. This was almost as painful as her words, but it also marked a breakthrough. Little by little, Melanie began to relax with me. I was careful not to say much; Melanie's words were more important than my own, although I told her several times that everyone at the school cared about her and was worried about her. "You don't have to handle this all by yourself," I assured her at one point.

"Sure," she said with a hint of sarcasm. "There are lots of do-gooders around who want to help. Do you know what their way of helping is? They'll take me away from my mother. They've done it before, and all it does is make me and my mother cry. We cry and cry, and the people think they're helping us."Melanie's story was familiar—so familiar it was almost predictable. Her mother was an alcoholic, living with an abusive man. Someone advised Melanie to call the Children's Aid Society for help if things ever became intolerable at home, and so she had. The response of the CAS understandably was to remove the girl from the home environment. "They took me away from my mother," Melanie recalled through flowing tears. "They left her alone with that guy and put me in a foster home with a bunch of crappy people who sat around and smoked and drank all day. *And I'm supposed to be helped by this?"*

I sympathized with the CAS staff, who I knew were understaffed and trying to do their best for the children.

"I'll tell you right now," Melanie went on. "If you call my mother or the CAS or anybody and tell them I said those things just now, I'll lie. I'll say I never told you those things, and you know what? My mother will back me up."

"But you also told me things were terrible at home," I reminded her. "Sure they are!" she agreed. *"But why should I leave?* I want him to leave, but my mother is not strong enough to kick him out and… and she loves him."

She made a good point, identifying a serious flaw in the system…A weak woman invites an abusive man into her life, is unable to eject him for one reason or another, and society's answer is to remove the child from the situation, making the two innocent parties miserable. In response, Melanie appointed herself her mother's protector.

When Melanie calmed down somewhat, she began negotiating like an adult. "I'll make you a promise that I'll eat tonight," she said, "if you promise not to call my mother. I agreed, but not without some conditions. "The trouble is," I pointed out, somewhat appalled to discover myself bargaining with a twelve year old, "you'll know if I kept my promise, but I'll never know if you kept yours. I have to trust you to keep your word. If you say you'll eat dinner this evening, I'll count on you to be truthful."

Her reply was typically direct—and convincing, thank goodness. "I wouldn't say so if I wasn't going to do it," she said. "I don't need your approval."

Melanie was not, I realized, being disrespectful to me. She was simply determined to be in control of her situation and not be a victim. I don't know for certain if she kept her promise to me that evening, but I do know that she abandoned talk of starving herself to death. When we passed in the halls, I would smile and ask if she had eaten that day. Sometimes she would answer and sometimes she would simply smile warmly back at me, which was answer enough.

Melanie's attitude reminded us welfare agencies alone are not the answer to the problems of our students. For one thing, their finances and staff always seem stretched to the limit. Just as problematic, however, is the "one size fits all" approach many agencies are forced to take due to heavy caseloads. We need to find a method that acknowledges the unique needs and personalities of our children.

Finding effective answers to this enormous problem involved more from the participants than just the presence of parents, schools and social agencies. It needs a community-wide effort, and we were slowly demonstrating this fact at South Simcoe. For many years a kind of social regression was occurring, and generation after generation were being further entrapped in the poverty cycle.

Bobby, Melanie and the rest were not statistics. They were bright, innocent children who did not seek the situation they encountered day after day, and could not alter it except by employing drastic measures. You could not solve their problems by tossing a few pennies in their direction and mumbling a few promises. They needed a totally different approach, an approach that showed them how to take charge of their lives, make wise choices and achieve their dreams. They also needed to be surrounded with and nurtured by caring adults. You could see it in their eyes. There are many theories worth considering when dealing with social problems and their impact on children. But as Bobby and Melanie and many others proved, theory alone is simply not enough. It certainly wasn't enough for Barbara, a bright grade eight student who was moody and lethargic but, interestingly enough, always neatly dressed and well groomed.

Barbara often arrived late for school, without having completed her homework. Many days she didn't arrive at school at all. She seemed not to care about school, appeared to be steadily losing weight and denied the existence of any problems at home. This, of course, was not true. Barbara had many problems at home, but she simply refused to acknowledge them out of shame or out of fear that, like Melanie, she might be sent off to a foster home. Foster families may be safe and comfortable, but they aren't home to these children. As hard as they work and as dedicated as foster parents might be, most children we encountered, preferred living with their biological parents.

It took time, but the total picture of Barbara's life eventually became clear to us in all its poignant detail. Both of Barbara's parents worked long hours in their struggle to raise six children, and when the parents separated, Barbara was saddled with responsibilities at home. Washing her clothes, as well as the clothes of her younger brothers, was Barbara's job. Some days she was unable to complete her laundry work and was too ashamed to wear dirty clothes to school, so she simply stayed home. She also played more roles than being her brothers' laundress; in many ways she was their nanny, often dressing and feeding them, as well as a housekeeper, responsible for sweeping floors and performing other cleaning duties.

As if that weren't enough, Barbara's mother took in boarders, and the tenants often entered her room when Barbara was at school, stealing her belongings and invading her privacy. One of the boarders, a man in his twenties, frequently made lewd suggestions to her. With no lock on her door, she slept fitfully, afraid he might enter her room at night.

Being frightened and overworked was just the beginning of Barbara's trials. Her chores at home left her no time to socialize with friends at school. She grew more isolated than ever, a condition made worse by her lingering pain over the breakup of her parents' marriage. She loved her father deeply, but saw him only two or three times a year, even though he remained in the city. Barbara's father favoured her older sister, a preference he never attempted to conceal. To top if off, Barbara's sister achieved an excellent academic record, a feat Barbara was made aware of through repeated comments such as "Why can't you be as smart as your sister?", or "Your sister would have no problem doing that!"

It does not take a degree in social work to recognize that Barbara's situation needed more than a standard-issue dose of welfare. Her already low sense of self-worth sank even lower, and she erected barriers to avoid suffering more pain from any source. When the full measure of Barbara's situation became apparent, we all reached out to assist her. Many times our efforts were rejected. "I don't want your help," Barbara would say.

"I'm too stupid. Leave me alone. Don't try to help me. I hate all of you." At other times she might call us a bunch of "do-gooders" who only wanted to help her in order to make ourselves feel better. Then she might toss a book against the wall.

Once more: *You don't give up on children.* You don't write them off just because their actions are annoying and hostile. You get to the root of the problem and help them find a solution.

We refused to give up on Barbara. We began by reassuring her she could take all the time she needed to talk about her problems with Teresa, our social worker. Some days her need wasn't an opportunity to talk. It was a chance to cry, all alone, for ten minutes in a closed, quiet room before emerging, ready to face the balance of the day. We grew determined that South Simcoe would be more than a school to her; it would be a safe refuge.

Things started to improve. Barbara became more trusting and perhaps more confident, although she suffered a setback when a boy began spreading false rumours about her. The boy even threatened to have his older sister, a high school student, physically assault her. While we helped her deal with that concern, we noticed Barbara was eating barely enough to keep herself alive, another symptom of self-worth problems.

Noting Barbara's exceptional problem-solving skills, we encouraged her to work with and help our younger students. She became an excellent source of help for them, and their response to her, along with our own words of thanks and encouragement, helped to restore her self-respect and self-confidence. She needed that desperately. What she did not need were words of criticism about her lateness or poor attendance.

We had three years to address Barbara's dilemma before she moved on to high school. During that time, we were able to help her see she did have strengths, she was capable and others looked up to her. All of this helped Barbara to gain confidence and a belief in herself and her capabilities.

Barbara slowly began to gain weight and to blossom. To top it all off, she was selected as the valedictorian for her graduation class. Barbara's problems seemed overwhelming to her, a mountain of difficulties she felt incapable of overcoming. Had we simply criticized and disciplined her for her late attendance and failure to complete her work assignments, we would be adding to her burden and misery. Instead, we offered care, concern, and love, and she used these as a foundation to build her inner strength, become more resilient and to improve her life in ways she once believed were impossible to realize.

LEADER'S REFLECTION

It is important to analyze and learn from your failures. Innovation often comes from perceived failures.

- How do you learn from perceived failures?
- How do you take failures and turn them into innovative and creative futures?

CHAPTER 8

The Right To Be Respected

Our guiding principle: *Everyone has the right to be respected and shares the responsibility to respect others,* was our compass, our point of reference for our focus on creating respectful relationships. We wanted to help our children to develop emotionally and socially and to have safe, caring and healthy relationships with one another, based on mutual trust and mutual respect. The principle defined the way we strived to conduct ourselves day-to-day, teacher and child alike, (respect was a two-way street). It helped the children to understand the importance of developing a strong and grounded character, which would be fundamental to their success in life. We wanted them to understand the kinds of relationships necessary in a vibrant and well-functioning team, as well as the requirements of their roles as leaders.

In moving this principle of mutual respect into practice, we made agreements about the type of nurturing and caring environment we were all working to create. We were conscious and consistent about the language we used. We developed our respect language, phrases and words, "a common language," that was used first throughout the school, then later in homes and in the wider community. We were explicit and specific about what we expected to see and hear from people who were being respectful to one another. When the children were disrespectful, in addition to kind, firm and fair consequences, we asked them what happened, why did they dishonour the agreements. We wanted to understand and we encouraged them to

151

talk openly about their feelings, so we could all understand what thoughts and feelings precipitated their behaviour, exactly what words or actions triggered those feelings and why. We reassured them that it was okay to feel frustrated, upset or angry, but it was **not** okay to physically hurt someone or put them down emotionally because of those feelings.

Once students were able to recognize and name their feelings and understand what had triggered their inappropriate behaviours, (this was the real hard work), they focused on learning and practising strategies that would help them to identify their feelings and deal with them, instead of being controlled by them.

Little by little, students learned self-discipline. They learned how to remain focussed on the positives, ignore or walk away from challenging situations that, in the past, might have ignited an angry response; redirect the thoughts that triggered their negative emotions, and change their personal state. This was no easy task. It took a great deal of time, effort and strength to control the impulse to hit or lash out in some other negative way, and to reach a stage where they were in charge of their emotions. All this came more easily to some than others.

This emotional learning was a transformational process. We provided support by continually telling the children we loved and cared for them. They could count on us to always respect them just as we were asking them to respect themselves and others. We monitored and measured this area of learning just like we did for academics. Goals were set daily, strategies were taught and practiced, and results were measured, graphed and became a part of the child's portfolio. In the more difficult cases, think sheets, daily anger logs and other tried and true anger management strategies were used, and progress was documented at very short intervals. This helped the students to stay on course.

The growth and development of Respectful Relationships was graphically depicted as a series of concentric circles (inspired by the lesson of my grandmother, of course) with Respect for Oneself at the centre. Radiating from this were other circles, representing Respect for Others in the Family, the Classroom, the School, the Local and Global community, and Respect for the Environment.

We knew we needed to focus on more than just correcting the children's behaviour, what they said and what they did: we needed to address the cognitive and affective domains as well: what they were feeling and what they were thinking. If we could help them to think differently, we could really make long term change, by teaching them a new way of being. Setting and achieving social and emotional goals as well as academic goals became a part of the daily classroom routine. We used a system of task analysis and focussed on setting very small goals, that were easy to achieve. Once the children experienced the feeling of achievement, they quickly warmed to the process and we were able to take small incremental steps towards the higher goal. For every goal, we specified what achieving the goal looked like, sounded like, felt like and what was in their mind.

How many of our children really knew what it felt like to be respected and respectful? We talked about what thought was in your head and what feeling was in your heart when you treated someone with respect. If you thought everyone had the right to be respected, then the next step was to take that thought and take action to convert it to reality. We explained that respect for yourself demonstrated strength of character, it influenced the way you dressed, the way you talked, the way you walked and carried yourself, the things you put into your body, the way you treated others, and so much more.

The children loved the idea that respect worked both ways, that we would be respectful to them and that we expected them to be respectful towards us. They understood the right to be respected brought with it the responsibility to respect others, and they quickly grasped all the implications of this approach to understanding and dealing with their emotions and behaviour.

Respect for others, for example, meant carefully listening to someone else's point of view. It meant using care and compassion when dealing with the feelings of others. It meant empathizing with others by putting yourself "in their shoes" to better understand their feelings and concerns. It meant responding with assistance when someone was in need, managing conflicts peacefully and solving problems respectfully, instead of resorting to bullying and fighting.

Respect for others in the local community meant treating people as friends, as neighbours, as people we cared about and would treat in the way the children wished to be treated themselves. We specifically focused on vandalism and shop-lifting, two areas we definitely wanted to eliminate..and respect for others in the global community meant accepting and appreciating the fact everyone is unique and worthy, so teasing and taunting someone for their differences was simply not acceptable.

Remember Melanie, the anorexic, wise to the world girl who rejected help from social agencies? She grew more and more confident as an individual, strong in her beliefs and in her expectations for herself and others. During her last year at South Simcoe, Melanie's physical development caught up with her mental maturity. To put it bluntly, Melanie was drop-dead gorgeous, a quality made even more striking by her new found confidence.

One day early in Melanie's first year at high school, I received a telephone call from her new, and very agitated, principal. I knew this man well; most of our students attended his school after graduating from grade eight. He understood and supported our efforts at South Simcoe, and was always courteous and amiable. This time he sounded perplexed at best.

"What the heck are you teaching your kids down there?" he said jokingly, but with a distinct edge to his voice. It took me a moment to respond. "What do you mean?" I asked.

"I have one of your former students here in my office," he said, "who just told her teacher where to effing go. When the teacher sent her to my office, she called him every name in the book. I asked why she spoke like that to her teacher, and she said he wasn't being respectful to her. She said she's a human being and has the right to be respected by everybody. Where the heck did she get all that stuff?"

That was Melanie, of course. Fiery, mature, don't-mess-with-me, younger-than-she-appears Melanie. "We teach our students they have the right to be respected," I assured him. "But we also teach them they have to respect others as well. Obviously, she did not handle herself in a very respectful manner."

I asked to speak to Melanie, who came on the line sounding angry and depressed. I told Melanie we missed her at South Simcoe, and in my brightest, most cheerful voice I asked how she was doing. Melanie was having a bad day, which was hardly news after hearing the principal's comment. According to Melanie, she arrived in class that morning without completing her work. This wasn't the first time for Melanie, and the teacher responded angrily, refusing to accept her excuse. When he raised his voice, Melanie believed he was not showing her sufficient respect and raised her voice back at him. Unfortunately, she also added a few colourful and totally unnecessary words of her own. "I lost my temper," she agreed.

"How could you have handled this differently?" I asked.

"I know, I know," she mumbled. "But he wasn't respecting *me!*"

"Two wrongs never make a right Melanie, now you've backed your principal into a corner," I said. "You haven't given him many options to deal with this situation. The bottom line is that you made a choice to swear at a teacher. I hope you understand there will be consequences to your choice. I'm asking you to accept them and learn from them. And please remember this: if someone is disrespectful to you, it does not give you the right to act disrespectfully towards them, and when you stand up for yourself, you must demonstrate self-respect by the way you handle the situation. Always try to do so in as respectful a manner as possible.

Melanie assured me she understood, and reluctantly agreed to apologize to both the teacher and the principal. She also promised to finish the assignment that launched this whole incident, and to make amends, if the teacher agreed, by doing another assignment suggesting ways to handle situations in which you do not feel you are receiving the respect you deserve.

She also promised to try very hard to be respectful to the teacher in the future. Melanie stopped by to visit me at South Simcoe a few days later, where we had a pleasant talk about high school, and how to deal with people who failed to respect us, and about life in general. I invited her to speak to the students about her own recent experience, so they too could learn from her mistake. She reinforced the importance of mutual respect and managing your anger to avoid such confrontations. When she finished, we hugged and wished each other good luck.

Unfortunately, Melanie needed more than luck. I discovered later that she dropped out of school in grade eleven, although she did return as a part-time student. I know they say you can't win them all, so you should just try to save as many as possible, but we all wanted so much more for Melanie..

We didn't win with Jared either, we simply learned the limits of our ability to steer all of our children away from disaster. A tall kid with an annoying swagger, Jared was transferred to us from Newfoundland and attended twelve different schools by the time he landed at South Simcoe. He and I chatted together on several occasions, and whenever his attitude became too grating and aggressive, I found I could soften it with a gently scolding word or two.

Jared's constant relocation between schools was disastrous for his education, among other things. Enrolled in grade seven late in the school year, he was unable to read at the grade one level, even though he was almost fifteen years old. The die was cast on much of his life. He began to hang out with older kids in the evenings and on weekends, many of whom were charged with stealing cars and petty thievery. There were also rumours of drug dealing. Eventually, Jared ceased attending school completely, boasting to his friends he was earning as much as a thousand dollars a week by selling narcotics. Although the police, the CAS and Jared's father were involved, it was virtually impossible to enforce any ruling designed to return Jared to school.

Within a few months of leaving South Simcoe, we heard rumours Jared was working the streets of Toronto as a prostitute to support his drug habit. The news shocked us terribly. We never had a student fall so far, so fast. Jared represented the limits of our ability to help the children. Even applying all we learned by then, kids like Jared suffered so deeply and for so long our best efforts were not enough.

Jared demonstrated that self-respect and self-worth cannot be acquired overnight, even from a program that was proving so effective with many other children. To be most effective, they have to begin the process at a very young age. Sometimes there was so much pent up rage in a child and they lashed out with so much intensity, we were at a loss as to how to deal with it.

Brenda was like that. Her moods ranged from sullen and morose to near out-of-control bedlam, and she was in and out of various treatment programs over the years. At her most violent, Brenda would heave her desk and all its contents onto the floor before charging out of the classroom, and sometimes out of the school. Or instead of fleeing, she would lie down and scream at the top of her lungs, sharing her anger and agony with the entire school. At times like these she sounded like a wounded animal in pain, and when the screams finally subsided, she would curl into a fetal position and sob uncontrollably like a lost baby.

Nothing in our training prepared us for this kind of behaviour. It was doubly frustrating because her moods were totally unpredictable. "Maybe it has something to do with a full moon," one of the teachers suggested, half seriously.

The moon had no effect on Brenda, but food did. We closely monitored Brenda's behaviour and noted on days when she arrived at school without breakfast, she was more prone to losing control. Once we realized this, we made sure to check with Brenda to see if she was hungry, but Brenda soon caught on and rejected our direct efforts to reach her. So Jacki suggested an indirect approach: Jacki recruited Brenda to assist in distributing milk and healthy snacks to other children in the school. In this way, she could help herself to food without feeling we intruded into her life. Brenda felt good about helping others and ensuring they were well fed. Accepting the responsibility of helping to ensure other children were fed, also improved her sense of self; she was now a valued helper. Sometimes Jacki invited Brenda to the staff room to help wash dishes. Doing chores seemed to calm the girl, and gave her an opportunity to talk with someone who cared.

It took tiny steps, and we made progress slowly, and Brenda began to trust Jacki.

Once, a student burst into my office to announce he found Brenda lying in the middle of the busy roadway in front of the school, causing a major traffic tie-up. He tried to persuade her to get up, but she swore at him and refused to move, claiming no one really loved or cared about her. Like Melanie, Stephanie and a few others, Brenda exhibited suicidal tendencies. In the midst of one of her outbursts she would scream, "I want to die!" and the agony in her voice would be almost too much to bear. "I don't know why they put me on this planet," she might wail. "I don't want to live anymore. I just want to die."

With help from Debbie and Teresa, we learned how to handle Brenda's crises at school, while they worked on getting her more specialized help to look into the situation at home. Brenda always needed to hear her feelings of anxiety would pass and things would get better. She depended on her teachers to reassure her of this, to the point where she began calling Jacki at home during summer vacation. Jacki invited her to do this if she needed to. Her voice would be very low, she would sound so horribly alone and she would repeat her wish to die.

One evening, she called Jacki at home, crying over the telephone. In the background Jacki could hear shouts of anger, and what sounded like someone thumping on a door or wall. "What's that noise?" Jacki asked, and Brenda admitted she locked her mother out of their apartment. Jacki suggested she unlock the door and let her mother in.

Brenda finally agreed, but not until she explained her actions to Jacki. Her parents, Brenda complained, did not respect her. They also, it became clear, failed to live up to Brenda's rules of behaviour. As Brenda explained it, she completed her housekeeping chores that morning in order to be permitted to attend a dance that night but her mother broke her word and informed Brenda she could not attend the dance after all. To thirteen-year-old girls, this simple incident can assume massive proportions of unfairness and disaster.

To Brenda, it represented yet more evidence of a corrupt world, one in which she no longer wanted to live.

Investigations by the police and CAS revealed extensive drug use in Brenda's home. Charges were laid, and Brenda was made a ward of the Children's Aid Society, placed in a foster home and transferred out of our school area. It was Brenda who eventually revealed what was going on in her home and reported her own parents to the police.

Lack of a decent breakfast intensified Brenda's rage through the day, and this was not unusual among the children we encountered.

Steve Ramsanker taught me to recognize the connection between an empty stomach and emotional outbursts, something he learned early in his career in Edmonton, where he introduced nutritious snacks and lunches as a key element of his school's program.

Those two needs—for food and affection—may appear unrelated, but they are primary nevertheless. Those of us who have never experienced intense hunger in the midst of plenty may have difficulty understanding such angry outbursts. Brenda's need for both food and affection were unsatisfied. Others might have chosen a more passive reaction, but Brenda took a dramatic, aggressive posture.

So did thirteen-year-old Brad. Brad arrived in mid-term during my first year at South Simcoe, and he provided one of my earliest lessons in handling very violent children. During his first week with us, Brad was almost invisible, sitting quietly in class and taking part in a few activities with other kids. This wasn't unusual for new students. Many were being moved constantly from place to place at the insistence of one parent or another, and it often took them some time to build close relationships among their peers.

One day, Brad emerged from his shell. Or more correctly, a furious and violence-prone adolescent appeared. Brad's anger exploded, triggered by another student's word or gesture, and he threw a chair against a school window, cursed his teacher and everyone around him, and stormed out of the classroom and into the hall. Alerted by his teacher, I went looking for Brad and encountered him in the hallway, walking back from the washroom towards class.

His temper still raging, he was punching walls and kicking snow boots and other items down the hall ahead of him.

I said hello as he approached me. "Leave me alone, you bitch!" he practically spat at me. It was time to show authority. "I beg your pardon," I said in my sternest principal's voice. "Do you know who I am? I'm the principal."

Brad was clearly unimpressed. "So what?" he snarled. "I don't care who you are. Just get out of my face, you stupid bitch!" I was stunned. Over my years in education I endured insolence and rudeness from students now and then, but never with this much hot anger fuelling the words. Brad was not going to respect me for my title alone, and short of suspension, no disciplinary action came to mind. I realized I precipitated this response by breaking a cardinal rule; confronting an angry student. So, I made a decision to let him cool off before I dealt with the situation—something I should have done in the first place. I turned on my heel and walked towards my office, leaving Brad standing there, looking for a fight.

Taking care to keep Brad in sight, I reached for the phone and called Rodger a former colleague who recently retired as a principal. I considered him a mentor and often asked his advice on handling situations such as this one. By this time, as luck would have it, Brad followed me and was standing outside my office door, not sure what to do and almost challenging anyone to approach him.

"It's nearly lunchtime," the former principal pointed out. "Why not get his lunch from his classroom, take it to your office, and let him know when he wants lunch, he can get it from you there. Tell him he cannot go back into the classroom until the two of you have a talk."

It worked. On my way past Brad, I casually mentioned I would have his lunch in my office, and that when the school bell rang at noon, he could come and get it, and in the meantime he could have a seat and think about what he did. "Because you threw the chair," I said, "I cannot let you back into the classroom until we deal with that."

A few minutes after the lunch bell sounded, Brad knocked cautiously on my office door and asked if he could have his lunch. I cheerfully pulled out a chair, handed him his lunch bag and invited him to sit down, as though nothing had happened."Let's eat our lunch together and chat," I said. My invitation and cheery manner surprised him; he was obviously prepared for a tongue-lashing or at least some hint of immediate discipline. He sat down rather tentatively, and I watched, horrified, as he withdrew nothing from the paper bag but a canned soft drink and a package of soda crackers.

Does it make sense for a thirteen-year-old boy to become violent and aggressive as a result of hunger and malnutrition? Only a starving thirteen-year-old boy feeling a little lost and dislocated is qualified to answer that question with authority.

"You know," I said casually, unwrapping the sandwich I brought for my own lunch, "I had something to eat earlier this morning and I won't be able to finish this sandwich. I hate to waste food. Can you help me out and take half for yourself?"

"Sure." Brad actually smiled at me. "I don't mind helping you out."

I expected to review Brad's unacceptable behaviour after we ate our lunch. But the gratitude on his face, the way he wolfed down my sandwich and the apple I offered him, made me change my tactics. Instead of discussing respect and our expectations of him, we talked quietly and struck a deal. The next time Brad felt himself growing angry, he could walk out of the classroom and use one of the school's designated safe places to cool off. "You have the right to be angry," I said. "But you don't have the right to use your anger to hurt or insult other people or throw furniture." I added there would be consequences as a result of throwing the chair against the window and breaking it. Brad nodded his head in acceptance and agreement. Funny how a decent lunch can deactivate so much fury in a child. Or maybe it's not funny at all.

During the weeks following our encounter, I made a point of seeking out Brad, to offer him a smile and a word of encouragement, and to ask if I could see his work. Brad needed three things. He needed a decent, regular diet; he needed to know we cared about him, and he needed behavioural boundaries. We could never be successful with behavioural boundaries until the first two needs were met. Are hunger for food and hunger for affection really so different from each other? Maybe not.

There was no immediate transformation in Brad. Other incidents fuelled by anger and rage popped up from time to time, but they became less violent and occurred less frequently.

When I began to examine Brad's life in more detail, the source of his rage and frustration became obvious and understandable. In addition to a challenging home situation, he often went for entire days without having much to eat, and the sight of other children eating their lunches must have driven him mad.

He wasn't alone. Some children caught shoplifting in stores in the mall across the street were stealing cookies, potato chips, soft drinks and candies because they were truly hungry. Was it wrong? Of course it was. Was it understandable? I leave it to you.

In response to our children's need for food, we decided to make sure food was available in the school. We had breakfast food and healthy snacks. With help from nurses in our local Public Health department, we learned about nutrition, what foods gave us energy and helped to avoid the mid morning and afternoon slump, and what foods to avoid. We learned about reading food labels and looking for bargains so we could get the most for our money.

One class took the leadership role for planning, organizing and implementing the day-to-day aspect of the Healthful Happenings program, (formerly known as Healthy Snack). The children would do a daily school survey to determine who wanted a snack. Then the surveying students had to decide how much food was needed. If for example, the snack was apples and cheese slices, a half of an apple was served to the younger students since they usually only ate a half. (Of course they could always ask for more if they were still hungry). So if seventeen children requested requested the snack, the students conducting the survey had to translate this into the number of whole apples they would need. This gave them an entirely new perspective on the concept of fractions and measurement, which of course tied neatly into their math studies. Not only did this initiative help the children to improve in math, it also helped to improve their self-confidence and most of all it helped them to develop healthful eating habits.

The practical benefit to the staff was identifying the children who needed daily snacks in a manner that did not single them out. This initiative also provided us with the opportunity to teach the children how to plan, shop for and prepare healthy snacks.

At the start of the program, snacks were provided by staff members, who paid for the food out of their own pockets. I realized we couldn't continue to fund things in that manner, so we turned to our Kiwanis Club partners for help. They became involved, along with St Vincent's Kitchen, and soon the children were munching on bagels, cheese and fruit, washed down with milk. If a child needed breakfast, it was provided for him or her as part of the school's everyday routine.

Why didn't the children receive decent meals at home? There were many reasons, most of them familiar and beyond resolution by the school alone. Many young mothers simply didn't know how to manage a household budget, or how to make inexpensive and nutritious meals. You could almost trace the income cycle of many families. At the beginning of each month, when funds were plentiful, the children arrived with full stomachs and ample lunches. As the month progressed, the lunches grew leaner, until, during the last few days before the monthly cheques arrived, they would often bring no food at all.

Some parents, whose incomes were strained by numerous expenses, were taking money from the food budget to buy clothing for their children. When it came down to providing either full breakfasts and lunches or a warm winter coat and hat, they chose the latter. This was something we could address with a clothing drive, so twice a year we "sold" clean used clothing collected from staff, family, friends, business partners and other sources. For ten cents or an item donated to the food bank, children and parents alike could choose whatever they needed, and every garment that left the school was, to us, a potential meal fed to the children in their homes. This was neither a sale nor charity; it was simply a method of distributing clothing to those who needed it, without offending their dignity.

Using the Respect principle to guide our efforts, was working! We were modelling and teaching the behaviour we expected, setting personal management (behavioural) as well as academic goals daily in every classroom, giving the children every opportunity to practice, carefully monitoring and measuring their progress, then celebrating their accomplishments at our monthly assemblies. When we showed the children the graphs depicting the dramatic **decrease** in vandalism, fighting and bullying, as well as those depicting the equally dramatic **increase** in respectful behaviour, the senior students said to us that we should make "a bigger deal" of all of this. Naturally we agreed; we wanted to find a way to celebrate these accomplishments. Together we decided that we would invite our entire community to celebrate with us, after all they all helped us and had all been positively impacted by the respectful behaviour. This would give the community an opportunity to show how much they too appreciated the children's efforts.

The students themselves came up with the idea of a Respect Lunch, something we probably would not have thought of on our own, but then food always seemed to work for us. The mood of the entire school moved to one of excitement in the days leading up to the Respect Lunch. It is this effect on particular children I remember most clearly—children like twelve-year-old Roger, who arrived at South Simcoe late one spring from Toronto, bringing a long history of problem behaviour with him.

Roger was extremely disruptive in class during his tenure at other schools. He mimicked teachers and students, was frequently absent for days on end, and was considered a handful at the best of times—not the kind of student you want dropped into your classroom towards the end of the school year, when classes are running well.

Regardless of his behavioural record, however, Roger quickly let us know how much he loved what he heard about the school's focus on respect, and how much he was looking forward to enjoying the Respect Lunch. By this time, news of our Respect Lunches spread and we were attracting people from outside the school who were volunteering to act as servers, including the Chief of the Durham

Regional Police Services. "I'm going to be the most respectful person you have ever seen. This lunch thing sounds great," Roger announced to his teacher, the day after he arrived at school. We really could not envision a child with a record like Roger's being able to change his behaviour so quickly. We had barely two months remaining before summer vacation. Roger didn't care. He was determined to enjoy that lunch before the year was over.

His actions seemed to prove it. Every few days, knowing Roger's troubled history, I would check with his teacher to ask how he was doing. Each time, the response was more than encouraging—in fact, it was positively effusive, not to mention a major surprise to everyone who knew of Roger's school history. "I can't believe it," his teacher exclaimed at one point. "If all my kids were as well-behaved as Roger, my job would be such a breeze!"

Our focus on Respect worked to help other children to improve their behaviour, we knew that, even so, Roger's response was spectacular. Here was this really tough kid, who might be expected to view what he referred to as "the respect thing" rather cynically, changing his entire attitude and carriage. And he was a newcomer as well; our other children had more time to understand and appreciate the concept of Respect for oneself and others, but Roger grasped it immediately.

I called Roger into my office one day for a chat, I really wanted to understand the background to his motivation. "It's simple", he said, after settling himself in a chair, " I hear you guys cook a really good lunch,"

"And I hear you've been an especially respectful and responsible student," I said, "a model in fact." I told Roger I was very impressed with his work and behaviour. I also promised that if he continued this wonderful behaviour, I would personally cook his hamburger at the Respect Lunch. The lunch, I reinforced, would be served by our business and community partners and officers from the Durham Regional Police, plus parents and teachers.

His face lit up with anticipation. "You will cook my lunch, and the police will serve it to me? It's a deal," he said, and practically bolted from my office, anxious, I'm sure, to boast about my offer to the other children.

Over the next couple of weeks, Roger continued to be respectful and responsible, even working with some of the younger children, in the playground, helping them to play games, wait their turn and solve small problems. He was, quite simply, a model student, always wearing a pleasant smile and telling everyone how much he enjoyed "this respect thing," as he put it. Then just two days before the Respect Lunch was scheduled, Roger's teacher stopped me in the hall. "Something's wrong with Roger," she told me, looking distressed. "He's not the same, he's acting strangely this morning."

I asked her to send Roger to my office, and the boy who entered looked very different from the one who was determined to sit down to a Respect Lunch. This Roger hung his head, spoke in a low voice and carried himself as though he were about to flee, strike out or simply break down and cry.

"Roger," I said when he was seated, staring at the floor, "what's wrong?" "My father was hurt last night," he said. "They took him to the hospital."

"What happened?" I asked. "Tell me about it."

I expected to hear about a traffic accident or an industrial mishap, perhaps a tumble off a ladder in his home. Instead, Roger blurted out, "He was hit with a machete, and they took him to the hospital. I don't know if he's OK or not."

I felt sick to my stomach. Suggesting I talk to his mother, I went to another telephone, called Roger's home, left my name and my reason for calling on the answering machine, and awaited a reply.

A woman who identified herself as Roger's mother called back a few minutes later. Instead of hearing the voice of a distressed parent, I found myself speaking with a woman who was annoyed with me and upset with her son. "Why are you bothering me now," she snapped, "I'm in the middle of this mess," "What mess?" I asked "Don't you people listen to the news?" she asked. "Didn't you hear about the murder last night?" I already told Roger that Stan was dead. I don't know what he is so concerned about, it's not like he was his father or anything.""When did you tell Roger?" "Before he went to school this morning. Obviously, he wasn't listening, so what's new?"

I asked who Stan was and what she meant by he saying that he wasn't Roger's father. Who was this guy?

"He was just a boarder who lived in the same house as us. He moved out a few weeks ago."

Only a few years earlier I might have judged this woman for her harshness, and for her apparent insensitivity towards her son's feelings. But my experience with South Simcoe families had taught me a lesson about jumping to conclusions, so I kept talking to her, letting her lead the conversation. Gradually her voice became more emotional, and at one point, when I told her I understood her feelings, the line went quiet for several seconds. Then she began to cry. Whatever the relationship between her and the former boarder might have been, he apparently was kind to Roger, taking the boy fishing and generally filling a father's role, for a short while.

"If Roger didn't understand that he's dead," she said between sobs, "I can't talk about it now, not when I'm like this. Will you tell him for me?" she pleaded.

I had a brief moment of trepidation, before I went back to Roger. With all my experience, I had never broken the news of the death of a parent to a child before. I told Roger I was speaking to his mother about his "dad."

"Is he OK?" Roger said.

"People who get hurt as badly as he did," I said, "don't always turn out OK."

He pondered that for a moment. "Is he dead?" he asked."Yes," I said. "He is." I waited for the news to sink in. "Do you know what that means?" I said finally.

"Sure," Roger said. "He's gone to heaven."

To encourage him to release his emotions, I began talking as two saddened individuals, not as a principal and student. "Roger," I said gently, "my father died recently and it was a terrible loss to me." We talked for a while, long enough for Roger to describe the things he and his "dad" had done together.

"When my father died," I said, "I couldn't concentrate for a while. So you tell me: what do you want to do this morning? Go back to class? Maybe work on the computer for a while? Help the younger students? Or just stay here?" Roger said he would like to work on the computer until lunch, which sounded like a fine choice to me.

Roger went home for lunch and did not return to school for several days. Messages from me to his home, left on the answering machine, generated no response, and I feared we had lost him. We grew so close in such a short time, Roger and I, and my heart ached at the pain and sadness I knew he was suffering. I was surprised to see Roger appear on the day of our Respect Lunch. He remained subdued, but talked easily with me when I told him how pleased we were to see him. "You worked hard for this meal," I said at one point.

"It wasn't just for the food," he admitted. "I wanted to eat lunch with everybody and be a part of the group. To tell you the truth, I really wanted to see if the police would serve someone like me "

Watching him during the meal, I realized how important it was for Roger to feel part of this special group. He needed to feel he belonged. What else could he ask for, the principal prepared his meal (yes, I cooked Roger's hamburger, exactly as he ordered it), and while smiling police officers and community partners served the other children, the Chief of Police served Roger his lunch. Roger wanted to prove that he was good enough to be included; he wanted to prove he was worthy of belonging; he wanted the warm and loving feeling that comes from experiencing acceptance and belonging.

We never saw Roger again. Sometime during the following summer he and his mother moved out of the South Simcoe area, as so many children did. I took comfort in the thought that we made a difference in Roger's life, if only for a short time. Whatever trials he faced through the rest of his childhood, I hoped he would carry the warm memory of that special Respect Lunch with him, and remember what it felt like to be respectful and respected.

Was it wise to honour and recognize children for respecting themselves, others around them, the community and the environment?

I never doubted the wisdom of the idea. We needed to break a cycle of negative behaviour among South Simcoe children. It's difficult to maintain your self-respect, or your respect for others, when you are the innocent target of abuse, denial and neglect. We needed to demonstrate to the children they could change their behaviour and feel good about doing it. We needed to model the actions we wanted to see, and provide the students with the opportunity to strengthen their character by practicing being respectful and respected..

During one of our Respect Lunches, Staff Sergeant Bill Temple of the local police force talked to the students while they ate their lunch. Towering over the children in his service uniform and flashing a warm smile, he told them, "You must always try to respect yourself and other people because it's a good thing to do," he said. "Most times in life, no one will even notice what you do. You keep doing it because it's the right thing, and doing the right thing leaves you nothing to apologize or make amends for, it keeps you in harmony with your principles and values and enhances your sense of self, by demonstrating self-respect. This is what life is all about—feeling good about yourself for doing the right things, being strong inside, and helping others to feel the same way."

I couldn't have said it better myself.

LEADER'S REFLECTION

The new leader has a heartset and mindset of trust and mutual respect. This leader encourages the development of healthful and inclusive relationships where everyone feels accepted, appreciated, valued and included.

- What systems do you have in place to facilitate the development of healthful and inclusive relationships?

- How do you model the heartset and mindset of respect for yourself and others?

CHAPTER 9

Programs And Progress

Our school, family and community approach to improving student behaviour and strengthening their character, by focusing on what we wanted, healthy, safe and caring relationships, based on mutual respect, was working. We were creating a strong social and emotional foundation for learning and behavioural change . As you walked around the school, you would hear: "please, thank you, good morning, may I help you, I apologize if I have hurt your feelings, how can I make amends for this?" and you would see smiling faces, children opening the doors for others, older children helping the younger ones. All this might be considered normal in other schools, but for us, it was a huge shift from where we were previously. There was a vibrant energy and atmosphere you could feel; it was wonderful to experience. The most significant change was in the attitude of the children and the positive impact this was having on the teaching and learning process.

Since our children came from many different backgrounds and in some cases, different cultural groups, they did not have a commonly held set of standards for appropriate behaviour, or beliefs about what "good behaviour" was. In order to develop these needed standards and reach a common understanding of the behaviour expected in "a respectful relationship," we worked together, students, teachers, families and community members to define what respectful relationships were, then we jointly established relationship agreements, instead of imposing rules. By doing this, the children became active participants in the behavioural change process instead of passive recipients. As a result, we had fewer power struggles when dealing with inappropriate or 'disrespectful' behaviour. In order to arrive at the 'relationship agreements,' we began by taking our guiding principle, *Everyone has the right to be respected and the responsibility to respect others,* discussing what it meant and how we could take action and work together to move this principle into practice. This helped to ensure that we were creating an environment of collaboration,where everyone clearly understood and had input into what was unacceptable as well as acceptable and expected behaviour. We found respect and responsibility meant different things to different people, so we needed to spell out clearly the difference between appropriate as well as inappropriate behaviour. Reasons for particular behaviours were discussed, debated and clarified, so there was a clear understanding of the behaviours, as well as the attitudinal shift needed and expected in a healthy, civil, respectful and caring learning community.

This unified effort resulted in the children taking greater responsibility for learning how to manage their own behaviour. For us, this meant a greater chance for long-term change. In most cases, the simple questions, "what happened, was that what we agreed to?" was all that it took to refocus the children, then we were able to move on and deal with the situation.

Over time, the teachers, relieved of much of the energy and attention usually dedicated to enforcing rules, discovered they had more time available to enjoy the children, to individualize their teaching to particular needs and share in the wonder of the students' growth and development. Classrooms and the school as a whole were functioning well, yet behavioural problems persisted on the school yard. We were still experiencing incidents of violence, including bullying and fighting, and the more we improved the atmosphere inside the school, the greater the contrast with what was happening on the school playground. The problem was not exclusive to South Simcoe, of course; similar incidents were occurring elsewhere, growing almost as prevalent among girls as among boys.

Several studies suggest schoolyard bullying is not only more prevalent than in the past, but is also growing more violent and dangerous. A generation ago, schoolyard fights were conducted with fists; today they can involve knives and other weapons. Similarly, schoolyard bullies are no longer rogue kids, strutting around a playground to demonstrate their physical supremacy, like male lions defining their territory. Violence in schools can include entire gangs of children who may swarm their victims, goading each other on to more and more vicious actions. None of this, by the way, is confined to at-risk communities; the sad truth is, these incidents can occur anywhere in the world.

What's causing all this terrible violence and cruelty? I knew the playground violence was only a small part of the larger pattern of violence occurring outside the school. I knew many children witnessed on-going violence modelled in their homes, and that bullying was more than a school problem, it was a societal problem. Bullying was even occurring in the workplace and seemingly condoned by the fact that it was not being dealt with. We didn't have much control over those factors but as always, we focused on what we 'could change,' and we knew we could change the way we dealt with bullying at our school.

Stricter discipline and harsher consequences were not the answer for us; these would be a quick fix and short-term solution that could even exacerbate the problem by driving the bullying underground. We didn't believe the solution lay in "giving them a taste of their own medicine," either. Our children were young and we knew if we took a more gradual, deliberate and deeper approach, not only would they learn how to control their impulses and correct their behaviour, they would learn how to replace the negative behaviours with new and positive ones. They would change their thinking, strengthen their character, their sense of self, and move to a conflict resolution, negotiation and problem solving way of thinking. This could ultimately break the cycle of violence.

We were insistent, however, on bullies having meaningful consequences to their actions, making amends, repairing the harm they did to those they bullied and restoring the situation. They had

173

to be accountable, to take ownership of their problem, work with us to correct their offending behaviour, and manage their emotions in a more positive way. Our focus was always on getting to the root of the problem and not only intervening to deal with the problem but also taking steps to prevent it from recurring.

Reducing bullying, fighting and other forms of violent behaviour by increasing a child's sense of self, who they were and who they could become, some said was a muddle-headed theory. We proved other wise. Children who have a strong sense of self, respect themselves and others, neither bully nor accept others bullying them. Strengthening a child's sense of self, strengthening their character and helping them to develop healthful, inclusive and caring relationships, ensures you reduce not only the number of bullies but also the number of children they target for their aggression.

We proved this time and again at South Simcoe with children like Fred. Fred was new to our school and we soon found out he was a playground bully. He was a grade eight student who took pleasure in taunting, teasing and bullying other children for his own amusement. He especially delighted in targeting younger girls, making offensive remarks to them, and ridiculing them until they burst into tears. Sometimes, he would threaten to harm them if they did not kiss him. He would then walk around the playground pretending he did nothing wrong.

Fred's basic problem, we read in his records, was his "inability to interact with others in a socially acceptable manner." He simply could not make friends; no one wanted him near them. He was convinced nobody cared about him, and his actions seemed dedicated to proving this true. In working with Fred to help him replace his bullying behaviour with respectful and responsible behaviour, Kim, Fred's teacher, discovered more….

Each Monday, after spending the weekend with his mother, Fred appeared at school with a clean shirt, well-pressed trousers and freshly washed socks. From Monday to Friday, while he lived with his father, he would remain unwashed and would begin to smell. By the end of the week, his clothing often reeked of cat urine, his hair was unclean and uncombed, and his socks would become so filthy that the fabric on the soles would harden like cardboard. In the classroom, children avoided sitting next to Fred because of the foul odour that floated around him like a cloud.

Kim, and Susan, Kim's teaching assistant, after repeated unsuccessful attempts to contact Fred's father, decided to take matters in their own hands. They found a way to address the problem without singling Fred out from the rest of the children. They decided to hold a special session on personal hygiene during their weekly Health class. No one needed this more than Fred, of course. During this class they were very explicit about how you should keep yourself clean. They demonstrated how to scrub their feet and even how to trim their toenails with clippers. During one class Kim shampooed Fred's hair and Susan, a former hairdresser, cut and styled it for him. When they finished, the other children actually complimented Fred on his appearance, oohing and aahing over him. Some actually told him he was handsome.

This admittedly had nothing to do with the traditional "three R's," (but then neither were so many of the other things we did in order to engage our students. Maybe it is time the three R's are updated). Kim and Susan felt it was the only way they and the other students could survive with Fred in the classroom. Incidentally, the other students began to take more pride in their appearance as well. And this made everyone feel good about themselves. The impact of the personal hygiene lessons went much further than anticipated. The first time Fred saw himself with clean, well-groomed hair, he blurted, "I look so good, I feel so good. I feel like a king! I am going to keep doing this!" After this, Fred began to make friends, especially with the girls, and most of the problems were over. If only a class on personal hygiene could solve the bullying problems of all the other children, wouldn't that be wonderful?

Another risk factor linked to the rising number of incidences of schoolyard bullying and fighting is the excessive unsupervised time children spend watching violent television programs and playing violent video games. While this does not necessarily trigger direct acts of aggression, or spontaneously turn a good child into a bully, some programs can make violence appear more acceptable by desensitizing children.

To deal with the problem of bullying, I read the work of Olweus, one of the pioneer researchers in the field of bullying. He had found that bullying could be reduced in schools by tackling the problem head on.

In the past this issue was largely ignored, for many years, bullying was looked upon as a normal part of growing up, a necessary evil as it were, which would 'go away,' if ignored. Now, thanks to the work of researchers in the field like Debra Pepler and Wendy Craig, we know better, we know how devastating the consequences of bullying can be. We know that bullying, if not addressed in the early years, can progress to many other negative behaviours such as date rape, spousal or elder abuse and even criminal behaviour. Sometimes people who are bullied get really desperate and commit suicide.

We also know about the terrible emotional scars that bullying can leave; scars so deep they can get in the way of a person developing healthy relationships over the course of a lifetime. All the more reason for taking a long-term perspective.

To begin to tackle the problem, we needed to make sure that we understood what bullying was, the different types of bullying and what was already proven to be the most effective ways of dealing with it. It was clear that in extreme cases, a school would need support; some children would need clinical counseling from mental health professionals to change their behaviour, a solution far beyond the means of public schools.

It was time. If we were to succeed in creating a healthy, safe and caring learning community for our children, we had to maintain what we already had in place, then take the next step and eliminate or at least reduce, bullying and fighting on the playground. As with everything else, we continued our focus on a school- family-community-wide approach, and used our guidingprinciple, *Everyone has the right to be respected and the responsibility to respect others,* as our compass to keep us on course, and serve as a standard applied equally to all. We enlisted the help of the police, the parents and some of our older children and we developed very specific 'respectful playground agreements.' The police officers explained to the children that bullying behaviour can literally poison a school. They explained there were many forms of bullying, and bullies deliberately and intentionally seek to hurt those they see as weaker or more vulnerable than themselves, and they get a sense of power and pleasure from this. Bullying, the police went on to say, is not only absolutely cruel but can also be a serious offence. It is damaging to both the bully and the person being bullied. And both parties need to get support.

The police chatted casually with the children, talking about the dangers of gangs and the reasons behind bullying and fighting. They told the students how words, as well as fists, could hurt or heal and cautioned them to stop, think, then choose their words carefully, so as not to be bullies themselves, or be perceived by others as a bully. Sean Fitzgerald, one of the officers, said: "I want you to remember three important things always;

-Co-operate with others, rather than fight
-Stand up for yourself
-Stand up for others

He engaged in role playing activities with the children, demonstrating how bullies can be discouraged from their behaviour; how to stand up to a bully; how to avoid becoming a bully's victim; how to avoid being a bully, and how important it was to develop empathy and compassion for others.

Sean encouraged the students to continue to practice all of this in front of a mirror, to build confidence in their abilities to stand up to a bully's challenge. His final words to them were, NEVER give the bully the audience he or she craves. This takes courage, the hallmark of a strong character, but time and again it proves effective. People who stand up for themselves and others in a respectful and responsible manner are the real heroes in the world, he explained.

"When you do nothing to stop bullying, you are a supporter, an enabler. You can be an active supporter, by following or joining in with a bully or gang leader, or a passive supporter, a bystander, by providing an audience for bullies while they attack their victims. Understand clearly, the presence of an audience is a major incentive for bullies. When children witnessing the attack are silent bystanders, they, in fact, are supporting and condoning the bully's actions. Stand up for others. BE A PLAYGROUND HERO!"These sessions alone reduced the number of incidents of bullying observed and documented on the playground. But there were increased numbers of incidents being reported. When we investigated further, the children told us in both cases this was because they did not realize these actions were classified as bullying. Many children simply needed to understand the seriousness of bullying and fighting, how it was not harmless play, but very hurtful behaviour.

Violence should definitely not be regarded as an inevitable experience in childhood, but as unacceptable behaviour that needs to be understood, addressed and stopped. We have a duty to protect our children from violence, while teaching those who are violent more socially appropriate behaviours as well as new ways of being. In the long-term, we want to create an environment where violence is unconscionable.

Teresa and Debbie assisted us in developing and refining strategies to deal with bullying. The link was clear: as children develop a deeper sense of self, a stronger character, they develop compassion and empathy and are better able to respect themselves and others, therefore, bullying and fighting decrease.

When creating our 'respectful schoolyard agreements,' everyone decided it was necessary to make a concerted effort to banish bullying, not just reduce it. This included forms of bullying like teasing, taunting, and name-calling. Anything that could cause emotional pain and anyone involved in that kind of behaviour, by definition, dishonoured the 'respect agreements.'

A new student caught breaking the agreement, for example, would be asked to explain his behaviour and have a discussion with his teacher, to ensure he understood how his actions were perceived. He would then receive a warning. If it happened again, I would call the student to my office for a serious discussion about dishonouring the agreements, and explain that such behaviour was unacceptable. "That is not the way to respect others," I would say, "or to respect yourself." When necessary, we suspended the student and probed aspects in his or her life that might be causing the behaviour. Then, the teachers and I would begin to work with the child in a more in-depth way. There was always a better outcome if the child was with us long enough for us to develop a relationship with him, before an incident occurred.

I was determined to eliminate or drastically reduce incidents of bullying and fighting on the schoolyard, because of the amount of time I had to spend laying down the law to the kids. When there was a serious incident on the playground and teachers had to go back to their classes to teach, they expected me to take over and deal with the problem.

That was fine with me, except I found so much of my time being devoted to this single problem I couldn't find sufficient time for dealing with curriculum matters, far less for all the paperwork that comes with the position of the Principal.

The school, family, and community-wide focus on developing respectful relationships proved to be the answer to my predicament. As we progressed, with the children slowly taking more and more ownership for their own behaviour and teachers, parents and community partners reinforcing their efforts, things began to change. Over the course of my first two years we were able to reduce bullying and fighting on the school yard by 60%, and as the years went on, even further.

In addition to teaching about the need to eliminate aggressive and violent behaviours, we also focused on teaching the children the behaviours we wanted to replace bullying, fighting and other forms of aggressive behaviour.

We changed how we supervised the school yard, since we learned many instances of bullying go unnoticed on the school yard. We were more active and vigilant, carefully observing how the children interacted with each other. We paid specific attention to schoolyard 'hot spots;' areas on the playground where a bully might be less visible, just as we paid attention to the bathrooms and lunch rooms in the school. We taught the children how to play, how to take turns, reminding them they already knew how to co-operate in the classroom so it was simply a matter of transferring those skills on to the playground. We taught them how to make friends and how to resolve conflicts peacefully, how to solve problems, and how to demonstrate strength of character by courageous actions.

When the older children told us they wanted to teach the younger children games so they would have something to do rather than getting into difficulties and we needed to have some new equipment for the younger ones to play with, we raided our own children's collections and took equipment to school, to get us started right away. We ensured we were easily available to the children; we would ask "what happened?" then listen to what they said. Each person had her particular version of events, and needed to be heard. We empathized, gave love and support, but did not judge or assign blame. We tried to understand and appreciate the emotions the children were experiencing and dealing with, anger, frustration, pain, etc. If they were not in an emotional state where they were ready to work on resolving the conflict, we gave them the choice to withdraw quietly to a previously agreed upon, 'safe place' to calm down, or take part in some calming activity, with the understanding when they were ready they would come to us to discuss and deal with the situation, by working to resolve the conflict, or solve the problem and repair the harm caused by their actions. We taught them to:

  -recognize what triggered their anger
  -talk about how they acted when they were angry
  -think about good ways to deal with their anger as well as not so good ways

The more challenging the behaviour, the longer and sometimes more frustrating this process could be, but we were determined to persevere. Once we had a group of children who mastered the process, they were able to help others to do the same. This multiplied our efforts, and there seemed to be a kind of snowball effect. We were making huge progress.

A short-term solution that worked especially well with children who were younger, those who were more tactile learners or needed more concrete reminders, or children new to the school, was an incentive system. We focused on 'catching them' behaving appropriately and recognized them by giving them what we referred to as 'a respect ticket.' They would receive these tickets on the playground, then when they went back to class, they related to their teacher what they did to receive their respect ticket and why it was an important thing to have done. The tickets became a very powerful teaching and learning strategy, using positive reinforcement to anchor the new respectful behaviour.

Later, when this program spread to many other schools, some people questioned why we would want to use a positive reinforcement system for behaviour? Some were very critical of this approach. My response was, and still is; the tickets work. They are an effective visual reminder of the child's appropriate behaviour. If a child was learning a new and unfamiliar behaviour, they really made a huge difference. My only caution to those using this system is it is a means to an end, not an end in itself. It is important to move the children to a point where they behave appropriately because it is the right thing to do, not because they got a ticket.

Diane, a principal from England visiting Dr. Bonnie-Larson Knight's school after she implemented the program stated that with all her years of experience and all the schools she visited, she never saw such a peaceful and pleasant school yard. All the children were playing, co-operating and having fun and when a problem did occur they would quickly move to a designated problem solving spot and sorted it out so they could go back to playing. "It was a joy to watch" she said.

There was no one size fits all solution; we had to respond according to the individual child and the particular situation presented. Was any of this easy or a quick fix? The short answer is no! The long answer is the results were worth every minute of our time and effort.

Some children posed major challenges; just when we thought we made a breakthrough with them, and we were ready to celebrate, they would do something totally unexpected. This was the case with Tom. He was a bully, then completely changed his behaviour. Now, after months, he joined with two other boys to again begin to bully younger children. Tom and his buddies wanted to create a neighbourhood gang because they believed, gangs earned "respect." They were basically good kids who discovered how to flex their muscles and use their age and size to intimidate some of our younger children, even while participating enthusiastically in our school programs designed to counter these same activities. I could not believe it!

I learned about Tom and his gang activities shortly before one of our Respect Lunches. Tom's behaviour throughout the school term was exemplary and he was looking forward to the lunch not only as a participant but also as a helper. Obviously this created a dilemma, after all, the lunch was a celebration of respectful behaviour. If he joined the group at the Respect Lunch, it would appear we were condoning or at least overlooking his bullying behaviour. If we excluded him, we would be negating all his previous efforts to be kind and caring to other children. He, like many of our children, experienced too many broken promises in their young lives; he didn't need another one from me.

So I compromised. Tom would have his lunch as promised, but he would not be included with the other children as a part of the school family. His choice to bully others, especially children younger than himself, was not what was expected from a kind and caring family member. As a consequence for this unacceptable behaviour, he would be excluded from the 'family,' he would eat lunch in my office, with me supervising.

And that's what we did. I served him with a smile, at a table in my office. While Tom ate, I explained while we were including him in the Respect Lunch celebrations, his bullying behaviour was so abhorrent we could not include him with the other children; he would not be able to enjoy their company. He finished his lunch in silence while I sat at my desk and read some reports. Then I asked Tom if he enjoyed his lunch. "Not really," he frowned. "It would have been a lot nicer if I was in with all the others. It was no fun eating by myself."

As much as anyone in the school, Tom needed and wanted acceptance, recognition and the family atmosphere of the Respect Lunch celebration, with his peers, teachers, parents and community partners. Tom was disappointed, but he understood and agreed with the reason behind our decision. He agreed it was fair. He went so far as to say although he knew his bullying might have these consequences, he didn't think he would feel so alone. He then came up with numerous ways to make amends to those he had bullied and was a model student for the remainder of his days at South Simcoe. He often went out of his way to help others both in and out of school.

Bullying and violence at South Simcoe were not restricted to boys. One of the most aggressive and angry students I encountered was Meredith, a bright grade seven girl with an angelic face and cold, hardened eyes. I don't recall encountering a child with both more promise and more rage than Meredith. She refused to be touched, either physically or emotionally. Just eleven years old, Meredith was already associating with much older children in the evenings and on weekends. Many of her friends already had arrest records for car theft and other crimes. Meredith was waiting for placement in a restricted facility but in the meantime, she was placed at our school and we did our best to help her.

Over time, I observed, in horror, Meredith's actions growing ever more intense. Her penchant for violence was shocking. On one occasion, Meredith, finding taunting and teasing was not enough to make her classmate cry, beat the girl up so brutally she broke the other girl's nose. Many of her attacks appeared totally spontaneous, without cause or provocation. Consequences meant nothing to Meredith. If she grew bored or angry in class, she would simply rise from her seat, walk out of the school and go home.

After numerous failed attempts to get Meredith to attend school regularly and on time, she was taken to court by the attendance counselor. When the judge began to admonish her for her behaviour, Meredith simply turned on her heel and walked out of the courtroom, right in the middle of the warnings and admonishments.

Much of Meredith's life was spent with various foster families, and she was receiving counselling arranged by a social agency. While Meredith attended South Simcoe, she resided with a woman in her thirties whom we assumed was her mother. She wasn't. The woman was Meredith's grandmother.

Although we quickly formed some suspicions about the source of Meredith's rage, there was much of her life we did not know for certain, and Meredith herself made it clear she would not discuss the matter. Yet we grew determined to help Meredith if we could. It was impossible not to feel sorry for someone so young, and with so much anger boiling within her.

The attack in which Meredith broke her opponent's nose was a clear signal the counselling efforts alone were not working. We could no longer risk injuries to other children.

When a child is a danger to others in the school, Home Instruction, where a qualified teacher goes to the home to teach, is an option, since by law, the child is still entitled to receive schooling.

I was concerned about sending a teacher to be alone with Meredith because of her violent outbursts. I could be putting the teacher in danger. What's more, Meredith's instantly negative reaction to the idea of a teacher entering her home made it even less practical.

Looking for some guidance, I raised our predicament with officials at the district office, who suggested we use a nearby library. Give me a break, I said to myself. Where was I to find a local library? There is no local library in this area. People don't realize how lacking in services some areas are.

A little later I happened to be chatting about the problem with Louis, the manager of the local Zellers store (formerly K-Mart), directly across the street. I expected to receive nothing more from him than a nod of understanding. Instead, Louis asked how often I would need space for Meredith's special instruction periods.

"About one hour, three days a week," I said.

"Why not use my office?" he suggested.

I was stunned, and deeply touched. Here was the manager of a major department store, who faced dozens of crises each day—including, unfortunately, the odd incident involving a South Simcoe student—and still he was willing to relinquish his office space three times a week. But Louis wanted to help the children, and he believed both Meredith and South Simcoe were worth it. His suggestion demonstrated how deeply engaged our business and community partners became. Kim began meeting Meredith at Louis' office for the special instruction Meredith needed.

Meredith's situation? You probably already guessed it. She was the victim of incest, a bright and attractive child who tried to balance her desire for a true childhood with her inner shame and self-loathing the only way she knew how—by lashing out at the world around her, especially anyone who threatened more pain and humiliation. My heart broke for her, and once again I was reminded of the practical limitations imposed on me and the school system generally. We simply could not solve all the problems we faced.

Meredith surprised us; she actually responded quite well to this one-on-one teaching from Kim in a corporate office setting. Just as we began feeling good about this small measure of progress, Meredith became pregnant, even before she experienced her first menstrual period, and she was removed from her home by the Children's Aid Society. I wish we had an opportunity to work with Meredith from an earlier age; I am convinced we could have helped her avoid so much tragedy and pain.

Nurturing the development of a sense of self in our children, teaching them ways to strengthen their character, manage their emotions, and create relationships, were all working and getting the intended results. As always, we continued to deepen and widen our efforts. Along with strengthening the children's sense of self, I wanted to strengthen their engagement with the school and with learning, increase their sense of belonging, and generate a collective sense of pride, in the safe, caring and healthy learning community we were creating.

We had our motto: *Together We Light the Way.* This expressed our comprehensive, collective and collaborative approach, school family and community working together to light the path of learning for our children. There was something missing, …some music perhaps? …A school song might do the trick, Sharon McLean said. So we all worked together to write the words and choose a melody. The song summed up, I believe, so much of the atmosphere we were trying to create, and the goals we set for ourselves, the children, and the community:

We are the children who are looking to the future,
Sharing pride and singing our school song.
At South Simcoe School, we're learning every day
If Together We Light the Way, we will be strong
We learn the skills that are going to shape our lives,
The sense of self that a good beginning gives.
And every day we're sharing with our teachers and our friends
Who will help us all become the best we can.

We are the children who are looking to the future,
Sharing pride and singing our school song.
At South Simcoe School, we're learning every day
If Together We Light the Way, we will be strong.
If Together We Light the Way, we will be strong.
So Together Let's Light the Way, and we'll be strong!

We taught our school song to the students, and each class began singing it every morning, immediately following the national anthem. I would walk from class to class, listening to the children in each room, and stop to congratulate those who sang lustily and well. Only the grade eight students tended to disappoint me, but that was understandable: by age thirteen or fourteen certain kinds of public display can be awkward for many children. I knew the younger students looked up to the grade eights as models, and I didn't want the reticence of the seniors filtering down through the grades. Singing the school song to us demonstrated the pride students have in their school, and by extension, the pride they have in themselves as students of the school.. Singing was a wonderful way of expressing that feeling. The school song was later recorded for us by Rick and Terry Johnson and became available as a DVD.

Our school chant, created by Michelle and her students, was playful and heartwarming, it went like this;

At South Simcoe
We all know
We're the best
Yes! Yes! Yes!
At South Simcoe
We will, we will
Rock you!

Each time I recall our school song, I think of Meagan, and a host of emotions wash over me. We were now holding regular school assemblies at the Legion Hall, and these were a confirmation of success to us. The behaviour of the children during our assemblies was exemplary. We used assemblies as an opportunity to teach and practice the behaviour expected when attending a formal performance. We expected respectful entry and exit just like at the school, we expected our audience to listen attentively while someone was speaking or performing and we expected appropriate applause to honour those who performed rather than hooting and hollering. Our children were better behaved than many adult audiences at major events in the city, and as a result, they were invited by our business and community partners to many performances and events.

We ended each assembly by having the entire school sing the school song with as much passion in their hearts as they could muster. When we first began to do this, again the senior students had difficulty overcoming their adolescent self-consciousness about singing out loud. Perhaps, I thought, they will sing if we invite them in small groups to lead the rest of the audience. So I asked for volunteers from their class to come up to the microphone and lead the school in singing our song. Among the small number who responded was Meagan.

I was taken aback. Meagan was a thin waif of a girl with huge, heart-breaking eyes ringed in dark circles, and the sad look of a fetal alcohol child. Sweet and good-natured, Meagan had never shown any such initiative in the past, and standing at a microphone in front of hundreds of classmates, leading them in singing, is not customarily an ambition for shy and introverted children. But Meagan seemed determined, and how could I refuse her?

After I introduced the song leaders at the next assembly, Meagan seized the microphone in her tiny hand, positioned herself in the centre of the group, and burst into song with a powerful bell-like voice, exhorting the other students to raise their voices with her, and they responded. She sang with such power and confidence we asked her to repeat the performance at subsequent assemblies. During one of them, CITY TV a Toronto TV station, with David Onley, the education reporter (who later became a Lieutenant Governor of Ontario) arrived to tape a three-part series on the school and captured Meagan's exuberant performance on television. From that time on, she explained to others that she was a TV star and she was; she had performed on television.

Meagan's family background was in sharp contrast to her marvelous onstage persona. On the occasions when Meagan and I chatted, she spoke sadly of her treatment at home, and complained of her parents' excessive drug use. Like so many children I encountered at South Simcoe, Meagan was forced to deal with a wide gulf separating her life at school from her life at home. School was a place where she could count on being loved and cared for, a place where she received recognition and admiration for her talent. At home, little attention was paid to her needs as a young girl; no one seemed interested in her accomplishments, and the pain must have been very real and very deep to her.

Meagan was not dealing with her situation alone, and that both encouraged and frightened her. The Children's Aid Society was aware of her home life, and case-workers were monitoring Meagan's treatment, supported by information we provided on request. Knowing someone was watching and caring for her may have been encouraging to Meagan, but she also knew there was a possibility of being removed from her home environment, and this alarmed her.

Finally, the day came; a decision was made to relocate Meagan, and when the CAS worker arrived at the school to carry out the order, Jacki and I sat with her as she received the news she would be sent to a foster family. Meagan rushed across the room and into my arms, crying uncontrollably. "You guys care about me!" she sobbed, begging Jacki or me to take her. "Why can't I stay with you? Why am I being sent away to some strange family?"

Jacki and I were on the verge of tears as we sat with Meagan while the CAS worker explained where she was going and why. Thankfully, the Society arranged for Meagan to continue attending South Simcoe so she could have some stability in her life and count on us to continue to love and care for her. Still, wrenching a child from her parents, no matter how necessary a move it may seem, is always agonizing to watch.

Once the pain of separation began to fade, the transformation in Meagan was gratifying. She arrived at school with clean, well-brushed hair and wearing attractive clothes, and she walked with more confidence than I had ever seen in her. Meagan missed her parents terribly, and she agonized over reporting their drug use, even though she knew she had done the correct thing. She continued to lead the school in singing, but with a hint of sadness and regret in her large eyes, one I suspected would remain there for a long time.

We wanted our children to return home at the end of each school day with a feeling of accomplishment, the knowledge they achieved something worthwhile. We felt if they left the school with this sense of accomplishment, they would begin to engage more with schooling and learning. They would see the school as the place in which they felt successful and therefore really look forward to returning to school the following day. It would also demonstrate that, while they had little control over what was happening at home, at school they were fully in control of the choices they made and the results that ensued.

So, we focused on moving another one of our guiding principles,into practice. *Everyone has strengths which must be nurtured and supported.*

We created a goal achievement system. Later, as our programs spread to other schools and countries, this became known as our Success Mapping and Achievement System. Every morning in every classroom (yes, even in kindergarten), teachers worked with the class as a whole, to set daily academic, social, emotional and leadership goals, (Academic, Respect (Personal Management), Teamwork and Leadership). With this as a guide, the students then set their personal or individual goals. Throughout the day, these goals were monitored and measured, then at the end of the day, students reflected on and processed, (reviewed or talked about) what they did to achieve their goals, the activities in which they were involved, the strategies they used and whether these activities and strategies helped them to achieve their goals or not. They documented their progress, graphed their results, then selected their focus for the next day. Would they try the same activity with a different strategy? Would they need a different activity and more assistance from the teacher? Did their goal need to be broken down into smaller steps? What would help them to succeed? This strength-based approach was a powerful motivator. Students always began the goal achievement process by documenting their assets and their strengths.

The daily documenting and graphing of their successes, however small, emphasizing what they accomplished over and over, day after day, layering success upon success, had an exponential effect, and the children began to see themselves as successful. Their graphs were evidence of this, and little by little, they were convinced they were capable of anything they put their minds to. Even when they experienced a setback, the students began to develop the self-confidence to pick themselves up, move forward and 'find their way.' After all, they now had a history of success, they knew what it felt like to experience success, and they strived to maintain that state. They were becoming more and more resilient.

As the years unfolded, we realized just how critical it was for the children to spend enough time reflecting on their day, processing their successes, taking the best lessons from their failures and integrating their new knowledge into their personal repertoire of skills and strategies.

Reflection helped the students to identify what worked, what did not work, and why not. They learned to change their strategy, change what did not work for their individual learning styles and embrace what did. They learned to understand themselves, their learning styles and patterns and thus became more independent learners and problem solvers. They developed the understanding that progress is always evolving.

Even when the students were not able to achieve the larger goal for that day, our focus on task analysis helped them to identify and focus on some small achievement. We wanted to keep them focused on the positives: (remember, FIND THE GOOD). Something good happens every day. We could not afford to let students take one failure, which they saw as a 'bad thing' and let it crowd out the many good things in their minds and leave them feeling depressed or frustrated.

The children gradually needed less and less teacher involvement in their goal-setting and achievement process. It was like teaching them to ride a bike; you don't need to run alongside them forever. Once they have their sense of balance and the feeling of being in charge of their own choices and outcomes, they are independent enough for you to let them go and give them time and space to practice. Our goal was always to find ways to sustain the students' interest and engagement in their learning, by helping them to think for themselves, figure out which strategies worked best for them, and help them to become more independent. They built on a series of small successes, each adding to the overall weight and impact of the others, to produce three major results: Students discovered they had capabilities, strengths and talents and could succeed at anything they put their minds to. Students experienced success. When they left school at the end of each day, they felt good about themselves, raising their overall sense of self, (who they were and what they were capable of achieving), and their engagement with schooling. Students learned about themselves as learners and took more responsibility for their choices and actions.

Many of the children still needed many things in their lives, and some were beyond the scope of our abilities to provide. Fortunately, a sense of self and self-respect, their most critical needs, were not. We were able to help the students to develop these. The impact of engaging their hearts and minds as well as igniting their spirits, and the self-confidence that resulted made all of our other achievements at the school possible.

LEADER'S REFLECTION

Thriving and successful organizations have practical and useful success mapping systems for goal achievement, that are asset-based and focus on creation versus elimination, and "finding the good."

- Do you have a goal achievement system that focuses on creation versus elimination?

- How do you create a culture of "finding the good"?

CHAPTER 10

The Circle of Love

Something unique was happening at our school, a change so profound and positive that one of our community partners called it *a revolution of the heart.*

As the skeptics grew silent, others grew intrigued and supportive. We relished and embraced assistance from many sources, and in at least once instance, the help proved literally life-saving.

One of the organizations that offered to assist us was St. John's Ambulance. Our friend George, one of our most enthusiastic partners, happened to mention that the Kiwanis Club funded a booklet used in a course on babysitting conducted by St. John's Ambulance. The course was being taught to neighbourhood teenagers on Saturdays.

It occurred to me that many of the children in our school could benefit from this training. I knew first-hand that children ten years old or even younger were being assigned to care for younger brothers and sisters. We couldn't change the circumstances that led parents to place so much responsibility on the shoulders of such young children, but we could help our students to acquire some basic safety skills that would assist them with this task. This would also help them to be more confident and better prepared, adding to their capabilities and sense of self. And if we could provide them with a job skill, wouldn't that be worth pursuing?

If St. John's Ambulance could teach a babysitting course in the neighbourhood on Saturdays, perhaps they could teach one to the students in school during the week. This would mean reassigning some time out of the school day for participants in the course—a noon hour activity perhaps? A decision to be taken only if the parents agreed that it made sense.

Our covenant to assess new ideas remained, *What's in the best interests of the children?* In this case, some basic training in babysitting would benefit everyone, and when the majority of parents said, "Let's do it!" we did.

Among the students who completed the course was Susan, an attractive 11 year old frequently called upon by her mother to babysit Susan's four-year-old sister and seven-year-old brother. One evening, Susan and another grade eight student were babysitting the children when the seven year old refused to obey a request from his older sister. Susan, in an attempt to persuade him to see things her way, threatened to complain to their mother, noting that the mother would likely remove the boy's bike-riding privileges. In anger, the boy pulled a large kitchen knife from a drawer and hurled it in Susan's direction, missing her but striking his four-year-old sister in the leg.

The blade nicked an artery. Blood spattered everywhere, and as the little girl shrieked in pain and horror, the training Susan and her friend had received from St. John's Ambulance kicked in. In seconds, they staunched the flow of blood, called 911, and rushed the child outside to meet the ambulance as it arrived.

At the hospital, surgeons noted that the little girl might easily have died from loss of blood had Susan and her friend not acted so quickly. The CAS persuaded Susan's mother to leave her job and accept mother's allowance, enabling her to care for her children herself, and her son was enrolled in a special counselling program. Susan, of course, had proven the value and wisdom of the babysitting course in a true life-or-death situation. It also validated my decision to take time during the school day for the course.

Education, I realized, could not begin and end at the playground gate. Nor could the demands of life stop there. They both worked best when integrated—when social issues reached into the school, and when education extended into the needs of home and family. The educational and social changes went hand in hand.

The number of our community partners, our extended family, continued to grow and, best of all, their level of engagement deepened. The children had come to value and rely on the community more and more. Various branches of Kiwanis, St John's Ambulance, several mall merchants, the local police force and the Canadian Legion had formed the early core of our supporters, and other organizations were being added month by month. It was uncanny; it seemed as if as soon as we realized that we needed assistance in some area, someone would show up to meet that need.

Within just a few years, South Simcoe Public School had become a symbol of change and improvement. We had begun our change process using the resources we had and doing what made good sense. As we progressed, our four guiding principles were the compass that steered all our programs and initiatives and they all supported and complemented each other. As we introduced new ideas, we made sure that they were either based on research and evidence of success over time, or were simply a natural and sensible progression from where we were. We did not discard traditions, a practice that is quite common in organizations, "throwing out the baby with the bathwater," this would have made no sense. Instead we kept the best of the old, and introduced what we needed from the new that would keep us moving forward, meet the needs of our children and work in our particular context. Our implementation strategy involved layering, integrating and weaving what worked for our children, into the very fabric of the curriculum and the functioning of the school. Everything we did was integrated into the whole. After all, we were not educating bits and pieces of a child we were educating the whole child; this also meant a focus on the 'whole teacher,' the 'whole parent,' the 'whole community partner' and yes the 'whole principal,' as well. Did this make the process more complex? In many ways, yes, however we wanted sustainable change, so we took a long-term view and built slowly and carefully over time. This was the secret to our success.

The result of all this was the creation of a multifaceted, muti-dimensional infrastructure encompassing academic, social, emotional and leadership learning and achievement. This was graphically depicted by pillars. Later, as our programs spread, some cultural groups used the graphic of circles instead of pillars, because they felt that circles represented an ecosystem, a more natural process rather than 'man-made concrete.' It really didn't matter, as long as the focus was not solely on academic. Major strategies, that moved us from vision to results, were;

- **Our success mapping and achievement system** that included setting and achieving goals in each of the learning areas, the monitoring, managing and measuring of these goals, documenting, maintaining and sustaining the achievement, as well as taking every opportunity to celebrate success.

- **Partnering with others** in order to provide a wider circle of support for our children. With strengthening the children and working together to increase the protective factors around them as our common goal, families and the community as a whole were also strengthened.

- **Inclusive Leadership**, we encouraged a participatory style of leadership, where everyone shared in the process, took ownership of and accountability for the entire change process.

We deliberately and intentionally worked to create a culture that supported all our efforts. It all became simply "this is the way we do things." "Leading and managing this system tested all my personal and professional skills. Using the guiding principles kept us all grounded as individuals and on course, keeping our focus on the humanity of the children. Creating and using the infrastructure of the pillars helped us all to manage the seemingly competing priorites that are a part of school and classroom life. We integrated and wove every activity and every initiative we undertook into the fabric of the whole instead of implementing in silos. . As educators, we sometimes think that we have to have all the answers, but in this case we didn't. We opened up our hearts and minds to this discomfort, just as we were asking the children to do. We learned as they learned; we developed and grew on a personal level as well as in our roles, as did the parents, the partners and the children themselves."It was a little like cooking several dishes at the same time," I explained to someone. "They're all bubbling away, and every now and then you have to pay attention to first this one, then that one, you stir one, you sample, you add some spices to it, then you move on to another." That's what leading and managing the various programs and initiatives at South Simcoe was like for me.

Our senior students had now become more involved in sports and other physical activities; they became very conscious about the importance of a healthful lifestyle and would monitor even teachers' lunches, to ensure that they were healthful and litter free. They were now actively involved in service activities in the school and in the community, they were inspired by all the service club members who worked with them, they had tasted success and were now more interested in pursuing academic achievement.

In order to keep the momentum of change moving forward, we collectively decided that we would honour and recognize the students appropriately for their achievements. Although we wanted them to work hard and achieve because it was what they should be doing in school, at this stage they still needed a great deal of support and encouragement to remain engaged with schooling. Anyway, who does not like being recognized?

We felt that a ceremony to honour and recognize their achievements would do the trick. Celebrating our Stars became one of the most popular initiatives for our senior students. At the ceremony, held at the legion hall of course, preparations were underway for the first celebration. Students were to be honoured for their achievements in the areas of Scholastics, Sports, School Activities, Service to Others, and Initiative, Innovation, and Leadership in any of these areas. Reinforcing that learning was important in all these areas; the intellectual, the physical, the social, the emotional as well as the spiritual.

The service category honoured students who had been of service to others, whether it was in the school and or in the community. This was a critical part of our effort to teach the concept of being a good citizen, by taking responsibility for one's community, being a kind and caring human being who gives service to others without waiting to be asked, and treats others in a way that you would want to be treated.

My approach had its roots in yet another lesson learned at my grandmother's knee. She taught me that we all have something to give, and that even if we have nothing to share in terms of material things, our time and love are the greatest gifts we can offer.

She told us that a wise man in India had said, "The greatest gift you can give is your time and your love." Years later I discovered that the man she referred to was actually Rabindranath Tagore, who won the 1913 Nobel Prize for Literature, and his actual words were: "The greatest happiness in life is in service to mankind." I have learned that children are quick to grasp the idea of giving their time. They love to play a role in the community, and they especially enjoy the good feelings they get from providing service to others.

Teachers and children alike worked together to brainstorm different ways of giving back to the community. Someone pointed out that seniors in the area had difficulty walking to the store for a newspaper or other items. They lacked the mobility and energy of youth, which the children possessed in abundance, so this was quickly identified as one kind of service to be provided. Another service might be shovelling snow from the sidewalk for someone who lacked the ability to do it herself. A dozen other ideas were proposed: visit someone in the hospital or at a nursing home, especially after major holidays. We learned that there are many visitors at holiday times but after those occasions, the numbers dwindle. They could collect and take non-perishable items to the food bank, join with one of our business partners who sponsored the annual Terry Fox Run to raise money for cancer research, or simply walk through the neighbourhood picking up garbage.

Activities in all categories were noted, and, at the end of each term when report cards were issued, each student was honoured with "Stars." A "Star" from three of the categories provided the student with 'Triple-Star' recognition.

The idea struck a responsive chord with the children for a reason that, frankly, had never occurred to us. "You know what I like about these stars?" a student said to me one day. "They are just for us. Report Cards are for our parents, this is for us. When all these important people come to see us, celebrate with us and applaud us, it makes us feel really good and it makes us want to do even better. All these people are here to show that they care about us and how well we are doing. They treat us like stars, we really are stars to them."

In order to keep our focus on moving forward collectively, we ensured that all students were encouraged and given the opportunity to be honoured and recognized during the assemblies. With a little effort, every child could qualify for at least one "Star," and they all did. All, that is, except Fred.

Fred had been gaining confidence and pride in himself as a result of the attention and assistance he had received with his grooming. But he remained a grade eight student functioning at the intellectual level of a grade one student, filled with enough anger and frustration to prevent him from participating in any activity that would involve him in the celebration. From time to time, Fred still insulted his teacher or threw a tantrum serious enough to send him to my office, where he would eventually mumble an apology and offer to make amends. During one of these sessions, I encouraged Fred to perform even one small act of service, do 'something nice' for his teacher or for another student. Fred had made no effort thus far to perform even the smallest act of service in the school, such as opening a door for someone or helping them carry something, far less do something in the community.

"And I won't," Fred almost sneered. "I'm not doing nothin' to help nobody."Fred seemed determined, which was unfortunate in my view. By refusing to build relationships in any way, he was alienating himself still further from the rest of the children.

One day, when Fred was walking down the hall towards a classroom, he passed a windowed door with a large smudge or smear on the glass. As I stood watching, open-mouthed, he stopped, unconsciously withdrew a tissue from his pocket and began wiping away the spot.

I couldn't contain my excitement; here was an opportunity that I had to seize. "Fred!" I shouted. "You're doing something nice for the school! You're performing an act of service! That's terrific!"

Fred froze on the spot; he wasn't sure what the heck I was talking about and equally unsure about what would happen next.

I called Fred's teacher, Alvena, out of her classroom, and Kim Hutchinson came running down the hall from the other direction at the sound of my voice. "Look," I said to them, pointing at Fred. "Fred is cleaning the window in the door. He's performing an act of service for the school."

Fred grinned a little and resumed polishing the glass. Kim ran to her room and returned with a cleaning rag. "Here," she said, handing it to Fred, "this will work better than that old tissue," and Fred took it from her and kept polishing. "You know," I said to Kim and Alvena as we stood back and watched him work, "Fred has definitely made a choice to do something good for the school. What do you think?" They agreed he had.

All right, it was stretching things a little, I suppose, but Fred was obviously proud that his name could now be included at the celebration assembly. Whether he had intended to perform an act of service or not was irrelevant at this point. Fred later began helping the school custodian, and what's more, he polished that particular pane of glass virtually every day for the rest of his time at South Simcoe. Fred had tasted success and he liked it!

Our first Celebrating our Stars ceremony was held in March, 1993, and no Academy Awards ceremony was orchestrated with more attention to detail and emotional impact. We created enough pomp and circumstance for a Buckingham Palace reception, and the children loved it. The formality, music, staging and speeches all made them walk a little taller and prouder, and to this day, the ceremonies in other schools that adopted the program maintain the same tone and atmosphere.

The youngest children in the school entered the Legion Hall carrying their class banners with their class names, in a processional, as the theme music from *Chariots of Fire* played through the speakers of the sound system. The students to be honoured walked slowly and solemnly up the aisle; they were escorted to their front row seats, (after all they were the guests of honour), then seated by grade six ushers who were formally attired. Next came two senior students who mounted the stage and slowly unfurled our new banner displaying our motto *Together We Light the Way* and our new symbol.. The audience sat in hushed silence, and the children's faces shone with pride.

Several invited guests, including our community partners and school custodians, were on hand to share in the celebration. I remember Sharon McLean reaching out to squeeze my hand. "This is it, Sandra," she said. "We're doing it, we are really beginning to make a difference now. Just look at them, look at their faces; you can tell how good they feel; this is the legacy we will leave." We both had lumps in our throats and tears in our eyes. The children were enthralled throughout the ceremony. The names of the first few children to be honoured, and the activities in which they had been involved, were read solemnly over the sound system. The audience applauded with enthusiasm as each student stepped up to the podium to receive his or her certificate.

The attention paid to them by the other students, the staff and the invited guests was obviously important to the children, as were the descriptions of their actions, which we took the time to describe in detail—"Joey helped at Parent Rap sessions by babysitting. He also performed acts of service in the community by shoveling snow from his neighbour's walkway"—These descriptions were important, they helped to clarify what was valued and they provided the younger students with ideas for their own activities. Why all the solemn formality? We had several reasons. We wanted everyone to recognize the importance of what the students had achieved and we wanted the students themselves to feel what it was like to be seated in the front row because they were the guests of honour; what it was like to walk onto a stage and be honoured and recognized for something that they had freely chosen to do.

We wanted to honour both the achievements of the children, and the support of our community partners. But most of all, we wanted to anchor this feeling of success and achievement. We wanted the children to remember the ceremony in detail, and remember the emotional high they felt so that they would treasure the joy of that day in their hearts forever.

At the end of the first celebration, we revealed our 'piece de resistance.' Kim Hutchinson, who was a great bargain hunter, had spent several days searching local costume houses for a shark outfit. It was not easy; a shark costume is not a common party outfit in our part of the world. She finally managed to find a costume so worn and moth-eaten that the rental company sold it for just a few dollars. With a little sewing, stitching and patching by her mother-in-law, Pauline, it was made as good as new. As our celebration was ending, we announced the arrival of a special guest: South Simcoe Public School's very own mascot, Sharkie. Kim appeared dressed in the costume as wild cheers exploded from the students.

Everyone wanted to hug "Sharkie", and almost every student did. At that point, we knew without any doubt at all that our dreams of creating connectedness, a sense of belonging, school spirit and achieving wonders at South Simcoe Public School were beginning to come true. These children, many of whom did not enjoy the opportunities available to students in other schools in more affluent areas, were now engaged with their school, proud of their achievements and, most importantly, feeling stronger inside.

When it came to community partnering and engagement, the initiative that seemed to give our partners the most joy and create the most enthusiastic response was our Circles of Love: Reading Together program. We knew that the simple act of reading to a child yields many wonderful benefits. It creates a love of books and reading in the hearts and minds of the children. I always said that it was as if the opening of a book was like opening the doors to a magical world where the reader and the person being read to shared the joy of their secret adventure. This made them both feel good and generated a special bond between the adult and the child.

Each time our community partners read to the children, it made the children feel that they were important and it made the adults feel needed and appreciated. The chemistry generated by this special bonding is difficult to describe. Perhaps Rob Pitfield, our partner from Scotiabank, put it best when he said, "It's like magic!"

Interestingly enough, many of the community partners who agreed to read to our children began to, or in some cases resumed reading to their own kids at home, even if they were older. One partner confessed that he thought reading stories aloud to his children ended when they learned to read for themselves. He changed his mind, however, and admitted that the experience of participating in our Circles of Love program prompted him to resume reading to his daughters, aged nine and twelve. These are sometimes difficult ages for father-daughter relationships; this was compounded in this case by the extensive travelling required by this man's work. Choosing books from the library, and reading from them to the girls on evenings when he was home, became a wonderful way of building and strengthening the father-daughter connection.

Everyone we invited to participate in our Circles of Love initiative, from parents and police officers to the mayor, the president of General Motors of Canada, bankers, politicians, school board officials, and the chief of police, responded with enthusiasm. We also encouraged our older students to read to younger children, nurturing in them a parenting skill, that we hoped they would someday put to use with their own families. It was one more strategy we used to break the cycle of poverty and the ensuing problems repeating themselves generation after generation.

We held Circles of love sessions in the school library every two weeks, and it was such a delight to watch the children snuggle up to our community partners, their eyes wide and shining, while they listened to the stories. It was especially dramatic when the person reading to them was a male business executive in a suit, or a policeman in full uniform. We welcomed male readers from our community because the South Simcoe neighbourhood had a high percentage of single-parent families. The majority of our single parents happened to be mothers, and this left many of the boys in our school without good male role models in their lives. We wanted the boys to experience men in a traditional fathering role, taking time from their business or careers to read stories and chat with them, because they were that important.

The presence of the men could never, of course, take the place of an absentee father or eradicate the trauma some of them had suffered. It could, perhaps, mitigate the effects of abuse from a live-in boyfriend. For that reason it was very important.

Among the male role models who proved especially popular with the children was one of the tallest uniformed police officers I had ever encountered. Colin Shaw stood well over six feet and arrived at the school in full regalia, including handcuffs, sidearm and billy club, and actually stretched himself full-length on the floor to read aloud to the children. In the beginning, they couldn't resist peppering him with questions about his weapon, his handcuffs, and if he had ever appeared on the TV show *Cops*. As time passed, however, they grew more relaxed around Colin. They loved to wear his hat, and the conversations they shared with him extended to include music, fashions, sports, movies—all the diversions important to children yet rarely discussed with adults, let alone a uniformed police officer. Eventually, the students didn't seem to notice the uniform at all, all they saw was Colin, a trusted friend and advisor.

Colin began visiting the school regularly to chat with children, often arriving in his police cruiser. Several months earlier, the sight of a police cruiser parked at the school signalled bad news to the children and their parents, who assumed someone was in trouble with the law. Now the sight of a cruiser produced little more than a shrug of the shoulders and the observation, "It's probably just the police reading to the children." And it almost always was. Later, this initiative expanded beyond the school. We held several sessions at local shopping malls and community libraries. These sessions were held during National Police Week, to bring a focus to the importance of community support in the development of literacy and, of course, the critical link of literacy to crime prevention and success in life. At these sessions, we invited children from other schools to join us to listen to stories read to them by the mayor and chief of police. In later years, this became an annual event in many municipalities. We were even invited to the nation's capital, Ottawa to hold annual sessions in the senate chambers at the Canadian House of Parliament.

We welcomed surprise visitors to our Circles of Love from all walks of life, and from all sources. When Curt Tingley, one of our community partners, encountered cartoonist and author Ben Wicks at an airport lounge and described our program to him, Ben agreed to visit us, reading to the students, drawing cartoons and often exaggerating his Cockney accent for comic effect.

Success truly does breed success. With the passage of time, word spread of our achievements, and of the growing number of local business and community organizations participating with us in educating and supporting the children. This encouraged others to join in. We were able to persuade them to help other schools as well.

While we welcomed offers of assistance from every source, we were careful to interview our potential partners to ensure they shared our concerns about the safety and security of our children. We also wanted to confirm they understood and would agree to abide by our guiding principles. These were:

- *Every one has the right to be respected and the responsibility to respect others.*

- *Every one is unique and has a contribution to make.*

- *Every one has strengths, which must be nurtured and supported.*

- *Service to others performed with caring and love makes a difference.*

Everything we did together was to advance the educational agenda.

We were so grateful for all the involvement pledged to us, but I remember we were especially touched by the assistance received from the owner of a small pizza parlour near the school. The young franchise owner was among the first business partners to offer his help, and I was amazed he was not only an enthusiastic supporter and he even found time to spend with the children. The pizza store was not a big money-maker for him; he was actually holding down two additional jobs, and he was certainly not a wealthy man, but he was a man who cared about children. He believed in the goals we were trying to achieve, he believed in community cohesion and he wanted to give something back to the community. So he visited the school regularly to talk to the children about setting and achieving goals, making wise and informed choices, staying in school and graduating from school, then doing something useful with their lives in addition to getting a job. This young entrepreneur was so impressive. He also helped to organize Thursday pizza days, paring his profit to the bone to make it affordable for our children to enjoy pizza for lunch one day a week. The pizza operator's contribution and generosity of spirit were what we wanted in a partner; he wanted to help the children simply because it was a good thing to do, and he asked for nothing in return. We declined, with thanks, offers of money to assist the school and its programs; sometimes we were offered large sums in return for using our children in advertising campaigns. The answer was always an emphatic "No thank you."

We partnered with people who understood that raising and educating children was a complex undertaking and to do this well involved not just the school but also families and the entire community, opening their hearts and minds to taking ownership of, and responsibility for, their education and well-being. We needed all the assistance we could get; we needed our extended family, the whole village.

In my third year at South Simcoe, I was so buoyed by the success of our programs and community partnership strategy I proposed we become more active, vocal and visible in our "thank you" to those who were helping us and what, I asked, is more active, vocal and visible than a parade of children?

Thus began our South Simce Community Parade. We would celebrate the beginning of the school year with a parade through the neighbourhood as a tribute to our community partners, reinforcing the connections we established with them and acknowledging their contributions to our children. It became, however, a much-needed celebration of the entire community. The school's success was making an impact on the community, and we sought to do more than say a simple "thank you." We wanted an impossible-to-ignore, in-your-face event that said to the community, *"Don't you just love us??!!"* and defy anyone to disagree.

Our first South Simcoe parade consisted of the children walking through the neighbourhood, led by school staff. The following year our community partners asked if they could join us, and GM added a truck to the parade. Parents also participated, along with partners like the Kiwanis and Optimist Club members, business mascots such as the Swiss Chalet Chicken, the Kmart Cougar, Marty, the Shoppers Drug Mart Shutterbug and the Pizza Pizza Doughboy joined in. One way or another, often juggling their busy schedules, the mayor and our Director of Education demonstrated their support of our efforts by participating as well. The entire procession was led by Constable Colin Shaw in his police cruiser, and the parade eventually became a community-wide event, as impressive as any in the city.

By this time, there was a strong sense of school spirit; children identified with the school and saw the school as a place where they could be successful. A strategy that contributed to this, was the choosing of names for every class. The class names were linked to the theme of light from the school's motto, *Together We Light the Way*. The children had a great deal of fun coming up with the names, we had names like the *The Grade Four Firecrackers, The Grade Five Flaming Eagles, The Grade Seven Shooting Stars* and even the *Kindergarten Kilowatts*. (I suspect this class had some input from the teacher, unless I seriously underestimated the awareness and vocabulary of our kindergarteners). The class names fostered a common sense of identity and further strengthened the sense of belonging and connectedness we wanted to create for the children. On one level, it was fun to see the high spirits of each class. But on another, deeper level, we knew our children were learning about the interdependence of people, of the school and its community; we knew we were strengthening the connection of the children with the school with each other and with the community. Children who feel isolated, and/or disconnected can become lost, and children who feel lost can drift towards problems—including poor school work, delinquency, sometimes even suicide.

During the parade, each class carried their banner bearing their class name. The children added their own decorative touches, wearing colourful balloons tied to their wrists and singing the school song as they marched, guided by staff and parents. Leading the way, of course, was our mascot Sharkie. Stopping in front of our business partners, the children would repeat the South Simcoe chant while waiting for the manager or owner to emerge. Then, two students from each class would hand the proprietor a certificate thanking them for their support and promising to return within a few days to perform a community cleanup around their place of business.

The first stop on the parade route was always the nearby Legion Hall, where the children assembled in front of the building to be greeted by the manager and his staff. After promising to return over the next few days for a neighbourhood cleanup of trash and garbage, with special attention to the area surrounding the Legion Hall, the children would launch into their chant.

The last line of the chant was delivered in lusty voices and with arms raised in the air, followed by laughter and applause. Then we would move on to greet the next community partner and repeat the process. Our route was not a long one, because many of the little legs in grade one couldn't handle a major trek. (The kindergarten classes rode in a school bus decorated with cat whiskers, provided by Laidlaw, one of our community partners.)

New supporters were constantly popping up throughout the community. One day in June, I received a letter from Dr. Frank Gold, a local dentist who occupied an office in the mall across the street. Hearing of our progress at South Simcoe, Dr. Gold congratulated us on the program and expressed a desire to get involved with us. Although we always welcomed new partners, we weren't certain of the potential role for a dentist in the program, and it was too late to accept his services for that school year anyway. In fact, we didn't even have time to reply to him before the onset of summer vacation.

During our parade in September, however, I got a rather mischievous idea. Instead of drafting a letter to Dr. Gold, thanking him for his support, why not do so in person? We made a short detour to Dr. Gold's office, assembled outside his door and began chanting his name—"Doctor Gold! Doctor Gold!"—over and over.

The sound of more than 260 voices shouting his name must have alarmed the poor doctor terribly, not to mention the bewildered patient seated in his dental chair. Dr. Gold appeared at the door wearing his white dentist's gown, holding a dental instrument in rubber-gloved hands and wearing an expression of confusion and concern. I quickly explained we appreciated his offer of assistance so much we chose to express our thanks with a visit from the entire school. He broke into a smile while the students applauded and cheered him, then excused himself to scurry back inside to finish treating his anxious patient.

Dr. Gold became yet another active partner in the programs at South Simcoe, teaching our children about the importance of healthy teeth and healthy bodies. He eventually confessed he was thrilled by our impetuous visit.

Most schools launched each new school year with a Meet the Teacher event. By our third year, Meet the Teacher no longer seemed appropriate because so many individuals from outside the school were also involved in the teaching/learning process, including a large number of parents, business and community partners, and special guests such as the mayor and local celebrities.

Instead of Meet the Teacher night, we renamed the event the South Simcoe Community Get-Together, held on the school playground following our parade. The Get-Together was our opportunity to forge relationships around a common cause, and it evolved into something close to a large family picnic. We dined on hot dogs and hamburgers provided by our friends at Swiss Chalet and barbecued by Kiwanis members, and drank iced tea and lemonade. Pony rides and jumping toys in the playground kept the children occupied and burned off excess energy, and the entire area was decorated with balloons and banners honouring our business and community partners.

Our Community Get-Togethers served many purposes. They provided a gathering time for everyone who partnered with us; they recognized the support of our community and business partners; and they celebrated our past achievements while setting the stage for new ones in the coming year.

By this time, even minor disasters were unable to spoil our success. For our first Community Get-Together, two teachers were in charge of lighting the barbecues and beginning the cooking of the hamburgers and hot dogs. The day was unusually windy, however, and neither teacher was able to get the barbecues lit.

Kim Hutchinson sprang into action. Seizing a cooler filled with raw hamburgers and sprinting across the street to the Swiss Chalet restaurant, she explained the situation to our friend Phil Lawson, and without a moment's hesitation he said, "Leave it to me."

We still don't know how he managed to cook so many hamburgers so quickly, in a kitchen equipped to broil chicken. As many patrons waited patiently for their broiled-chicken dinners, delayed by our hamburgers and hot dogs, Kim entertained them with stories of the accomplishments of South Simcoe students, adding that the children were very hungry and waiting patiently for their meal. It worked; when Kim sprinted out the door with the cooked hamburgers, several diners actually applauded!

A few months later, when Swiss Chalet announced it would be adding hamburgers to its menu, we jokingly remarked this minor revolution in corporate policy must have been launched because of our Community Get-Together at South Simcoe.

One morning in early November, several children came running to me before classes began, obviously distressed. "There's a fire down the street!" they announced. "And it's in a house where some of our kids live!" The blaze was a block away, and after confirming the children were safe and it would be unnecessary to evacuate the school, I investigated the circumstances. Three children, recently enrolled in the school, resided in the house. We discovered them, along with their distraught mother and a baby in diapers and a thin blanket, seated in a van nearby. It happened to be a bitterly cold day, and we could either wait for one of the social agencies to arrive or take charge ourselves. Jacki and I put our heads together and decided to take charge.

We went out to the van, met the family, carried the baby inside and made the mother some hot tea. Then we found a warm blanket and oversized woolen socks for the baby, and calmed the family as much as we could. The parents needed to talk with fire authorities, arrange for new accommodations, find a kennel for the family dog and reassure concerned relatives. We told them to leave the children, including the baby, with us.

Meanwhile, the other students began expressing their concern. The president of the Students' Council approached me and proposed a student meeting to discuss how best to assist the family. I agreed, and watched while the students took charge. They outlined the family's needs. "They have just had a real loss," the Students' Council president pointed out. "They are frightened and don't know if anything is left at their house. So what can we do to help them?"

Their response was wonderful. All the leadership skills they were practicing instantly materialized. With no direction from any teacher, they brainstormed ideas as to how best to help the family. Many returned after lunch with food and gifts of clothing. One child pointed out it wouldn't be fair for the older child, a girl, to miss classes because she needed to care for the baby. "Let's take turns babysitting," another proposed, and they quickly established a schedule. The rest of the day passed quietly, with the children constantly inquiring about the family's situation and, I realized, enjoying their role as a collective of heroes. Meanwhile, I felt as though I were about to burst with pride. It is one thing to learn and practice a skill under supervision, but it is quite another to watch a child step up and take ownership of a situation in need of a leader. The children reacted immediately to the situation. They took the initiative, assumed leadership roles and accepted responsibility with the confidence of individuals twice their age. (Incidentally all of this was filmed by David Onley and the CITY TV crew since they arrived around the same time to do a special three-part series on the school). Years later, when David became the Lieutenant Governor of the Province of Ontario, he asked me to join his advisory group for his Aboriginal Computer Literacy initiative. Saying: "Now I have the opportunity to practice some of the principles I learned from my favourite principal." I was honoured and deeply touched.

211

As things turned out, Pam, the mother was unable to return to retrieve the children until almost six o'clock that evening. I sent the rest of the staff home and remained alone at the school for two hours after the end of classes, playing the roles of principal, babysitter and fill-in mother. It seemed the three children were everywhere at once, keeping me busy changing diapers, offering reassurances and tidying things up while they demonstrated their energy and curiosity. Ah, the life of a public school principal...

Not surprisingly, both parents became exceptionally strong supporters of the school and its programs. More gratifying to me, however, was the manner in which the children responded to others in a time of need, just as the community responded to them earlier. During that one-day crisis, we saw the children of South Simcoe rise to the occasion. They began looking out for each other, spontaneously, in a loving and caring manner. There was no "What's in it for me?" attitude. Something simply needed to be accomplished by them. And it was. Was this a foreshadowing of the future? How wonderful it would be.

Look what we've all accomplished, I reflected in the days following the fire. Together, the school, families and the community fostered changes that would have been unimaginable a few years earlier. At one point, the students of South Simcoe Public School were considered the source of problems in the neighbourhood. Now they were self-confident, loving and caring children, who generated pride and affection among all who encountered them. Especially their principal.

LEADER'S REFLECTION

Wise leaders create a culture of inclusive and participatory leadership in the workplace.

- How do you include others and encourage them to participate in the leadership process?

CHAPTER 11

From Worst To First

B y my third year at South Simcoe, word of our success spread beyond the neighbourhood and the city of Oshawa. In the fall of 1994, I was surprised to receive a call from the Canadian Broadcasting Corporation, which was dedicating an episode of their award-winning *Man Alive* television series to the subject of resilient children. The network dispatched crews from Toronto to visit schools all across Canada in search of the most outstanding program for helping children to become resilient. When they arrived in Edmonton to discuss the project with Steve Ramsanker, he was amazed to see them. "Why did you travel all this way," Steve asked them, "when you have a wonderful example right in your own backyard, in Oshawa? Sandra Dean's system is the one you should be documenting.

For almost five weeks we shared the school with TV cameras, lights, sound equipment and TV crew members, as they captured our daily routine and ventured into some students' homes to interview parents and children. The show aired across Canada early in 1995, and within a day or two I received a telephone call from Jennifer, an executive with General Motors of Canada. GM was looking for someone from outside the automotive industry to share "leadership principles and strategies that get results" at their marketing conference, attended by managers from the company's Ontario zone. Jennifer asked me to come and chat with her colleagues, no formal presentation—no notes, no charts, no overhead projection materials.

"Just be prepared to answer questions; we are going to put you on the hot seat," she said.

I was hesitant: sure I did many presentations but I was concerned about my ability to make a presentation with no supporting material. What could I possibly say 'off the cuff' that all these business people would be interested in?

My nervousness quickly dissipated when the 150 GM managers rose to their feet and applauded as I entered the conference room. I couldn't understand why. I thought, boy, that must have been quite an introduction that they gave me! Later I found out Jennifer showed the Man Alive documentary and asked the question "How do you think she accomplished this? After several answers, she said "Why don't we ask her?" They didn't know I was coming: it was a surprise, that's why the standing ovation.

The time flew past quickly and easily. What's more, the audience seemed genuinely interested in what I said. They were also surprised a school principal could could share such effective team building and leadership strategies with them. They proved this with their thunderous applause at the end. Business can learn from education and vice versa.

Afterwards, Jennifer asked me how they could compensate me for my time and the advice I gave them; what could they do for me in return for the presentation—a monetary contribution to the school, perhaps?

No way! "It would be so easy for you to write a cheque," I replied. "But money is not the most valuable thing you can contribute. I want more than money, I want your involvement in my school with my children, I want your time. The children need to see that people like you are interested in their education and well-being. We need people who care about what happens to these children and who will be involved with them for the long-term. We need you to visit the school and get involved; after all we are just down the street from your head office."

My suggestion unleashed an outpouring of new support from the people in GM's Ontario Zone. Jennifer McDonald, Barry Kuntz and their staff joined our Circles of Love program, arriving regularly to read one-on-one with our children. They, also, brought along a number of their colleagues to participate in our annual session at the Oshawa Mall, involving the Chief of Police and the Mayor of the city of Oshawa. They became frequent visitors to the school and eventually got involved in many other aspects of our school.

Then something extraordinary happened. When Jennifer and Barry experienced our programs, saw the children in action, setting and achieving goals, and studied the strategies we used to build an effective team, they asked if they could bring a group of Ontario-zone employees with them on their next visit. Fascinated by our achievements, and how we were accomplishing so much with so little money, they were anxious to share these ideas with their zone employees. They were especially interested in the way we interacted as a team, how enthusiastically we pursued our common goal and how everyone did what needed to be done, without necessarily being asked. They wanted more than a "talk" from us, they wanted their people to job shadow us, observe us in action, to see if they could figure out our "magic formula for success," so they could apply it to their own respective situations. We agreed, of course; we were honoured to be of assistance to such a large and prestigious company. This would never have happened if I had taken a cheque from them.

Our visitors were intrigued by the way the whole staff participated in the leadership process, by our success mapping system, our goal setting and achievement process, where the children set goals at the beginning of the day, shared with the teacher the responsibility for monitoring and measuring their progress throughout the day, then noted and analyzed their successes, and reflected on what they achieved and what strategies helped them to achieve success at the end of the day before celebrating them. The GM employees were particularly interested in finding out how we managed to create a culture where respectful interactions, acts of service and partnering with others to do the job, performing with integrity and a strong sense of sense of purpose were simply the way things were done--an accepted norm. No lists of responsibilities, direct reporting, accountability and performance appraisal systems could create this.

We simply trusted each other to each do our part, and our children trusted us.

The GM group noted with interest the way we always focused on strengths and areas for growth and development, instead of weaknesses and deficiencies. They loved this asset-based philosophy. They appreciated our refusal to focus on things we did not have and our insistence on emphasizing and making the best use of the resources we had, however few. They marveled at our ability to achieve so much with so few material assets. They loved the way we supported each other on a personal as well as a professional level and wanted to hear more about the strategies we used to nurture everyone's spirit and show we cared for one another like our Bouquet Board in the staffroom, where we wrote compliments and good wishes (bouquets) to each other.

Many of our ideas found their way into the GM training programs, and when other GM zones grew aware of the lessons to be learned from South Simcoe, they too invited me to come and speak to their groups as well. As a result I travelled to B. C's beautiful Okanagan Valley, Calgary, Prince Edward Island and Winnipeg. The warmth of the hospitality in Winnipeg countered the January weather, as did viewing the *Man Alive* documentary on Resilience at South Simcoe, projected on a giant IMAX screen.

At each location, I asked my audience to find a way to get involved with a school or with children in their community. "Children need to know they are valued by people like you," I repeated. "They need people like you to coach and mentor them, to cheer them on and be there to believe in them and support their efforts. You *can* make a difference in their lives!"

What an amazing development! South Simcoe Public School, located in the heart of Oshawa's inner city, was teaching important lessons to employees of one of the world's largest and most dynamic corporations. It put an entirely new spin on the idea of schools "giving something back to the community."

Community support at its best is a two-way street, with each side taking turns at giving and receiving. We were proud Barry, Frank, Curt, Tom and other members of their team at GM valued our school both as a source of management and teamwork training ideas, as well as a place where they felt good about making a difference in a way they could see really mattered. They became like family, and we were gratified when they and other GM employees helped us turn a potentially tragic Christmas into a joyous event one year.

It concerned Penny and her children. Penny, a single mother struggling valiantly to better herself and her children, was determined to do everything she could to help them to succeed. Penny was a regular participant in Parent Rap and a strong advocate for our school, she would tell anyone who would listen, how we helped her son to be more successful in spite of the fact that he had ADHD. Penny moved out of the neighbourhood in search of better living conditions, yet insisted on her children continuing to attend our school because of the relationships they built and the success they were experiencing. To be able to pay a higher rent, Penny and her family shared an apartment with another family that included two teenage boys. With only mother's allowance as her income, it was a struggle, but Penny managed to set aside enough money each week so in mid-December, she was able to purchase some special food, treats and a few small gifts for her children to enjoy at Christmas. The holiday season meant a great deal to Penny, and she looked forward to seeing the smiles on the faces of her children on Christmas Day. They would open their gifts in the morning and share what would be for them a somewhat elaborate meal that evening. But it was not to be. A week before Christmas the other family's teenage boys raided the freezer, ate most of Penny's food and tossed out whatever they were unable to consume. Then they stole the gifts Penny had wrapped and hidden for her children, selling them on the street for money to play video games.

Penny was devastated. Life, which was hard for her for so many years, turned cruelly unfair. No mother's allowance cheques would arrive before Christmas. There would be no presents for her children, no modest feast, and very little joy.

Jacki Devolin heard of Penny's situation and passed the news on to me. Could we do anything to help the family? It didn't look very promising. All our normal sources of assistance at Christmas were already given to needy families; it was unfair to call them now, so close to the holiday. In quiet desperation I called Tom at General Motors, and quickly explained the situation to him. He recognized my description of Penny almost immediately. "Wasn't she in the *Man Alive* show?" he asked. I told him she was indeed. "A lot of people around here saw that broadcast and were moved by it," he said. "And some heard you speak here. I don't know what I can do on short notice, but I'll try my best.

What he did was virtually miraculous. When word spread throughout the GM zone offices where I made presentations, we became almost inundated with a small avalanche of cheques and cash donations to be used for Penny. In fact, we received enough money to replace the food and gifts stolen from Penny and also help a second family in distress.

Over the Christmas break I recalled the warm generosity of our new GM partners many times. We can count on them, I realized. They had become part of our extended family When we are in trouble, they come to help; when we need something we can rely on them for support, no questions asked. Just as if we were family. What a wonderful realization to have at that time of the year!

Barry heard someone in GM's Ontario zone refer to our school as "the Saturn of the education world," referring of course to the innovative and non-conforming approach of GM's former Saturn division. I was thinking of that remark when I spoke at a celebration of the school's eightieth birthday a few weeks later. Over six hundred visitors crowded into the school and onto the grounds, overflowing from the classrooms into the halls, and out of the halls on to the playground. I mentioned the comparison during my talk. "Actually," I quipped, "Saturn is the South Simcoe of the automotive industry." We both made our points.

The CBC *Man Alive* segment was aired on a number of occasions, and the day following a repeat telecast, someone commented that our story would make an ideal feature for *Reader's Digest* magazine. "If that is meant to happen, it will," I said. It isn't something I have time to worry about. Obviously, it *was* meant to happen. The previous evening a woman in Kamloops, B. C. named Lynn Schuyler was having difficulty dropping off to sleep and thought perhaps a few minutes watching TV might make her drowsy. What she began watching did not make her drowsy at all. It was the *Man Alive* telecast, and instead of preparing her for bed, the show alerted her to a perfect story idea for *Reader's Digest*. The next morning Lynn began tracking me down, contacting me barely two hours after my off-the-cuff response to the idea of a *Reader's Digest* article on South Simcoe. When Lynn introduced herself and the reason for her call, I burst into laughter. I have always believed if you are on the right path, the right things will happen and the right people will come along to assist you. Not surprisingly, Lynn's telephone call cemented that belief more firmly than ever in my heart.

I was invited to make an appearance on the CBC's immensely popular radio show *Morningside*, hosted by Peter Gzowski. Peter, besides being perhaps the best-known media celebrity in the country at the time, was also a strong advocate of literacy education. As the interview progressed, he grew more and more enthusiastic and supportive. "Tell me what you might need at the school," he said near the close of our talk. I asked him what he meant. "We're being heard coast to coast across Canada right now," he said. "If there is something you and the school can use for your programs, go ahead and ask for it."I was caught unprepared. "If I knew that you were going to ask me this I would have prepared a list," I said. However I thought quickly and did mention two things. Photographs, I explained, played a large role in our work at the school; we have a large 'School Portfolio' in our front hallway, where we display photos of the children, demonstrating their successes. This serves as a continuous reminder of their strengths and capabilities and encourages them to keep going, keep persevering. It acknowledges and encourages them. The children are highly motivated by the 'School Portfolio' so we want to take more photographs and include more children. We take so many photos, our printing and paper costs are mounting. Photographic paper is very expensive for us, so that's what I need help with.

Almost immediately, CBC received a call from Anne Hartling, marketing manager for Kodak, saying she was available to help us.

Anne had always wanted to get involved with school children but when she phoned the school in her neighbourhood and they heard her area of expertise was photography, they responded to her offer of involvement by saying they didn't need a photography club, maybe she could try the local secondary school. What a loss to them.

Anne's company worked with Colortron, a photo processing business in Stoney Creek, near Hamilton, Ontario, so that made it easy for her to help us. Anne visited the school the following week and quickly found ways to became more involved. She was so supportive of our work she not only offered cameras, photographic paper and photo finishing, she also brought two of her colleagues, Sue and Steve to help our children. The three of them worked with a grade three class who were focusing on a section of the curriculum that dealt with Colour and Light. They were able to enhance the curriculum and make it more meaningful to the students, by teaching them how colour and light were a critical part of the world of photography, thus blending the real world of the classroom with the real world of the photography business.

They also taught the students how to take photos, make prints, and mount them for display. Anne said she always dreamed about doing a project with children, about what made them happy. We were thrilled to help her make her dream come true. She gave the children cameras and asked them over the course of a weekend to take photos of whatever brought them the most joy, what made them happy. The children took all kinds of photos, their running shoes, cats, dogs, flowers, their teachers, some even took photos of candy. Anne was so thrilled with the photographs that she, Sue and Steve, enlarged them to poster size, then asked their business partner, Shoppers Drug Mart, to display them in their stores. You can imagine how proud the children were to take their parents and friends to the drug stores to see the photographs they took. The banner for the display told Anne's story and was titled, Anne's Dream Comes True. It proved to be a wonderful project, made possible by Kodak, Shoppers Drug Mart, and Anne's generosity and kindness.

I, also, mentioned to Peter Gzowski just how badly we needed a bus from time to time, for excursions. We wanted the children of

South Simcoe, many of whom had never travelled beyond their own city limits, to discover other nearby places like Toronto and Niagara Falls, even the neighbouring Bowmanville zoo, and transportation was prohibitively expensive for us. "Anybody out there got a bus?" Peter said. "Sandra Dean needs a bus!"

A few days later someone who was listening to the radio suggested I call one of our partners, the Tim Hortons doughnut chain. Sure enough, they were pleased to make their bus available for excursions, and later that school year, our students were visiting historic sites aboard a luxury air-conditioned bus thanks to the Tim Hortons Company and Peter Gzowski.

Professor Bob Ellis, Associate Dean at the School of Business and Economics at Wilfrid Laurier University, asked permission to do a case study on leadership at our school. This would be a case study he would use with his MBA students. He later told me this case was a favourite with his students.

The *Reader's Digest* story was one of a long chain of events that spread the word of our activities far beyond the South Simcoe neighbourhood. Our story spread across Canada, down to the U.S., then overseas to Europe and eventually all the way to Australia. Strangers began asking staff members about our programs and methods, once they found out where they were teaching. Mail and telephone calls arrived from more locations than I can remember, both foreign and local and requests for interviews and speeches became so numerous we were unable to handle them all. The pile of letters became so voluminous, in fact, I simply placed them in a box in my office until I could find time to read and respond to them. It was reassuring to see such an outpouring of interest, but I refused to let all the attention distract me from my prime responsibility, the children at South Simcoe.

Just a few years earlier, I walked in one direction to seek help from the Legion members and in the other direction looking for assistance from neighbouring mall merchants. Now the traffic reversed, and as *Together We Light the Way* began making an impact, others were coming to us, to learn from us. It was nothing less than astonishing.

I was asked to do a second interview on CBC since there were so many requests for more information about our school and our programs. I spoke on Peter Gzowski's radio show three times, and during the third show, a woman named Courtney Garneau, working in Communications with the Federal Justice Department, happened to be listening to the show and shortly after the interview telephoned and invited me to Ottawa, where I discussed our approach, our achievements and the way we engaged students at the school, with several government officials.

Violence in schools and amongst children was beginning to attract wide media interest in Canada, most of it focused on a "Let's get tough with the kids" approach. Our philosophy, of course, was based on a totally opposite approach, one of intervention, prevention, healing and restorative practice, one of school-family and community-building, where the school is the centre or hub of its community; where the community is involved and engaged in nurturing, supporting and educating the children, and the children are engaged in contributing to their community. A focus on creating an inclusive, safe, healthy, and caring school, family and community environment, based on respectful relationships, leads to trust, engagement and ultimately school and life success.

Courtney and the folks at the department of Justice were impressed with our achievements; they understood the importance of this kind of approach when dealing with 'at risk' children. They loved our strategic comprehensive, collective and collaborative, school, family and community approach, to educational and social change. They asked many long and detailed questions. This led eventually, to them providing funding under their National Crime Prevention Centre initiative to our District, so we could further develop our *Together We Light The Way* approach and transfer the principles and methodologies to other schools, not just schools in our district but also schools across Canada. Imagine that, South Simcoe School was lighting the path of learning for children across the country, what a legacy! Courtney Garneau remained involved as an advisor, mentor and guide throughout this process and remains involved to this day.

We made enormous progress building relationships with the community. It seemed that once we opened our doors, there were literally hundreds of people who wanted to walk through them, to help our children to succeed. Our business and community partners would always say how good they felt about coming into the school and doing what they were doing; they were helping to transform the school, the lives of the children and rebuild the community from the inside out. The school and the children were, in turn, helping them to transform their lives. The partners too, were developing a greater sense of self, who they were, and what giving a little of their time could accomplish. The partners felt more fulfilled, and, interestingly enough happier about their jobs, and more passionate about life in general. They began to refer to South Simcoe as the heartbeat of the community; a spiritual oasis for all who walked through its doors. Ours was a more community building instead of transactional approach to partnerships and it proved to be a win-win for all those involved.

We created a foundation of success on which to build the achievement of academic excellence, to be measured by standardized tests in reading, writing and mathematics. Unfortunately, these tests would/could not measure the less tangible foundational elements equally required for academic success; such as a feeling of personal safety, a feeling of emotional security that comes with being socially accepted, included and appreciated, and the change of thought pattern that was needed with children who had never experienced success in any aspect of their lives.

Our children were now coming to school regularly and on time. They were beginning to understand who they were, unique and capable individuals with strengths as well as areas for growth and development. The children knew what they stood for, they were young people who believed in honesty, justice, fairness, respect, responsibility and all the other values and attributes of character they were learning about, practicing, and by now were so much a part of the way they tried to function as individuals and we functioned as a school and a community.

With the help of our parents and community partners, our children were able to learn about, and in some cases even experience, some of the many work and life options open to them. Because of their exposure, the children could now envision themselves in the workplace, or pursuing further education. This was far beyond what they previously thought possible. They were becoming more resilient, learning how to bounce back after setbacks. Their parents now had much higher expectations for them, both academically, and socially (they now expected them to stay in school until they graduated so they could go on to college or university, some parents wanted them to get a job and work in the kinds of places they had visited, it was as if a whole new world of possibilities was now open to them); they liked the idea of their children contributing to their community and being appreciated by those they helped. Their children were now people to be reckoned with.

Parents were working with us to help their children grow and develop personally, socially, and academically. The most important thing was our children could now envision themselves finishing school, finding a job, or pursuing further education, thus breaking the cycle of generation after generation caught in the poverty cycle.

Academically, we knew from the evidence provided by our in-school monitoring and measurement, we were improving. Why were the huge gains we were making not reflected in the district-wide test scores? The task of raising a child's reading scores by three or four levels is not simple. Yes, as noted earlier in this chapter, we spent time getting them to attend school regularly and on time, they were now looking forward to coming to school and engaged with learning, feeling and knowing they could be successful, that they could set and achieve goals. Our teachers had a growing repertoire of differentiated skills and strategies to meet the students' diverse needs, they were definitely getting stronger emotionally and improving socially and academically. We realized that the tests simply did not measure these early stages of progress so critical to our growth and development as a school in our particular context. That made our in-school monitoring and measurement all the more important. There were so many prerequisites to gaining high scores on the tests, but we were on track.

I clung to these thoughts when studying the results of the region's first series of district-wide exams. Ours were dreadful. We lingered at the bottom of the list in every category. If someone were to judge the impact of all our hard work and commitment based on those results alone, they would be appalled. Of the 120 elementary schools in our district, South Simcoe was rated dead last, and I was principal there for the last two years.

As a leader, I knew we were on the right track, our school and classroom records and statistics demonstrated we were making good progress. Our graphs demonstrated that behavioural problems were drastically reduced, attendance had increased dramatically, and you could even sense an attitude of striving to learn in virtually every class. The children were smiling, confident and articulate, they loved attending school, and they were working hard to prove they belonged at South Simcoe.

The staff and I consoled ourselves with this knowledge, but we knew schools are judged on their test scores, and we couldn't help but wonder how our parents would react to these disastrous test results? Would they decide our noble experiment failed, that their children were doomed to reside at the bottom of the academic totem pole? Should we even discuss the results at the next Parent Rap session? Perhaps we could avoid the subject entirely and hope the question never arose.

We decided to meet the issue head-on. At the next Parent Rap session, I presented the results to the parents and awaited their response. To their everlasting credit, every parent stated flatly the tests were wrong. When I explained these were the kinds of tests made up by many people and used in many other places, they said they didn't care about these tests and their results.

"We know how hard you, your teachers and our children are working, and you know how hard we parents are working," one parent said, "and what's more we can see our kids are learning. Just look at them, look at their goal achievement books, their class test results and their report cards."

"My son is reading, and he used to hate reading," another added. "Now he enjoys it. He's even showing off how well he can read. So what if he's not at the grade three level yet? The way he's going, I know he'll be there by the end of the year."

Our efforts to build relationships with our parents, based on mutual respect and trust, and the time taken to help them understand the teaching and learning process, was paying off. They now had high expectations for their children's success, and they had also become advocates of the school and of our approach to change. They believed as we did that strengthening the children's sense of self, who they were and who they could become, focusing on their personal growth and development as well as their emotional and social learning, was a firm foundation for academic achievement.

It was a heart-warming response, and I left the session feeling more confident than ever that we were on the right track and making a positive impact on the lives of both our children and their parents. We raised their expectations of the school and their children, we raised our expectations of them, now we had to raise the school's academic levels. We could, and we would!

I have always loved the term "strengths" but hated the term "weaknesses." Ours was an asset-based philosophy and our Guiding Principle in the area of learning was *"Everyone has strengths which must be nurtured and supported."* We always thought and spoke in terms of strengths, in terms of assets and capabilities and worked with our children to recognize and nurture their budding strengths, but I refused to say to our children they had weaknesses. How could they have weaknesses? If they didn't know how to do something it was not a weakness, it was simply an area for growth and development, on which they could focus when they needed and wanted to. If you honestly believe in the concept of lifelong learning, how can you accept the term "weakness?" We stated emphatically our children suffered no weaknesses; we simply recognized that what they could not do or did not know were areas for growth and development.

We kept our focus on those areas for growth and development. We continued to work with our partners to *Light the Way,* and we continued to help our children to maintain and sustain their emotional and social gains, and the healthy, caring, and respectful relationships they created. We knew we had to find a way to demonstrate our academic gains on the region-wide tests.

We went over our in-school measurements of our progress, score by score, comment after comment. The evidence was there; although to us the strides we were making academically were huge, they were not large enough to demonstrate this growth on the standardized tests; these strides had to be greater. "Maybe they should create a new kind of test for the early academic gains of children in these circumstances," I quipped to my superintendent one day.

We continued to strengthen and refine the programs and initiatives already in place. The social and emotional improvements our children were making meant teachers spent far less time on correcting and redirecting behaviour and therefore had more time to spend working on academics and with individual children with so many learning gaps, probably due to their constant moving from school to school and never staying in one school long enough for the teachers to give them the help they needed.

Our goal achievement process monitored by both parents and teachers, (through the goal achievement booklets that traveled to and fro, school to home and back), meant children were beginning to take more responsibility for their own learning. The students were now working with the teachers rather than opposing them, and this took a great deal of emotional stress off the shoulders of the teachers.

Our relentless pursuit of teaching and learning strategies so we could meet the needs of all our children and making these strategies transparent so the children knew which strategies were helping them to achieve, meant our children had another set of tools to help them to take more responsibility for their own learning. Again, this was another way of working with, instead of against, the teacher.

Our business and community partners were working with our children to help them to understand and appreciate that the academic, social, emotional, and leadership skills and strategies they were learning in school had relevance outside the school. These skills were needed in the work place, as well as in college or university and most of all in life in general. The partners coming in to answer questions about their businesses gradually evolved into them coaching and mentoring the students. The students loved to hear their explanations or go to see first hand how what they were learning in the classroom had relevance outside the school. This motivated them in ways we never anticipated. The partners were definitely enhancing the curriculum, and helping our children become more engaged and dare I say, even passionate about their schooling. There was a sense of energy and enthusiasm in the school. It also meant both staff and children loved coming to school.

The children's contributions to their community, meant even those who did not work directly with the children were still cheering for them, still championing their efforts and wanting them to succeed.

We produced handbooks documenting our programs so they would be easy for new staff members to follow and we continued our journey. We did not choose a 'quick fix' approach, that would give faster results; we chose the path that would lead to long-term change and sustainability. It was going to take more time but, oh, what a legacy this would be for us all!

Our Circles of Love reading schedule was swinging into high gear, to the delight of both the children and the adults reading to them. Business people and educators alike were asking us to share our team building, reculturing, success mapping, and goal achievement system with them, and our Parent Rap members were being invited to visit other schools, where they explained the importance and benefits of their involvement. We, also, took comfort in the continuing support from officials at the district office, who understood that elevating our academic levels would not be an overnight miracle. They knew we were making progress, and were always saying how much they appreciated the changes we were making. As a reflection of their belief in our programs, we were persuaded to apply for an award from the Conference Board of Canada.

These awards, presented every year to recognize partnerships between schools and business, were highly prized and hotly contested by schools all across the country. If South Simcoe Public School could win recognition in that forum, it would go a long way to proving that schools, businesses, and communities partnering and working together to help children learn was an approach that brought with it results, not just in the academic area, but also in the social and emotional areas. What more could we ask for?

With the encouragement and financial support of my director and superintendents, I attended that year's Conference Board event and returned filled with enthusiasm and resolve. Our school, I was convinced, stood a good chance of being selected for recognition at the next event. This wasn't simply my own personal evaluation but the opinion of others as well. They encouraged me to continue to do what we were doing and submit an entry the following year.

All of this activity, the long hours, together with the day-to-day demands of my role as principal, were taking a toll on my energy. The truth is I was growing mentally and physically exhausted. Between acting as principal, supervising programs, maintaining contacts with our community partners and conducting media interviews, my work became a seemingly endless procession of meetings, discussions and decision-making. I usually loved every bit of it, but even happy work can be too much for one person. I was paying a physical and emotional price for the long hours and weekend work, even if I refused to admit it.

That summer, both Ishwar and the boys insisted I take an extended vacation in Trinidad. I returned to Trinidad frequently to visit my family and friends, who were unfailing in their pride in my accomplishments and their encouragement. But this trip was somewhat special. I spent long hours in conversation with people who helped to shape my values as a child, and the experience was truly a spiritual renewal. Then, Ishwar and I went to Tobago, where we spent our honeymoon so many years earlier, and I whiled away many long, languid days soaking up sunshine, catching up on my sleep, walking on the beaches and generally recharging my batteries.

When I returned to begin the new school year, I discovered a new reservoir of energy, and I applied it towards raising our academic levels to match our other achievements. More than ever, I saw our community partners as a special extended family, capable of providing spiritual sustenance to the children just as my family and friends back in Trinidad provided for me. I grew determined to shine our light so brightly no one could ignore it.

Around the same time, we began to document our initiatives and successes in preparation for the Conference Board of Canada's submission for the award for Excellence in Business and Education Partnerships. From the first day of school in September, with the invaluable help of Pauline Langmaid, a board facilitator, Tamara Gattie, and Kim Hutchinson, two of our teachers, we described our procedures, recorded our achievements, demonstrated evidence of our accomplishments and gathered testimonial letters from our community partners. We were assisted along the way by senior officials at our board office who wanted to see us succeed. Then, near disaster. On the day we were to courier our submission to the Conference Board for arrival the following day, we realized some of the information on the application was inadequate. Rewriting large sections of the submission meant missing the one-thirty courier pickup, but we refused to send in an inadequate presentation, so we set to work on major revisions. The next pickup time was five-thirty, but by mid-afternoon we realized we wouldn't make that one either. We found a company that agreed to pick up the presentation at nine o'clock, and we worked through the dinner hour, by now practically staggering with exhaustion. Still the work went on, and we had to cancel even that late-hour courier, finally settling on a company that promised same-day delivery, the next day, for a hefty fee.

We somehow found the energy to finish the submission and finally wrapped things up at eleven o'clock that evening. By that time, we were all so weary and my eyes were extremely sore. They still were sore the next morning, so I couldn't even put on my contact lenses. The arrival of the courier service the next day, was quite literally, 'a sight for sore eyes.' We worked so hard, and now everything was in the hands of strangers who, I prayed, would see our successes, not just as numbers and graphs, see our children not just as statistics, see our parents and community partners not just as 'do gooders,' but really look closely at the comprehensive, multifaceted and measured effort to reach goals many others once considered impossible.

The call arrived in February. Tiny South Simcoe Public School, the school that sat at the very bottom of the Durham District's test results one year earlier, was declared the best of all Ontario's elementary and secondary schools in the competition for Excellence in Business and Education Partnerships sponsored by the Conference Board of Canada.

We whooped, we hugged and we laughed. Then I shared the news with the school over the PA system, which set off such an explosion of cheering by the students I wondered if it could be heard ten miles away, at the school board offices. I followed this up with visits to each classroom, where I explained in detail the meaning of the recognition and why they should feel proud, because the award was more theirs than anyone's.

The National winner would be chosen from among the provincial winners at the formal presentation, which was to be held in Saint John, New Brunswick, later in the spring, and this posed a problem. The Conference Board would make travel arrangements for me to attend, but I felt it would be terribly unfair if I were the only representative from the school to attend the awards ceremony. None of our achievements would have been possible without the hard work and sacrifice of the teachers as well as everyone else who worked in the school, and of course the support of our business and community partners; they all deserved to share the honour and recognition. A team effort won the award, and the team should be on hand to receive it.

In a meeting with Pauline Laing, my director, I explained my dilemma and made an impulsive promise. "If you can arrange to make time available for the teachers to attend," I said, "I'll arrange the rest." Meaning, of course, the expense of flying our entire staff to New Brunswick.

Pauline came to the rescue. If the parents agreed, a Professional Development Day could be shifted, providing the time needed. The parents enthusiastically supported the idea. Now it was time to raise the money to cover travel and accommodation.

The support from our business partners was nothing less than inspirational. When word spread we needed funds to send the staff to New Brunswick, parents, trustees and community partners went to work, and soon contributions of five, ten and twenty-five dollars began arriving, along with congratulations and fervent beliefs we would be selected best in the country. Substantial amounts came from surprising sources: the neighbouring Kmart, (Zellers) where a few years earlier some of our students were considered rampant shoplifters sent a generous sum, while Mike Nicholson, our school trustee, drummed up support from the entire board and even convinced Doug Ross, another trustee, to contribute as well.

We invited all our partners to attend and be recognized, including members of the police force. The chief of police responded by sending Colin Shaw and his partner in a brand new police van to drive the nine hundred kilometers from Oshawa to Saint John.

The event was much more than an awards ceremony. Each regional winner set up booths and displays in a conference hall where over six hundred attendees, most of them educators, milled about looking at photographs, examining records and exchanging knowledge with representatives at the booths. Constable Shaw helped at our booth; this drew a few curious comments from visitors, who may have wondered why a uniformed police officer was a necessary player in all our activities.

Everyone seemed intrigued by our initiatives and impressed with our accomplishments. They loved the photographs of the children we used to decorate the booth (provided by Anne, Steve and Sue), and they were impressed by the partnerships we forged among members of the community, especially with the fact we asked our partners, even huge corporations like G. M. and G. E. for a contribution of their time instead of their money. Still, none of us dared to hope we might be chosen the winner from all the school and business partnerships in Canada.

Then the moment for the formal announcement arrived. We held our collective breath…crossed our fingers…then erupted in more joy and noise than I ever expected a small group of teachers and two police officers could express.

When the pandemonium settled down, I wanted everyone who supported us back home to hear the news. The school board, I knew, was holding an evening meeting at the board office. We had to call them and share the excitement. But no one was at the building's main switchboard at that late hour. There was simply no way to get the word to the meeting room—until Constable Shaw said, "Leave it to me." He called police head-quarters back in Oshawa and had a police cruiser dispatched, complete with flashing lights, to the board office, where the officer managed to rouse someone who admitted him to the meeting room with the good news.

I have always wished, in a small way, I was present that evening when the Durham District School Board, probably deep in a discussion of budgets and curricula, was suddenly interrupted by a police officer arriving with, I'm sure they expected, news of some near or imminent disaster—only to discover that South Simcoe Public had just won a prestigious national award.

The conference Board of Canada presentation was not the first award to South Simcoe, but it was the first award made *outside the school system,* which validated the significance of our programs beyond the school walls. It was also our first national award as well, and one that recognized our success at making, as Ken Leithwood put it, simple—*but not simplistic—changes* with very few resources and very little money. A good deal of our success was admittedly a result of our comprehensive, collective and collaborative approach to working with our community and sharing the responsibility for raising and educating 'our' children in the South Simcoe community. We could have never achieved our goals alone. But really—aren't partnerships and sharing the responsibility for raising and educating children something every community, every society should expect from its members?

We received numerous requests from other educators and school districts, to visit our school, learn about our programs and strategies and why they were working so well. We did our best to accommodate these visits. My dear friend and mentor Ken Leithwood was conducting a case study on Teamwork in schools; he surveyed a number of schools to establish relative levels of enthusiasm, commitment and morale among the staff. The results from interviews conducted at South Simcoe, he told me with astonishment, went right off the chart; they were so high they unfairly skewed the data obtained from other schools in the survey.

Things had certainly changed at South Simcoe Public School, now, we all loved our work.

The children too, enjoyed the growing attention being paid to their school. Little Meagan, whose singing voice stirred hearts at every school assembly, seemed to take special pride in welcoming visitors. She would rush to greet them, thrust out a tiny hand and say "Welcome to South Simcoe!" Her positive attitude and her pride in her achievements was impressive. It took only the barest hint to encourage Meagan to display her personal portfolio, to anyone who happened to visit the school. She would quickly pull out her 'anger logs' and show how she learned to manage her anger. She would then show them evidence of all the academic goals she accomplished, then ask if they wanted to hear her sing the school song. Her success summed up so much of what we strived to accomplish, and set the tone for many tours by visitors.

It occurred to me Meagan was unconsciously teaching us a lesson. We all need encouragement, support and assurance that our presence on earth is valued and appreciated, and Meagan needed this as much as anyone. Her family situation prevented her from savouring the joy and satisfaction that comes from being loved and appreciated at home.

Many children react to this kind of situation with rebellion and alienation. But Meagan chose to find acceptance elsewhere, first from the teaching staff, and later from visitors to the school. Some visitors arrived as skeptical strangers, but they usually departed the school totally beguiled by this little girl's enthusiasm and poise.

In August 1995, I was asked to present our programs and share our ideas with other educators at The Learning Partnership's conference in Toronto. (This was a huge deal for us). We gathered together a team of school staff and community partners to prepare and deliver the presentation. Since all of this was being done during our holiday time, we decided to treat ourselves by pitching in twenty dollars each and hiring a stretch limousine, complete with uniformed chauffeur, to drive us there and back. On the way we toasted our new celebrity status with non-alcoholic champagne!

Even our now-lovely gardens were attracting attention. In September that year, South Simcoe was declared the winner of the 'Looking Good Award', given to the school judged to have the most attractive grounds of all 120 schools in the region.

But good looks, I kept reminding myself, can take you only so far. Our bottom-of-the-barrel rating for reading, writing and mathematics still felt like a millstone around my neck. Two things kept raising my spirits. First, we had no direction to go but up, as I kept repeating to the teachers, over and over. Second, we knew we were slowly and steadily making academic progress and our standing in the previous series of board tests was a thing of the past.

When the Ontario Ministry of Education announced it would conduct a provincial standardized test two years later, I knew we would do much better; after all, we could hardly do worse. Sally Roberts and Joanne Blohm, the grade three teachers, were confident in the abilities of their students. When the results finally arrived, virtually the entire staff gathered in the staff room to share in the news.

It was amazing. South Simcoe Public School was no longer at the bottom of the barrel, or even in the middle of the pack. Our results were substantially higher than the average for all elementary schools in the entire province of Ontario. The following year, we were the top school in the province. We managed to rise dramatically in the ratings for reading, writing and mathematics. The gardens, the awards, the recognition and the media coverage all paled in comparison.

Our children were not only more capable, more confident, more respectful, more resilient and more articulate than before, they were also academically outstanding students and the proof was there for all to see, in their dramatic rise in academic standing.

LEADER'S REFLECTION

Resilience is a key success factor in business and in life as a whole. It is important for individuals as well as organizations to develop reslience.

- How do you work to make yourself more personally and professionally resilient?
- How do you help others to develop resilience?

CHAPTER 12

The Gifts They Gave Us

Through 1996, South Simcoe gained international recognition. Early that year, we were informed our board of education was nominated as an entry in a competition to honour excellence in school systems, sponsored by the giant Bertelsmann Foundation of Germany. Although the nomination process asked for one school to be used as the example for the district, Michael Fullan, then the Dean of Education at the Ontario Institute for Studies in Education, (a part of the University of Toronto), included South Simcoe Public School as an example of great change made on a shoestring budget with very few resources. This all meant our school was included in the international competition and would be added to the tour being conducted by the Bertelsmann judges.

The criteria for the competition required the jury to assess a long list of qualities, including each school system's concern for learning and life chances; originality and evolution; employee potential; innovative school leadership; participation of pupils, parents and other agencies; co-operation between individual schools and external decision-makers; evaluation and quality assurance; and a framework to support similar development on a national level.

We readied the school for the visit and added a few extra touches for the Bertelsmann Judges. The judges' visit included the lunch hour and we were asked to recommend a restaurant for them. When we learned that they would be touring other schools all over the world for three months before arriving at South Simcoe, we decided instead of recommending a restaurant to them, we would prepare a special home cooked meal for them—we figured by this point, they were probably growing tired of restaurant meals. Jane Hallett, one of our classroom assisants, suggested we prepare a home-cooked European meal, complete with freshly baked bread, a European favourite.

Alvena, a super chef when it came to baking, made fresh bread, and its heavenly aroma wafted towards the judges as they entered the building; Jane cooked and served her favourite casserole and we all contributed to dessert. We invited Phil Lawson, our Swiss Chalet partner, and Curt Tingley from General Motors to join us to talk about our partnerships and discuss our successes from the perspective of business people.

Before they began their tour of the classrooms, each judge was provided with a summary of our school terminology for different programs, so they would be using the same language as our children. We felt this was a practical way of demonstrating the importance of using a common language to create and sustain respectful relationships, as well as all the other changes we made. This also enabled the judges to become more involved with the children, instead of merely observing them. They were able to see first hand, the glow of pride in the eyes of the students when they praised them for their accomplishments.

We went from classroom to classroom, with the judges growing more impressed by the minute. In Sally Roberts's grade four class, they inspected the student portfolios and asked one girl to name her best subject.

"Reading," she said without hesitation. "I'm a really good reader."

One member asked how she knew that.

"Easy," the girl replied. "I'll show you."

As the judges watched, she withdrew her portfolio from her desk, opened up the academic section, then showed them examples that illustrated her level of reading in September and her current level. What a tremendous leap! She also showed them the graphs depicting her progress. She progressed three years in reading levels in less than one year, and she demonstrated it with poise and pride.

Downstairs in the kindergarten class, Nancy was reading a story to the children when the judges entered. After the judges introduced themselves, one asked the children if they were proud of their school. "Yes!" the children responded, almost rattling the windows with their voices.

"You show them," Nancy suggested to the class, and the youngsters spontaneously exploded in the loudest, most enthusiastic South Simcoe chant ever delivered by a group of five year olds.

At the end of the tour, the judges expressed their surprise and pleasure at the staff's enthusiasm and dedication, and at the confidence and pride of students. They also went on to praise the consistency of our programming. "In every classroom," one of them commented, "from kindergarten to grade eight, the teachers and students are clear about the goals of the school, their classroom goals and their personal goals. They can clearly articulate the agreements they have made about speaking and behaving in a respectful manner. They can also talk to you about how they work to develop respectful relationships based on mutual respect. What's more, both teachers and students have personal portfolios divided into the areas of professional growth, (academic for the students), Personal Development, their growth and development as individuals, their emotional learning, teamwork, their Social Growth and Learning and Leadership, how they have participated in the leadership process, how they have taken charge without being asked, how they use their strengths and capabilities to make improvements. They can describe the strategies they used to help them to succeed, and they can demonstrate how they measure their progress and goal achievement. The most significant point is that they are consistently achieving the goals they set for themselves."

The judges were impressed—so impressed that a film crew arrived from Germany in May that year, to spend two days filming at our school, and two days at Sinclair Secondary School, the "showcase school" for the award. The presence of the film crew was evidence that we did more than simply impress the Bertelsmann judges, and in September it was made official: Durham District School Board, represented by Sinclair Secondary School with South Simcoe Public

School 'also showcased,' won out over all the school systems in Hungary, New Zealand, Norway, Scotland and Switzerland, to be declared the best, most innovative school system in the world. To this day, I believe the aroma of the freshly baked bread worked in our favour.

Linda Scott, from the Conference Board of Canada, asked us to host a group of visitors attending an International Partnership Conference in Toronto. Since we were the previous year's winner, a number of people wanted to visit the school. I watched as one visitor, Ola Risnes, a dour Norwegian, moved through the school taking videos of everything without exhibiting any apparent response to all he saw and heard. I feared he actually disapproved of our programs, or was disappointed in some way, but later that year, when I encountered him at an educational conference in Calgary, I learned he was, in fact, very impressed. I, also, discovered he was the head of the Norwegian Confederation of Business and Industry. As a result of his visit and that meeting, he invited me to make the keynote address at the International Partnership Conference in Norway the following summer.

Other invitations began arriving from international destinations. I was delighted to be invited by the Royal Bank in Trinidad and Tobago to return to my home country, where I spoke about the development of business and educational partnerships. The Prime Minister opened the event and, needless to say, the experience was immensely flattering to the entire South Simcoe family. For me in many ways, it was like coming full circle. It enabled me to reach back to my roots, to the region and the culture that shaped me and shaped so much of what happened at South Simcoe School.

Shortly afterwards, the prime minister of Grenada invited me to Grenada to launch a partnership initiative with school principals, teachers and business people. I made several visits to Grenada to do this, all funded by Rob Pitfield from Scotiabank. During this time, the prime minister's first annual awards for excellence in partnerships were held. After the ceremonies, I was invited to address the prime ministers of the other Caribbean nations.

Shortly afterwards, I set off for Jamaica upon an invitation by Bill Clarke, head of Scotiabank to speak to his bank managers at their annual training conference.

Later, I was invited by Margaret Gourley, Vice-Chancellor of the University of Durban in South Africa, to give the keynote address to a conference centred on the importance of the community supporting children and their education. The people I met in South Africa, where there was such hunger for knowledge and so few resources to provide it at the time, were thrilled to hear the message *Together, We Can Light the Way*. They needed to know a small school facing many challenges in far-off Canada developed an asset-based philosophy and succeeded in spite of limited resources, by creating cost effective and innovative programs and working with their community. If we could do it, I assured them, they could as well. I stressed the need to believe in the strengths and capabilities of the children and to work with them to help them find their strengths, then nurture and encourage them to apply their skills and talents to improve their own situations as well as their communities. I explained that with the support from partners in their community, all this was possible.

"Not simply support from their wallets," I emphasized. "Support from their hearts as well."

I explained how a large number of people, each giving just a little of their time, can make an enormous impact on the lives of children. I talked of the critical need to teach respect for self and others, the value of innovation, teamwork, and initiative, and the importance of participating as leaders with those involved in the change process. I described the struggles faced by children such as Melanie, Meagan, Bobby, Leonard, Cathy, Barbara and so many others we encountered, and how we helped them to become resilient and deal with the challenges they faced. I explained that significant academic gains were made by breaking tasks down into very small steps, setting a goal to achieve each step, carefully monitoring and measuring progress and always celebrating achievements. Accompanying this was the careful and deliberate selection of the teaching and learning strategies that would best facilitate the achievement. It was important to make these strategies transparent so not only the

241

teachers but the children too would clearly understand how to use them on their own; this would assist them to become independent learners. The conference participants loved the concept of schools, families and communities working hand in hand learning and growing together, and collaborating in the raising and educating of children, the importance of believing in children and nurturing and supporting them in a protective circle, as it were, until they grew and developed and believed in themselves enough to stand on their own. I assured my listeners they should begin their own journey by making positive choices, finding their own paths, and not waiting for someone else to do it for them. "If we change the way children *think* about themselves then we can change the way they are *being* as individuals. We can show them new ways of being in the world, and change their lives forever. Then the world becomes a better place, not only for them but also for others."

One day, in the spring of 1998, I returned home from school as usual and checked my voice mail. All but one were the familiar kinds of messages, spoken in familiar voices by people with familiar names. One was anonymous. I could not recognize the voice. "Sandra," it said, "I'm someone who cares about South Simcoe School, and I want you to know this. The school is going to be closed. I don't want you to be shocked by the news, because I know you have said that it would only close over your dead body."

That was all. They hung up.

I felt as though I had been kicked in the stomach.

It could be just a crank call. Who would leave a message like that without mentioning their name? But the words were delivered with such authority that I knew they were true. Due to governmental cutbacks, school districts everywhere were being forced to reassess the economics of operating buildings that were small and costly to maintain. Like South Simcoe.

I didn't mention the telephone call to any one at the school. A few days later, when I was at the board offices, hoping against hope that the rumour was untrue, Grant Yeo, the director, called me into his office for a chat. He closed the door behind us and I knew instinctively what he was going to say.

"We're going to be announcing the closure of your school," he said in a solemn yet kind and caring voice, like a physician announcing the death of a relative. "I want to handle this in a manner that won't create a negative impact on the community, and I need your co-operation."

Thanks to the anonymous telephone call, I managed to remain calm while he explained, in a sweeping cost-cutting plan, the Durham District School Board would be closing eleven older schools, most of them in heavily urbanized areas, and constructing twelve new schools in developing neighbourhoods.

It was not something anyone wanted to do, but every possible way of keeping the school open had been explored. There was no real alternative. Grant encouraged me to look on the bright side of things. I always despaired that South Simcoe lacked a gymnasium, a large library and sufficient washrooms for the children. Moving the children to a newer, larger school would provide them with all of these facilities. I knew the children would gain in so many ways. I tried, but I simply couldn't accept the closing of South Simcoe as a step forward for the children.

Things grew worse when, soon after my talk with the director, I had to sit through a meeting and listen as someone read aloud the names of all the schools to be closed. Through the list they went, moving closer to the revelation I knew was coming but found difficult to acknowledge, and when they called out "South Simcoe Public School," it was as though someone plunged a knife into my heart. I sat frozen in my chair. I may have been a dedicated educational professional and a member of this important and influential group, but I was blinking back tears. How could this be the fate of a school that was praised as a beacon of hope for other schools all over the world, and as a spiritual oasis for the entire community?

When the meeting finally ended, I managed to rise from my chair, walk to my car, drive the long distance back to the school and break the sad news to the staff.

By this time, I resigned myself to the reality. Drawing on my leadership training, I began concentrating on ways to help the staff and students deal with the news. At the school, I did what was expected of me professionally and took the official board position, explaining the logic of its decision to the hardest-working, most dedicated group of teachers I ever was privileged to know, while they dabbed tissues at their eyes or stared blankly into space. "This is not entirely unexpected," I pointed out. "We did wonderful things here, and made a difference to so many children. Unfortunately, the building is old, it is costly for the district to operate, and there is no room for expansion on the lot to accommodate a gymnasium and other things we need." I asked them to remember the importance of working together to make the change as easy as possible for the children.

In June, the day before our Community Day and the celebration of the school's eighty-second anniversary, the decision was made public. At the end of the next school year, South Simcoe Public School would be closed and shuttered, left to await demolition or sale. The press practically stormed the school in the middle of the festivities, with five local and national TV stations dispatching cameras and reporters to cover the story. Fortunately, I anticipated the media response. Ann Hartling and Linda Sinclair helped me prepare a statement regarding the closing of the school, and I read it over and over again to reporters and interviewers throughout the day. The joy of the celebration, of course, dissolved in the reality of the school's imminent closing.

That's one reason I remember the day so vividly. The other reason? It was the only time in all my years at South Simcoe that we had rain on the school's Community Celebration Day.

With the word now made official, I personally visited each class, explaining to the children they deserved better facilities than we were able to provide at South Simcoe. It was a fine old building, but its time had passed. "Nobody enjoys closing a school," I said, "least of all its principal." Least of all *this* principal, I might have added.

And that October, in the midst of a beautiful autumn, the final autumn in the final year for South Simcoe Public School, a remarkable thing happened. Once again, the Ontario Ministry of Education conducted standardized testing to determine abilities in reading, writing and mathematics among grade three and six students in all schools in the province. This time, we didn't open the results with the same breathless excitement as before; but we were stunned, nevertheless.

The findings were clear and unequivocal: South Simcoe students were performing at the top two levels in reading and mathematics, and 94 percent of our grade three students achieved the top two levels in reading, writing and mathematics skills. South Simcoe was no longer merely above average in its academic performance; on the basis of these tests it was the most successful inner-city school in the entire province. There was more.

According to an ensuing district report, "a remarkably high percentage of South Simcoe students attended school regularly and on time, and the overwhelming majority of our grade seven and grade eight students earned at least two A's on their report card. Once notorious for incidents of vandalism and shoplifting," the report noted, "South Simcoe now enjoyed the steady support of twenty-six business partners and community agencies. And the school that once could entice only three parents to each Parent Rap session now drew at least one out of every four parents to its meetings, and the parent group was cited by The Royal Commission on Learning as "a model for others to follow".

Upon hearing the news of the school's closing, some of these same parents resolved to save the building. Their presentations, letters to the editors of local newspapers and outraged telephone calls to local politicians all repeated the same theme: How could they close a school that won the national award from the Conference Board of Canada, a school that helped the district to win their international award, a school that became a beacon of hope for so many other schools in so many different countries? They can't just shut down a school that did so much for so many in the South Simcoe neighbourhood.

Well, they could, and they did.

Towards the end of 1998, I accepted the decision intellectually, if not emotionally, and was determined to handle the situation with as much grace, dignity and decorum as I could muster. Still, it seemed as though irony kept piling atop irony.

During the same week in December 1998 that the decision to close South Simcoe Public School was declared binding and irrevocable, the federal justice department, along with The Ontario Ministry of Education and Training, announced a spending commitment of

$1.8 million to fund the expansion of our programs to schools all across the country. This was announced at one of our Celebrating our Stars student achievement ceremonies, held at the Legion Hall and attended by a host of federal members of parliament, members of the provincial legislature, plus several business and community partners. It was a huge celebration. Every staff member, every student and every interested parent we could squeeze into the hall was invited to attend. I reminded each class that not only did they succeed but now they were role models for others all over the world.

I was asked to head the justice department's initiative to be called *"Creating Safe and Caring Learning Communities*, using the *Together We Light the Way* Model." Yes, *Together We Light the Way* was now a model. The work we did, and the lessons we learned, could now make a difference to untold numbers of children everywhere in Canada and beyond. We helped to make a difference to an entire community; now we were being given the opportunity to make a difference to an entire country, and even other countries beyond Canada.

The ministry's description of our program, as contained in a news release of December 16, 1998, managed to sum up all we conceived, refined and practiced over the previous seven years:

Together We Light the Way…*is a school-based intervention model that builds resiliency and responsibility in young children and relies on the commitment of teachers, parents and the community for its success. The model reduces risk factors affecting young children and increases protective factors.*

Why would the Department of Justice make use of our program? Because t*he elementary school setting provides perhaps the only consistent access to large numbers of children.*

My final day at South Simcoe fell immediately before the Christmas vacation period. During my years at South Simcoe, we maintained a tradition at the school of "clapping out" grade eights who were moving on to high school. On their final day at the school the grade eights would walk along the lower corridor, which was lined with all the other students. As the senior students moved towards the door for their final exit, the remaining students would shake their hands and applaud them. This was our "clap out", and it proved so moving and popular that some grade eights would exit and scurry around to re-enter the school from the other side, just to be "clapped out" again.

I always dreamed of leaving in the same manner. But it would be both inappropriate and too emotional. So there was no clapping out for me. My final day ended with the usual rush of telephone calls, a raft of documents to be signed and a long walk, alone down the hall and out the door.

During this walk I considered something I did not give much thought to in the past. Our aim was to make South Simcoe a safe haven and a spiritual oasis for the children. We wanted them to know they would be loved, respected and cared for within its shabby old walls. Yet, over my last few years there, I felt I was the one who was loved and cared for. If I had become sick, someone would have watched over me; whenever I needed a kind word, someone spoke it for me. I genuinely loved the school, the staff, the students, the community, and all they represented. I also recognized the changes that took place within me. Like the children I, too, grew, both personally and professionally. Like them, I too became more resilient. I was both stronger and more centred as a person. The physician, in seeking to heal and care for her patients, found herself also healed and cared for in the same process.

I did not, and still don't, enjoy goodbyes. So, that night, filled with a maelstrom of emotions and recalling all the school meant to me, I got into my car and drove home.

Times and situations change. Teachers and students alike must understand and accept this fact of life. When I was assigned to South Simcoe, it was a place I didn't want to go to; now it was a place I didn't want to leave. The children helped me find a strength I never knew was within me, and I am forever indebted to them for it.

One of the foundations of wisdom, I believe, is the awareness of universal themes, concepts of belief that are equally valid everywhere in the world. Among the most important of these universal themes is the one my father first taught me when I accompanied him on his visits to distant villages, seeking people who needed assistance.

You have to guide people towards the opportunities in their lives, explain how to use them, support them as they learn, then when they grow more confident, they will discover new opportunities for themselves. Then they will assume the role you undertook earlier; they too will find opportunities for others—and so the cycle continues.

Respect for self and others is another universal theme. I believe every society must nurture this value in children.

Hope may be the most valuable universal theme of all. With hope, children embrace a vision of better things for themselves, and realize they do not have to settle for the same conditions into which they were born.

We gave the children of South Simcoe a realization of the opportunities available to them; an awareness of the importance of having a strong sense of self, respecting themselves and others; hope that they could continue to grow and seek happiness, success and fulfillment in their lives; and knowledge that these represent the foundation of a happy, healthy and fulfilling life in an inclusive healthful, safe and caring community.

They gave themselves better grades, a more promising future and permission to pursue the unlimited potential within them.

The things they gave me and my staff are beyond measure and description.

LEADER'S REFLECTION

The health, well-being, and life success of the people in your family, workplace, and community depend on your thoughts and actions as a leader.

- Are your thoughts and actions congruent?
- Do you consciously and consistently work to harmonize your mind, heart and soul so you have a whole new way of being?

THE WAY FORWARD

Visit Sandra's website for an exciting sneak peak at the way forward, what's coming next. Successes since South Simcoe School closed and how its story continues to light the way for schools all over the world, watch for the educational version of her book, Hearts and Minds: A Public School Miracle, A Blueprint for School and Classroom Success, with a foreword by Michael Fullan and contributions by Ken Leithwood.

For trainings seminars, speaking engagements, personal and organizational consultations and a look at her new Virtual Training Institute, go to www.21stcenturyleadershipstrategies.com or contact her at deansandra@gmail.com

www.ingramcontent.com/pod-product-compliance
Lightning Source LLC
Chambersburg PA
CBHW031244090426
42742CB00007B/308

* 9 7 8 1 4 5 2 5 0 0 1 4 0 *